The Sullivan Institute/
Fourth Wall Community

Recent Titles in
Religion in the Age of Transformation

1st published in 2003

The Sullivan Institute/ Fourth Wall Community

The Relationship of Radical Individualism and Authoritarianism

Amy B. Siskind

Religion in the Age of Transformation
Anson Shupe, Series Adviser

Westport, Connecticut
London

Library of Congress Cataloging-in-Publication Data

Siskind, Amy B., 1953–

  The Sullivan Institute/Fourth Wall Community : the relationship of radical individualism and authoritarianism / Amy B. Siskind.

    p. cm. — (Religion in the age of transformation, ISSN 1087–2388)

    Includes bibliographical references and index.

    ISBN 0–275–96878–2 (alk. paper)

    1. Sullivan Institute/Fourth Wall Community (New York, N.Y.) 2. Therapeutic communities—Case studies. 3. Cults—Psychological aspects. 4. Control (Psychology) 5. Social control. 6. Collective settlements—Case studies. 7. Utopias. I. Title. II. Series.

RC489.T67S56   2003

362.2—dc21   2001058944

British Library Cataloguing in Publication Data is available.

Library of Congress Catalog Card Number: 2001058944
ISBN: 0–275–96878–2
ISSN: 1087–2388

First published in 2003

Praeger Publishers, 88 Post Road West, Westport, CT 06881
An imprint of Greenwood Publishing Group, Inc.
www.praeger.com

Printed in the United States of America

The paper used in this book complies with the
Permanent Paper Standard issued by the National
Information Standards Organization (Z39.48–1984).

10 9 8 7 6 5 4 3 2 1

Copyright Acknowledgments

The author and publisher gratefully acknowledge permission to use the following material:

Interview of Michael Bray by Richard Ofshe, Ph.D. for the Bray/Dobash custody case used with permission of Michael Bray and Michael Cohen.

The edited chapter "One Step Away From Mother: A Stepmother's Story" by Alice Neufeld, which appears in *Women and Stepfamilies: Voices of Anger and Love*, by Nan Bauer and Maglin and Nancy Schniedewind. Reprinted with Permission of Temple University Press and the Author. © 1989 by Temple University. All Rights Reserved.

Contents

Acknowledgements

It is a privilege to be able to acknowledge all the people from different parts of my life who contributed to the conception and execution of this book. My mentor at the Graduate Faculty of The New School, José Casanova, was enthusiastic and extremely supportive from the beginning. His extremely comprehensive knowledge of the sociology of religion, and his research on authoritarian groups and governments made him an ideal supervisor for this project. Robert Lifton and Charles Strozier, with whom I studied at CUNY Graduate Center, were in on this project from its earliest inception and pushed me to "make something of it." Their studies of "thought reform," of fundamentalism, and of the impact of totalizing ideologies on the individual contributed immeasurably to this dissertation. Donald Scott of the Committee on Historical Studies at The New School commented on several pieces of this dissertation in the seminar on Knowledge, Power, and Culture, and subsequently as well. Arthur Vidich encouraged me to participate in his dissertation workshop and to draw out the connections between the founders of the Sullivan Institute and the New York intelligentsia. Jeffrey Goldfarb contributed his expertise in sociology of culture.

Vera Zolberg expressed her interest from the point of view of cultural studies. Tom Robbins and Arthur (Larry) Greil showed their interest and support by asking me to write a chapter in their volume on religion and the social order and to present at the Association for the Sociology of Religion and the Society for the Scientific Study of Religion. Susan Jessop read several drafts of chapters and made extremely useful comments. Ed Levy read chapters, talked to me at length about various issues, and supplemented my bibliography. Michael Cohen provided me with at least half the data used for the analysis, as well as reading and commenting on most of the chapters at length. His unique position as both an ex-member and a psychologist was invaluable in contributing insight and inspiration.

Many people who were involved with the Sullivan Institute/Fourth Wall Community agreed to be interviewed and generously supplied me with information and commented on drafts of some chapters. Not only did they help me in this way, but they also helped immeasurably by reacting so positively to my writings on this subject. I have felt throughout this process that not only might I contribute to a body of social scientific and historical knowledge through this work, but also to the self-understandings of many of my fellow participants in this experience. This has been an incredible source of strength and fortitude.

I also want to thank Bruce Friedman and Ellen Streger of the New School administration for making this one of the most painless interactions I have ever had with a bureaucracy. There were so many times when I needed something at the last minute—instead of making it more difficult for me, they went out of their way to make it easy.

My staunchest supporter and most severe critic throughout this project has been my husband, Michael Cohen. He contributed more time and energy to this project than any other individual, and constantly cheered me on. Michael Bray also contributed a great deal of time and effort in both supplying me with data and in lending a sympathetic ear during times of frustration and despair. Ruggiero de Ritis, recently deceased, provided cheerleading from across the Atlantic Ocean. Margaret Heide, Randal Hepner, Susan Pearce, and Polly Smith provided criticism, support, and camaraderie. Barbara Cohn Schlachet had to listen to every complaint and fear I had about this process. And my daughter Laura had to put up with a stressed-out, tired mother. Coming home to give her dinner after a day of writing was (almost) always a treat.

My grandparents, Joseph and Lily Salwitz, didn't live to see the completion of this project, but made it possible with their unwavering faith in my abilities from my earliest years. Additionally, there are many ex-members of the Sullivan Institute/Fourth Wall community—some of whom are friends and others who are not—who helped make this book possible, either by agreeing to be interviewed, or by expressing their interest in and satisfaction with the work. I have had numerous telephone calls from people asking for copies of the dissertation. Now it will become much more easily obtainable in book form.

I dedicate this book to:

my brother Paul, who died at the age of twenty-nine, one of those who did not survive the mistakes made in the group;

Ruggiero deRitis, who succumbed to illness before I could complete the project he so persistently and caringly supported;

and finally, to the children and grandchildren of the members.

I hope it helps them to understand our legacy.

Chapter 1

Introduction

This is the story of the rise and fall of a radical therapeutic community—a community that founders and members believed was the beginning of a new society. In the United States of the late 1950s—a time of optimism about the future and dissatisfaction with traditional social forms—the Sullivan Institute/Fourth Wall community offered an alternative to the Leave it to Beaver U.S. family ideal. This alternative would liberate the individual from the constraints of obligation and repression and provide the means to the end of personal fulfillment and creativity. This goal was achieved for many participants, but not without significant personal, social, and financial costs. Although it focuses on a small group that was idiosyncratic in many respects, the Sullivan Institute/Fourth Wall community can also be viewed as a microcosm of the cultural and political issues that engaged large segments of society during a particular era in U. S. history.

The following chapters are not only descriptive, although they do describe particular events and individuals. They also examine the significance of particular social movements, specifically the psychoanalytic and the Communist movements, for U.S. history and social structure. This is done by using a combination of individual life histories, observations of community life, and documentary evidence that remains ex post facto. While hindsight is being employed here, I have also attempted to convey the electricity of the moment. For anyone who has been involved in a charismatic movement, had a personal religious experience, or experienced other similar moments of social transcendence, this ineffable feeling could not be left out of any complete account.

In 1957, Jane Pearce, M.D. and Saul Newton—who had been affiliated with the William Alanson White Institute, a well-respected psychoanalytic institute in New York City formed the Sullivan Institute for Research in Psychoanalysis. At first, the Sullivan Institute was structurally similar to other psychoanalytic institutes in the United States Over the next ten years, it would evolve into a utopian psychotherapeutic community that existed for over thirty years on the Upper West Side of Manhattan. This community arose in the context of the social, cultural, intellectual, and political ferment that was taking place in American society in the postwar period. Although it never claimed more than 400 members at one time, its impact was far greater than its numbers. The membership of the community consisted mostly of middle- to upper-class intellectuals, artists, and professionals, reflecting, to a large extent, a segment of the demographics of the Upper West Side at that period in history. Many of these individuals were teachers, writers, performers, and academics who had considerable influence in their respective fields. The Sullivan Institute/Fourth Wall community counted among its number individuals who were in the forefront of the psychoanalytic, political, and cultural avant-garde in New York City.

One of the singular achievements of the political and cultural movements of the 1960s was the transformation of the notion of political action from an isolated sphere of activity, practiced in political clubs and voting booths, to a way of life. The conception of the personal as political radically changed the forms of political activity from the time-honored institutions of the campaign and the caucus to those of the march, the demonstration, and the political collective, among others. The Sullivan Institute community was part of an earlier social and cultural avant-garde that included the Beats, C. Wright Mills, the neo-Freudian theorists (Fromm, Horney, Thompson, Sullivan), and the abstract expressionist painters. When the mass movements of the 1960s began—the civil rights, anti-war, and countercultural movements—the Sullivan Institute community came into its own.

In the 1960s the community consisted of a tiny band of psychotherapists and their patients, some of who were already living together and engaging in relationships that breached the traditional professional boundaries between patient and therapist. Most of these members were in their thirties and forties. In 1970 the directors of the Sullivan Institute established a training program designed to enlarge the number of patients that could be seen under their auspices. With the introduction of inexpensive psychotherapy practiced by young radical therapists, many young people who were seeking personal growth in conjunction with a radical political perspective were attracted to the Sullivan Institute. The membership of the community grew from approximately fifty to seventy in the late 1960s to approximately 400 in the early 1970s.

After the political and countercultural failures of the late sixties, many individuals who had been involved with these movements entered what Greil and Rudy (1990) have referred to as Identity Transformation Organizations. These organizations attempted to trigger radical shifts in world view and identity (1990; 227) among their members. Some of them were religious, like the Zen Buddhist communities that sprang up around the United States during this period. Others were secular, like Synanon, which drew its membership from the many individuals who were adversely affected by the drug use of the late 1960s and early 1970s. Additionally, as Steven Tipton (1982) suggests, these organizations provided a means through which young people who had dropped out of mainstream society could find a road that led back in, or at least a way of life that mediated between their own radical divergence from mainstream values and the society that still professed those values. The Sullivan Institute/Fourth Wall community served this purpose for many people over its life span of approximately thirty years. Although it has rarely been written about in academic publications, the community was well known among Manhattan's Upper West Side intelligentsia from which it sprang, and included many prominent individuals in the artistic and academic professions.

FROM LIBERATION TO SUBORDINATION

The Sullivan Institute/Fourth Wall community developed from a porous, somewhat hierarchically oriented group whose primary concern was with the liberation of the self, into an isolated community with a highly authoritarian internal structure whose mission was the political enlightenment of mainstream society. The personal fulfillment of the individual—self-realization and gratification in the present—ceased to be a goal. Instead members were required to give up their money and free time for the good of the community and its mission. The transition from a postmillennial belief system to a premillennial one was made. In other words, during the early years of the community's existence, members believed they were the living embodiment of a utopian future. In religious terms they had already been, or were in the process of becoming, saved. In later years an apocalyptic vision emerged. It was thought that the end of the world could result from nuclear holocaust, environmental contamination, and finally, AIDS. Therefore no time could be wasted in frivolous pursuits such as art, music, or general enjoyment of life.

This book addresses the seeming paradox in the original stated goals of the community and its later transformation into a rigid, authoritarian group with little room for individual expression or decision making. Therefore, what is being studied, at least in part, is a consistent gap between theory and practice, as well as changes over time in the relationship of theory to practice within the group. Although certain characteristics of community life, such as the directiveness of the therapists and the regulation of childbearing and child rearing, existed from the beginning, they continually intensified. The justification put forth by members and leaders for the gap that existed between the libertarian goals and the authoritarian reality of daily life was promulgated in several forms, but was not often addressed directly by either group. Just as the overall ethos of the community changed over time, the daily life also changed drastically. Whereas many individuals left the community over the years, almost no one openly voiced disagreement with the direction that the group had taken. The original reasons for joining the group for many, if not most, individuals had been the desire for a life that included a higher degree of self-realization and actualization than was deemed possible in mainstream society. Over the thirty-year life of the group, the life of individual members became *more* restrictive than life in mainstream society in several specific ways.

Beginning in the early 1980s, the size of the community decreased and the living arrangements became increasingly centralized, making surveillance more pervasive. All individuals who were in the group as of 1978 were required to join The Fourth Wall Repertory Company, which was described by leadership as a political theater company. Members were expected to donate large quantities of time and money to the theater company and to the documentary films that Joan Harvey, the artistic director of the Fourth Wall and one of the four training analysts who formed the leadership of the community, was making. Beginning with the Three Mile Island nuclear accident in 1979, every member was required to account for his or her whereabouts twenty-four hours a day to the Emergency Communications System. The AIDS restrictions were enacted in 1983, prohibiting all members from having sexual relations with any nonmember. Politics classes began, and members were required to read assigned books and to discuss them in house meetings, beginning in approximately 1984.

These actions were justified with reference to a potential nuclear, environmental, or plague-type apocalypse. An unforeseen consequence of the AIDS restrictions was that the community's ratio of two female members to each male member resulted in many of the women being without sexual partners or potential fathers for their children. For many women, especially the older ones who had regularly chosen sexual partners outside the community, the termination of this option created an untenable situation. The issue of childbearing, while not considered by most women who joined the community in their early twenties, became a serious consideration for many individuals who were in their thirties and forties in the 1980s. While restrictions on childbearing and child rearing had always existed within the community, it was not until this time that they were directly experienced by a large proportion of the membership.

Initially, for many patients, the therapeutic relationship seemed liberating. Patients were encouraged to sever ties to their families and to choose careers and sexual partners as they pleased. In 1971 the inception of the training program, which recruited young people with either bachelors or no college degrees as therapists, instituted an almost automatic system of surveillance. Young trainee therapists told their supervisors about the statements and actions of their patients, who then took any critical information directly to the leadership. Many patients reported to their therapists about individuals who criticized the leadership, were dissatisfied with life in the community, or violated group norms. Therapists would then report anything deemed important to the leadership. With the inception of the Fourth Wall theater company in 1977, the surveillance system became even more ubiquitous because stage managers and stars, as well as work-crew leaders, provided additional conduits of information about members' activities to the leadership.

This book attempts to answer the question of not only why a community whose professed ideas were the ultimate liberation of the individual became more authoritarian than mainstream society, but also *how* this happened—the processes through which the life of the individual was constrained, and the theoretical/ideological justifications that were put forth for these practices. I believe that some of the conclusions reached here will be applicable, at least in some respects, to mainstream society as well as to other utopian/therapeutic communities. The high degree of control over membership was exerted using extremely sophisticated techniques. While this experience also echoes (in some respects) those of the people who lived during the Stalinist and Maoist periods in the former USSR, China, and in parts of Eastern Europe, it is more similar in several ways to the experiences of other small cults, such as the Center for Feeling Therapy and the Democratic Workers' Party in California.

In order to answer the questions I have raised above, several specific aspects of the Sullivan Institute/Fourth Wall community will be examined. In chapters 2 and 3, I examine in what manner the founders of the SI/FW community combined Marxist and neo-Freudian psychoanalytic theories in their attempt to create the perfect society. This entails clarifying the relationship of Jane Pearce and Saul Newton to the psychoanalytic and leftist communities, both theoretically and personally. I also discuss the relationship of the Sullivanian phenomenon to specific historical developments in U.S. culture such as the Beat movement and its eventual transformation into the countercultural movement, the civil rights movement, the New Left, and the women's and gay liberation movements.

Chapter 2 also places the Sullivan Institute/Fourth Wall community in the context of a historical tradition of utopian community experiments in the United States, many of which were concerned with restructuring the economy and the family. Prior to the most recent period, the 1960s and 1970s, the period from approximately 1840 to 1880 was a period when hundreds of communities of all types (religious, socialist, even anarchist) were founded. Like the communities of the 1960s, many of these were short-lived, but some of them lasted for decades. This raises questions about the similarities between the earlier period and the more recent one.

Chapter 4 describes what I refer to as the halcyon period of the community— the period of expansion between 1969 and 1979. This was also the period during which the distinctive social structure was both expanded upon and institutionalized. A good deal of this chapter is devoted to describing these unique structures, such as dating, group apartments and summer houses, and childbearing and child rearing. This period ended rapidly with the Three Mile Island nuclear accident in March 1979.

Chapter 5 is a detailed investigation of the role of the patient-therapist relationship, both in realizing the theoretical/ideological goals of the community and in the formation of its hierarchical structure. Through this relationship, patients developed altered self-conceptions; one could even argue that they developed totally new selves in the sense that their self-concepts were radically changed. Sullivanian therapists handled the transference, commonly accepted by most psychotherapists as one aspect of the patient-therapist relationship, quite differently than most other mainstream psychoanalytic psychotherapies. One of the keys to the efficacy of this self-transformation is the complete reevaluation of the patient's history and relationship with his or her parents. This reevaluation is then reinforced by the group living situation and the social isolation from family and outside friends. This process is the key to the high degree of control exerted by the leadership of the Sullivan Institute/Fourth Wall community over patient-members.

Chapter 6 discusses the transition from the hedonistic or halcyon period to what I refer to as the revolutionary period (1979–83). An important source of information about this period is the plays of Joan Harvey. The plays are didactic in style and pedagogical in their intent. While they may not be important from a literary point of view, they are extremely important to any understanding of the ideology of the community, particularly in the later period (1979–92) of the community's life cycle. The leadership did not publish any statement of purpose, theoretical or practical, during this period. The plays give the reader a detailed understanding of the ideology and the actual events within the community during this time. The transition from a hedonistic to an ascetic revolutionary ethos is quite clear.

In chapter 7 the decline and final dissolution of the group is documented through interviews, court transcripts, and journalistic accounts. This chapter utilizes the accounts of several ex-members to supply both information and the flavor of this period of uncertainty, and finally, chaos. When Saul Newton died in 1991, the community split into two opposing factions, each led by one of his ex-wives. Although Newton had been extremely ill for some time and unable to exert much control over activities within the community, his presence seems to have had some unifying effect. The dissolution of the community was quite rapid after his death.

In chapter 8, I attempt to draw out the reasons that the community was so attractive to relatively large numbers of educated and creative intellectuals, political activists, and artists. The eventual dissolution of the community is discussed in the context of its relationship to the current crisis of Western rationality. How do the world decline of Marxist/communist ideology and the current skepticism about the psychoanalytic paradigm relate to the eventual decline of the SI/FW community? What phenomena that existed in extreme forms in the group can also been seen in other parts of contemporary society? Since Marxism and psychoanalysis were the most radical projects of the enlightenment, what conclusions can we draw from their use (in some form) by the Sullivanians to create a restrictive, repressive community?

I have also attempted to determine whether the SI/FW community was successful because it addressed specific social structural needs that existed in society at that time. Did it address individuals' need for structured alternatives to the traditional nuclear family? Did it provide young adults with a holding environment' within which they could integrate themselves into adult society? Was it, as Tipton (1982) suggests, a means by which those who had been involved in the counterculture could reintegrate themselves back into society? Did it fulfill a need for new types of male-female relationships? If it did satisfy some particular structural gaps in society, what caused its decline and eventual dissolution?

SOURCES

I became a member of the SI/FW community at the age of five, when my mother joined; therefore some of the information in this book is based upon my experiences and observations. When recounting certain periods of the group's life cycle, the emphasis is on my participation; for others it is on my role as an observer. During the years from when I was five to sixteen, I lived with my mother, my brother, and some other community members. I have used data from my own experience to describe some of the flavor of the community during those years, but I have also interviewed some older members in order to get detailed information about the organization of the community, the relationship between therapists and patients, and so on. For the period of time from 1974–85, when I was an adult member, I have used my own experience as source material, in addition to interviews of ex-members, class notes from the Sullivan Institute training program (1972–81), scripts of Joan Harvey's plays,[1] Fourth Wall phone lists, and some court documents. After 1985, when I left, until the dissolution of the community, it was necessary to rely upon interviews of individuals who stayed until the dissolution of the community, or who remained for some time after my departure. The almost complete disintegration of the community in 1992 has made this task much easier.

Due to my long-term membership in the group, I was personally acquainted with most individuals who were members during the years I was there. This has resulted in my ability to obtain access to ex-members more easily than a researcher who is a total stranger. The interviews were structured along the lines of a clinical interview which allows the researcher to follow any line of questioning that seems likely to provide useful data. While certain information was directly requested, interviewees gave in-depth descriptions of their personal experiences in the community that were not completely directed by the interview questions. This approach enabled me to obtain individuals' subjective experiences of the community with a minimum of prompting.

There are places in this book where events that took place in the community are discussed. Wherever I have used either interviews or written material as the source of this information, these sources are cited. If no source is cited, it can be assumed that I either witnessed the event firsthand or that the information was common knowledge to all members of the group.

RESEARCH CONDUCTED

I conducted thirteen in-depth interviews between 1988 and 1994. Some of these interviews are quoted extensively in the book and the initials of the interviewees are cited. Initials have been changed to ensure the privacy of all informants, with the exception of M. B. (Michael Bray), who did not request that his initials or name be changed. I also used three interviews that were made available to me by Richard Ofshe, Ph.D., who was hired as an expert witness by Michael Bray and S. P. in their custody cases. Those interviewed by Ofshe were myself, Bray, and L. C. For a list of interviewees see Appendix B.

The estate of Isaiah Rochlin, M.D, gave me a number of tapes of Sullivan Institute classes. I had some of these tapes transferred to cassette from reel to reel, but their utility was limited due to the poor sound quality. I also used court documents generated by custody cases involving the Sullivan Institute: *Hoy v. Pappo*, *Bray v. Dobash*, and *Sprecher v. Agee*, held at New York State Supreme Court and presided over by the Honorable Justice Shackman.

Michael Cohen, a student in the training program at the Sullivan Institute for Research in Psychoanalysis for fourteen years (1972–84), gave me access to his class notes for those years.

As stated previously, I used my own observations during the time of my membership in the Sullivan Institute/Fourth Wall Community—the years 1959–70 and 1974–85.

THEORETICAL APPROACH

In an attempt to provide a comprehensive analysis of the data, I look at the SI/FW community from both micro- and macro sociological points of view. On the micro sociological level, the phenomenology of everyday life within the community will be described and analyzed. The analytical perspective to be taken will combine psychological and sociological approaches in an attempt to understand how members actually thought about their commitment to the community, their experiences before joining, their involvement with the theory, and their experience of the therapeutic relationship. These approaches have already been combined by theorists such as G. H. Mead and more recent social scientists following a Vygotskian model on the cognitive level. On the psychodynamic level, I will use a self-psychological approach, incorporating the work of Heinz Kohut and Robert Lifton. Self-psychology theory lends itself readily to an interface with cognitive psychology and with sociology.

On the macro sociological level, I attempt to place the SI/FW in a historical context, both on the theoretical and empirical levels. In the theoretical realm, I discuss the close connection between the theories of Erich Fromm, Frieda Fromm-Reichman, R. D. Laing, and other theorists of the postwar United States and the founders of the Sullivan Institute—Jane Pearce, M.D. and Saul Newton. Additionally I examine Pearce and Newtons' involvement with the Communist Party and connect this to the formation of the SI/FW community and their later theoretical positions. The connection between the sudden surge in community membership and the rise of the counterculture is not accidental. Many individuals who joined the SI/FW had previously been involved with either the New Left or the counterculture. While the group drew much of its ideology/discourse from the same sources as the counterculture and the New Left, it also differed from both of these movements in some respects.

From a historical point of view, this work demonstrates the continuity between the SI/FW community and earlier U.S. intentional communities, such as the Oneida community, the Owenite communities, other nineteenth century socialist and religious groups, and contemporary countercultural communities as well. Additionally, the implications of the use of psychoanalytic and Marxist theory to create an authoritarian community will be examined. As stated earlier, I attempt to place the failure[2] of the SI/FW experiment in the context of the failure of what I have referred to here as universalistic reason. In order to accomplish this, I will use the Foucauldian concept of discourse to analyze the means that were employed to realize the Sullivanian goal, and Habermas' attempt at a reconstruction of critical theory to show that the belief in a unitary subject of history contains some inherently repressive implications. Not only is intersubjectivity required as a replacement for enlightenment rationality, but also individuals who are able to think critically.

THE PERSPECTIVE AND BIASES OF THE AUTHOR

The position taken in this project is not be that of a detached observer— although that ideal is, I believe, impossible and undesirable for any chronicler of human events, it is even less possible for myself. While I do not view this as a limitation, the fact of my membership in the community has both positive and negative ramifications for this study. The positive aspects have been mentioned; the negative ones have not. Due to the fact that I defected from the community, it was impossible for me to interview the few remaining individuals who remain in close contact with two of the ex-leaders of the SI/FW community. Nor was it possible for me to interview the founders and leaders of the group, although I have quoted them extensively. On the other hand, it is highly unlikely that anyone would be able to do this, as the leadership of the community attempted throughout its existence to either silence any press or academic accounts of their activities, or to ensure that only those aspects of their beliefs and practices that they wanted portrayed were revealed.

Nevertheless, I attempt to look at the inception, formation, expansion, and decline of this community with a relatively detached eye. I have tried to tell the story from the vantage point of the membership, the patients who joined the community in search of better lives. In doing so, I hope I will enable the reader to understand this complex social experiment. I believe that only by telling the story, and by understanding its implications, can some of the harm done to participants be redressed, and precautions taken for future social experiments.

NOTES

1. They are a particularly rich source of information about Harvey and Newton's ideas at the time they were written because they were intended for an audience of both group members and outsiders.

2. Failure here is defined as the conflict between the goals of the community and their realization—the goal being a person who was liberated from social control, and the actuality being a person who was subject to an extremely high level of social control.

Chapter 2

General Cultural and Historical Context

In order to understand the development of the Sullivan Institute/Fourth Wall community over a thirty-year period, it is necessary to understand the intersection of several social, historical, cultural and economic factors that came together in New York City in the late 1950s and continued on into the 1960s and 1970s, albeit in quite different forms. Due to the participation of Jane Pearce and Saul Newton in several aspects of New York intellectual life, the influences on their work and on their decision to found the Sullivanian community were numerous. One of the formative influences on both Pearce and Newton was their membership in the Communist Party (CP/USA), although this research has been unable to pinpoint the precise years of their membership. Newton had been a member as early as the 1930s, and had fought in the Spanish civil war. Their participation in the psychoanalytic community was connected to their Communist beliefs in the sense that they viewed Harry Stack Sullivan as the "missing link" in the attempt by Marxist theorists to understand how the creation of the ideal consumer comes about in Capitalist society through the nuclear family.

The fact that Sullivan wrote a good deal about the negative effects of the nuclear family on the individual had an impact on Pearce and Newton. They felt that the Communist movements in the United States[1], the Soviet Union, and other parts of the world had failed, partially because they did not attempt to change the fundamental nature of individual socialization. Until the individual had been socially engineered in such a way that he or she no longer needed the security of the nuclear family (either family of origin or family of procreation), the need for private property, and therefore for capitalist society, could not be abolished.

While neither the Sullivan Institute nor the Sullivanian community were well known, many of its members were (or became) important figures in music, art, dance, academia, and literary circles. Some of these included Judy Collins (singer), Clement Greenberg (art critic), Jackson Pollack (artist), Richard Elman (writer and teacher), as well as other talented professionals in medicine, academia, computer software design, and film.[2] It is clear from the above list that the appeal of the psychotherapy extended to a much larger intellectual community than might be assumed.

For any analysis of the Sullivan Institute/Fourth Wall phenomenon to be successful, it must contain some conception of not only which historical phenomena made it possible, but also of the societal dynamics that produced it. While it is difficult to conceptualize all factors at one time, it may help to envision the collision of mainstream[3] political and cultural beliefs with the political and cultural norms, values, and customs of certain subcultures and countercultures from which the "Sullivanians" drew both theory and members. The dynamics at work in the formation of both the Sullivan Institute and the community were also complex—the character of the interplay between these various sociohistorical factors and the individuals who were moved by them, but who also added their own personal idiosyncratic touches to the process, is difficult to both conceptualize and to describe.

One aspect of the success of the community was its timeliness in terms of particular currents in U.S. history. It has become a commonplace that post–World War II American society was experiencing a period of both optimism regarding the future, and of conservatism in its desire to return to the "normal family life" that the war had supposedly interfered with. At the same time, cataclysmic social and technological changes were taking place that would quickly result in the social movements as well as the political and cultural critiques of U.S. society that emerged in the 1960s. The United States was more affluent than it had ever been as a result of several factors; among them the return of relative prosperity due to business generated by the war, and its relatively undamaged situation after World War II, at a time when all the European countries, and Japan as well, were in a shambles. This economic upswing had many ramifications: it made relative affluence and education available to a larger number of people than ever before. This high level of affluence was also partially responsible for the rampant materialism and consumerism, which became the secular religion of the United States.[4] It also gave people more time for introspection and recreation—aspects of social life that had previously been scarcer.

The radical, antimaterialist intelligentsia, first in Greenwich Village in the early part of this century, later in California and other parts of the country as well, had for years been a source of resistance and a challenge to mainstream cultural norms and values. Although Greenwich Village has been declared dead on many occasions (Jacoby 1987, 20), it was still flourishing in the 1950s according to commentators such as Michael Harrington and Ronald Sukenick (1985). By the end of the 1950s, however, the Beats had begun to transmute themselves into the "hippies" of the 1960s, and by 1967 the "counterculture" went mainstream (Jacoby 1987, 40). The intellectuals themselves did not stop writing, but the locus of intellectual life shifted to the campuses. Academics such as C. Wright Mills, Herbert Marcuse, Philip Riesman, and others who practiced academic social criticism are examples of this shift.

The Kinsey Report, which (presumably) documented the decidedly un-Christian aspects of American sexuality, and the invention of the birth control pill were two events that dramatically affected the cultural milieu of the 1950s. Kinsey's conclusions—that there was a great deal more extramarital sex than was previously imagined among the general public, that masturbation was not harmful, that homosexuality was more common than had originally been thought, and that premarital sex often had a positive effect on marital outcome—were explosive in their impact on the U.S. public. His failure to condemn homosexuality, premarital sex, and masturbation brought him under constant attack by conservative forces, and eventually caused the Rockefeller Foundation to discontinue his funding (Halberstam 1993, 281). The birth control pill was not widely used in the 1950s, but its invention would have a stunning impact in just a few years. The widely touted "sexual revolution" of the 1960s had begun, and in fact reflected both a change in practices, and a change in attitudes about these practices that allowed individuals to make statements about themselves that they would have been ostracized for making just a few years earlier.

The "sexual revolution" was not simply recognition of sexual practices that already existed in segments of U.S. society. It also represented a rejection of the ideology of the family that had predominated in the immediate postwar period. While popular culture may have represented the post-1945 family as the bedrock of societal stability, various demographic and cultural changes were taking place that made this point of view the tip of an iceberg. The adjustment process for couples who were reunited after World War II was difficult and resulted in an extremely high divorce rate immediately after the war (Gilbert 1986, 57). While many women found themselves unemployed after the war, many found other jobs, albeit not at the same levels of income or responsibility. During the late 1940s and throughout most of the 1950s, the marriage rate increased and the divorce rate decreased. The infamous baby boom created a demographic anomaly in the history of industrialized countries, most of which had declining birth rates. As early as 1953, however, and earlier in the literary world, the U.S. family was attacked from two different points of view. One group of writers blamed the ills of society—especially increasing juvenile delinquency—on frustrated housewives. A Senate Judiciary Subcommittee convened to study juvenile delinquency faulted decreasing discipline and broken families for increasing crime rates among teenagers (Gilbert 1986, 73). Obviously Jane Pearce and Saul Newton were not the only critics of the "traditional" U.S. family.

The whole world did not suddenly change—people did not simply wake up one morning feeling less sexually inhibited or more critical of materialism or more in need of direct sensory experience of the world. In fact, only a small proportion of the population articulated any of these notions at first. The Sullivan Institute was part of this small critical subculture from its inception in 1957. It was one of the many indicators of the break from small-town U.S. life with its social strictures and prejudices into a more cosmopolitan world. The young psychotherapists who initially became students at the Institute were part of a progressive intelligentsia that had flourished in New York City since the turn of the century.

THE RISE OF THE COUNTERCULTURE AND THE EMERGENCE OF ALTERNATE RELIGIOUS ACTIVITY

In sociocultural terms, the period beginning right after World War II in 1945 and ending in approximately 1973 (the end of the war in Vietnam) was one of the most affluent and optimistic periods in U.S. history. While the United States had had such periods before, this particular combination of postwar optimism and prosperity with rapid technological and social change may qualify as one of the most rapidly changing periods in the life of this relatively young country. The sexual revolution of the 1960s, and the women's and gay liberation movements that followed it in the late 1960s, were also benchmarks of social change. Women's and gay peoples' changing expectations for their lives in both private and public spheres had an incalculable impact on social and cultural life. For heterosexuals it became acceptable in many circles to engage in premarital sex and to have more than one partner—if not simultaneously, then serially. Women were attempting to define themselves as both sexual and independent beings fighting stereotypes of sexual passivity and financial and emotional dependence on men. Gay men and lesbians were declaring themselves publicly, challenging antiquated laws that forbade particular sexual acts as well as standards of dress and socially acceptable behavior for men and women.

While 1973 saw the end of a political mass movement against the war in Vietnam, aspects of the counterculture were still thriving. The women's and gay movements were still in their infancy and the spiritual legacy of the 1960s had transmuted itself into a diffuse but numerically significant third great awakening (see Hammond 1992).

Many historians and social theorists have put forth hypotheses that attempt to account for this sudden surge of interest in self-realization and personal fulfillment (Tipton 1982; Gitlin 1987; Gilbert 1986). Tipton (1982) attempts to clarify the worldview of the counterculture in contrast to those of mainstream culture: "The counterculture begins its conception of reality with the individual, not as an agent rationally pursuing her own self-interest, but as a personality that experiences, knows, and simply is" (14). He also states, "The guiding value of the second revolution was the central cultural and personal value of self-realization and self-fulfillment" (312).

Based on this definition of the counterculture, Tipton attempts to show the interrelatedness of the counterculture (Roszak 1969; Dickstein, 1989) with the subsequent resurgence of alternative religious activity. Values such as antimaterialism, anticonsumerism, spiritual connection to the land, universal peace and cooperation, communitarianism, vegetarianism, rejection of chemicals and pesticides, alternative medical paradigms, redefinition of traditional sex roles, respect for manual labor, a valuing of honesty above politeness, and a polymorphous sensuality were all part of the belief systems of different collectivities within the counterculture of this period. Since one of the most important values was that of individual fulfillment, commitment to any collectivity was extremely difficult to maintain. Most of the communes of the 1960s were very short-lived—some only lasting a season or a few months.

The counterculture's own structural and moral fragility also contributed to its downfall. Because it relied on unregulated feelings to realize its values, it could not institutionalize them stably. Its attempts to transform utilitarian culture outright or to ignore it completely were bound to fail short of overthrowing technological and bureaucratic society per se, and uprooting its values from the rebels' own outlook. And these attempts at revolution or utopia did fail. Large-scale social change in the direction of the countercultural ideals of mysticism, communalism, and socialism did not occur, either by radical political transformation of the old order or by ever-expanding growth of the new psychedelic lifestyle. (Tipton 1982, 29)

Many alternative religious movements, as well as the human potential movement that had first come into existence in the late 1960s, attempted to institutionalize some of these values. Rather than act to change mainstream political and cultural structures, many individuals withdrew from them, joining groups with others who shared their values and with whom they could experience being part of a community. As Veysey (1973) points out,

What, then, about the relation between cultural radicalism and man's social condition in the specifically modern context? During the 1950s a number of social scientists linked what they called "extremism" with the concept of "mass society." Alerted to the possibilities of an alarming social breakdown, both by the Nazi experience and by anti-Fascist writers like Erich Fromm, they pointed to a growing absence of genuine community in modern industrial societies in a way that interestingly parallels the more recent statements of American radicals. In "mass society," the individual increasingly drifts without attachment to firm social roles, such as might automatically have been his in medieval Europe or in tribal cultures. He is isolated, detached, "anomic," lacking clear norms. He floats through life without knowing why. In such a state he becomes prey to radical ideologies, strange religions, groups which promise to restore meaning to his existence. (69)

Veysey, a historian, did both archival and participant-observation research among several anarchist and mystical countercultures in the United States in the late 1960s and early 1970s. In one small community of thirty people in New Mexico who saw themselves as the avatars of a new civilization, he found that members came from highly advantaged backgrounds and had attended high quality universities from which many had dropped out. He experienced them as a very bright group—exactly the kind of people who would have become leaders in the established order if the times had not been peculiarly out of joint (Veysey 1973, 348). Veysey's description and impressions of the individuals in this community are strikingly similar to those of many individuals who came into contact with members of the Sullivan Institute/Fourth Wall community.

Veysey also discusses the limitations he found in the commune members' ability to think critically or speculate freely about ultimate questions (Veysey 1973, 349). They had accepted certain basic precepts put forth by their leader and simply parroted them. He noted that:

The vision of the universe which dominated their inner realm seemed to me a dank chamber, far more airtight than the underground tomb which I had finished building as my living quarters. And in it lived the demons of self-hatred, which were defined as "negative emotions," "resistance," and "false personality." Inside the closed box within which they speculated, the people here were flagellating the "grosser" parts of their own beings as if they were Penitentes. (Veysey 1973, 350)

The parallels between this description and the struggles members of the Sullivanian community went through are very close, though the explanations offered were quite different. In the Sullivan Institute/Fourth Wall community, individuals viewed themselves as engaged in a process of struggling against a restrictive self-system created by their mothers' role of transmitting the repressive nature of the dominant culture. In order to recreate themselves and experience the potential for true happiness and productivity, they were told they had to suffer through the anxiety generated by challenging those limitations.

In sum, the Sullivan Institute/Fourth Wall community was one of many experiments in communal living and personal transformation that came into being during this period. In its case, currents within the psychoanalytic movement, the legacy of the Old and New Lefts, and a countercultural critique of mainstream society converged in a particular way. The inclusion of these elements into a (seemingly) unified discourse that shaped the thoughts and communication of members was an extremely important factor in the growth and cohesiveness of the community.

THE CONNECTION WITH THE OLD LEFT

The two founders of The Sullivan Institute were products of a radical political subculture that had existed in New York and in other parts of the United States for many years. In addition to their membership in the Communist Party (CP/USA), Saul Newton had been a member of the Abraham Lincoln brigade—a group of Americans that volunteered and fought on the Republican side in the Spanish civil war.[5] Some general historical information about the state of the CP/USA is useful for contextualizing the Sullivan Institute. During World War II the CP adopted a platform of what it called "Popular Front politics." This term meant that it was the policy of the party at that time to unite with other antifascist groups, regardless of whether these were explicitly socialist or communist. After the war, when tensions between the United States and the Soviet Union began to rise, the CP/USA became increasingly isolated. The Popular Front policy was abandoned for a "left sectarian" (Isserman 1987, 6) position that viewed war between the U.S. and the USSR as inevitable. The leadership of the Republican Party, as part of its campaign to regain political hegemony, launched a fierce anti-Communist campaign (Halberstam 1993, 9), attempting to link all leftists with the brutal excesses of the Soviet Communist Party. The general political mood of the United States moved significantly to the right, as the McCarthy period began in the early 1950s. In 1956, at the 20th Communist Party Congress, Khrushchev made public the details of the Stalinist period. All these factors coincided to make the CP/USA a pariah organization.

Although Pearce and Newton had been connected with the Communist Party, neither they nor most other members or ex-members[6] were anxious to publicize this fact. Nevertheless, they retained important aspects of a communist critique of U.S. society, viewing the psychological problems that Sullivan observed as the result of the alienation of capitalist society. These convictions formed a crucial part of their theoretical outlook, and resurfaced openly again in the late 1960s, when the political climate was more receptive.

Not only did Pearce and Newton retain many of their Communist beliefs; they also emulated the structure of the CP/USA in terms of the leadership of the Sullivan Institute and their de facto control of the community that formed around it. The leadership followed the form of the psychoanalytic institute, which in practice meant that a small elite group made the critical decisions about admission to the institute, patient referrals, formulation and teaching of theory, and clinical supervision. This structure would not have had much impact on the patients if the community had not been formed,[7] but the fact that patients began to see their therapists socially to some extent, and to know who the supervising analysts were, made for a rigid hierarchical structure. Additionally, there was a great deal of similarity between the attitudes of Communists[8] and the attitudes of "Sullivanians" towards the theoretical analyses that formed the basis of their worldview. Both groups established a lifestyle that was based on their interpretation of the theoretical precepts of Marx (in the case of the CP) and of Sullivan. The notion of a "correct line" is applicable here. In the CP/USA this referred to the requirement that all members publicly support the Soviet Union in accordance with the analyses of their leadership. In the Sullivanian community adherence to the theoretical formulations of Pearce and Newton was required. No disagreement with the basic precepts of their work was tolerated—those who were skeptical either left or were asked to leave.

Whereas the late 1950s in New York City may have been fertile ground for a radical psychoanalytic institute like the Sullivan Institute, the advent of the social movements of the 1960s made it possible for the community to go from a tiny elite group of upper middle-class intellectuals to a much larger and somewhat more heterogeneous group. While membership of the group was always predominantly European-American,[9] the patient-members recruited in the 1960s were younger, less educated, not necessarily professionals, and came from various parts of the United States, and in some cases, other parts of the world.

The notion of the "personal becoming political" was not accidentally incorporated into the Sullivanian ethos. It came from the same critique that galvanized the movements of the 1960s—the critique of formal political structures as ineffective and hypocritical, of capitalist society as producing an alienated individual with false needs for consumer goods. In one sense, politics itself was humanized during this period; the humanist declarations of the Port Huron statement and the leftist poetry of Allen Ginsberg injected an affective aspect into the political sphere. In another sense, the personal became political—one's way of life was in itself considered a political statement. That is why the counterculture could not be considered truly apolitical—by founding alternate institutions such as communes, food co-ops, alternative schools, crafts workshops, and others, "hippies"[10] demonstrated their desire to make lives for themselves that kept them out of mainstream society because they considered it evil and corrupt.

The civil rights and antiwar movements that gained momentum in the mid-1960s and then funneled into the New Left impacted upon the Sullivan Institute community in a few different ways. Historians and other social scientists (Cushman 1986; Gilbert 1986; Lifton 1987; Whitsett 1992 to name only a few) have discussed this period as a time of social and psycho historical turmoil and dislocation. They cite events such as the civil rights and antiwar movements, political assassinations, nuclear threat, and the cold war as potentially damaging to the social fabric, namely, the families and communities of the postwar United States and therefore the psyches of the "baby boom" generation. Self-psychologist Heinz Kohut (1976) discussed the decline of religion and the changes in the family as problematic for children coming of age in the 1960s and 1970s. He theorized that the inability of most children to see their parents at work led to the loss of idealizable figures in the immediate social environment, and therefore to a tendency to search for other strong authorities. This research suggests that there may have been specific aspects of the psychological makeup of the children of the European-American middle-class—referred to by Kohut and others as "narcissistic hunger"—that made the existence of communities such as the Sullivan Institute group possible.

The cultural scene also impacted upon and was impacted by these movements. Andy Warhol and his coterie, various forms of folk and rock music, and the writings of Jack Kerouac, Ken Kesey, Allen Ginsberg, and others contributed to a culture of rebellion and protest against the dictates of mainstream U.S. society. First, they enabled the dormant activism of the Sullivan Institute leadership to express itself in various ways. Second, they created a whole new cohort of potential patients—young people who were critical of mainstream society and who had been exposed to the New Left, the counterculture, or both. With the advent of mass media, what might have remained a relatively isolated phenomenon became part of mass culture. Allen Ginsberg, Jack Kerouac, and the other Beats were not initially famous, but by the end of the 1960s, they had mass followings. The writings of social critics such as C. Wright Mills, Philip Riesman, and Paul Goodman became popular through the universities. This was true for popular music as well; the phenomena of jazz, rhythm and blues, and finally rock and roll initially began as the music of African Americans, but were adopted by European Americans before they were repackaged for a mass audience. The combination of the existence of a large cohort of young people admitted into institutions of higher learning in larger proportions than ever before and being exposed to various aspects of radical critique was an extremely powerful one.

Another aspect of the sociocultural upheaval of the 1960s was the questioning by some at very fundamental levels of received academic learning, and, in fact, of the importance of all "book learning," as opposed to direct experience-based learning. The question could be interpreted as one of "relevance"—an issue that suddenly erupted at the level of educational reform, and also as a total challenge to the epistemology of traditional academia.

Although not every college student dropped out in the 1960s, a high proportion did in comparison to other affluent periods in U.S. history. Experiencing the world firsthand, rather than mediated through books, became an acceptable life choice for the educated middle class (much to the chagrin of many parents). This weltanschauung became acceptable for individuals who considered themselves part of the counterculture and became craftspeople or farmers, and also for radicals who dropped out of college to participate in community or factory organizing.

On the international level, perhaps the most well known and extreme example of this type of movement could be seen in China, with the enormous upheaval of society created by the government-led cultural revolution. Contemporaneous with the burgeoning counterculture and student movements in the United States, Europe, and in some other countries as well, the Chinese cultural revolution was directed specifically at intellectuals who held positions of respect and power. While there are aspects of the Chinese situation that are, of course, drastically different from the Sullivanian case, there are certain areas of similarity as well. One of these areas is the use by those who hold political power of an alliance with a younger generation to disable opposition from older, more educated and established intellectuals. In this way the leadership of the Sullivan Institute discredited its first and second-year students, who held PhDs or M.D.s in clinical psychology or psychiatry in favor of the "trainees," who held no advanced degrees. On the basis of a crude (mis)interpretation of Marxist thought, the ideology of this period held that any learning that was not based in physical activity or experience was not valid. Based on this assumption, many teachers and other intellectuals were sent out to the countryside to help the peasants or to perform other public-works projects. Many were permanently deprived of their jobs and required to submit elaborate apologies and confessions. Some were sent to labor camps for "retraining" in Maoist thought.

The Sullivan Institute, which had started as a small, exclusive group of analysts and their patients, became, by the early 1970s, a community of several hundred people. It never attained a mass following, as did groups like the Unification Church, Synanon, or the Children of God at that time. This was partially due to the fact that it remained based in the highly secular and highly educated intellectual world of New York City's upper West Side. There is also reason to believe that the founders and leaders of the Sullivan Institute/Fourth Wall community never intended, or desired, that it achieve a mass following. Their conception of the relationship of the community to mainstream society owed a great deal to the Puritan conception of the "City on a Hill;" that is, a small group of exemplary individuals who by their actions would show the rest of the society a superior way to live.

THE RISE OF THE EXPRESSIVE ETHIC

Any attempt to discuss general trends in U.S. culture is fraught with problems. How can we generalize about a culture (if it is one culture) that is so diverse, so large both in territory and population, and that is constantly changing? Furthermore, if it is one culture now, has it always been? One can argue quite convincingly that before the advent of radio and television, there were several regional (and ethnic) cultures. Or even that each immigrant group that has come to the United States (including slaves) has maintained something of a distinctive character. Therefore, in attempting to put the Sullivan Institute/Fourth Wall community into an historical context, is it appropriate to discuss Tocqueville, Whitman, Emerson, and Thoreau? Or should we be discussing Freud and Marx, the culture of the U.S. Communist Party of the 1930s and 1940s, or the New York intelligentsia of the 1950s? Unfortunately, while there is no answer to this question, one answer is certainly that all of these phenomena are relevant. How they have interacted is still more difficult to ascertain.

In the well-known (and much-criticized) work, Habits of the Heart (Bellah et al., 1985) on the "American" character, the authors point to the increasing relegation of values (or "moral life") to the private sphere in our daily lives, leaving the public sphere increasingly dominated by instrumental rationality. The rise of psychology as a popular discourse is viewed as a contributing factor in the ever-widening gulf between system and life-world (Habermas, 1984). Bellah et al. provide an important perspective on the widening influence of the psychoanalytic worldview:

When morality came to be associated with the role of women and the family, and religion to be largely a matter of revivalist emotion, the split between the utilitarian and the expressive spheres in nineteenth-century America widened. Nonetheless, theologians and moralists believed feeling had some cognitive content, some access to the external world, and Whitman certainly believed his poetry was expressing the truth not only of himself but of the world. But with the emergence of psychology as an academic field—and, even more important, as a form of popular discourse—in the late nineteenth and early twentieth centuries, the purely subjective grounding of expressive individualism became complete. (Bellah et al. 1985, 46)

As the self has become increasingly dominated by the dichotomy discussed above, Bellah and coauthors argue that it has become more difficult for us to feel that our lives have any meaning beyond that of attaining personal satisfaction. In other words, for many people in U.S. society, our connections to any larger entity, such as a community or a nation, are extremely tenuous. Self-reliance, an American goal as old as the first settlers, is still extremely important for a large number of people. Economic self-reliance is an important component of this ideal, and most Americans aspire to be self-supporting. Therefore, those members of our society who are economically dependent are almost automatically considered to be less than full citizens in certain ways. One of the results of this belief can also be a moral justification for a type of individualism in the sense of not feeling any responsibility as individuals, or on the societal level, for those who have not "done for themselves."

For many people raised in middle- to upper middle-class homes in the United States, the ethic of self-reliance meant "finding oneself" at the personal level. Often it also meant a rejection of the more traditional conceptions of responsibility and familial obligation.[11] This concern with self-discovery and self-expression in U.S. culture can be traced backward to Whitman, and to Emerson and Thoreau as well. During different historical periods in the United States, there has been greater or lesser emphasis placed on the ideal of the "rugged individual." In the 1960s the number of young people (mostly college students) who viewed themselves as engaged in the project of discovering their "true path," or unique destiny, was much greater than in previous generations which had faced the challenges of the depression and World War II.

The expressive ethic was cultivated in the university—especially in the liberal arts colleges. In these institutions a great deal of value was placed on knowledge for its own sake—an implicit critique of the predominance of instrumental rationality in the economic sphere. The New Left was born in the universities:

During the 1960s, the New Left became a student movement housed primarily in the largest and most prestigious American universities. Here, middle-class students, predominantly studying liberal arts subjects, joined organizations like Students for a Democratic Society (SDS) and demonstrated for civil rights and against the war in Vietnam. By the late 1960s, these demonstrations intensified into an assault on the university structure itself, and the ideology of the movement deepened into a call for revolutionary socialism. (Gilbert 1986, 256)

The counterculture and the New Left impacted upon the cohort of middle-class college and even high-school students with much greater strength than it did on older people or on younger people who did not share the same degree of social mobility as the middle class. As Bellah pointed out in an essay written in the 1970s, the combined impact of the civil rights movement, the brutality of the war in Vietnam, and the challenge to the values of U.S. middle-class culture by its sons and daughters was far-reaching:

A style of dress and personal adornment was beginning to appear that made a large part of the youth generation look like homeless vagabonds. Long hair became almost an insignia. By looks alone one could not tell whether an apparent hippie was a Buddhist or a Marxist. Attraction to rock music, psychedelic drugs, and group living arrangements united both political and religious radicals, even if an interest in Zen meditation, also pioneered by the beatniks, did not have quite so catholic an appeal. Clearly, by 1967, with the Vietnam War replacing, though not obliterating, racism as the chief crime of the United States government, the disaffection reached an intensity that was more than political, more even than cultural, and that for many could only be called religious in its breadth and intensity. (Bellah 1976, 80–81)

The repugnance that many draft-age young people felt for the war in Vietnam was exacerbated by the antipathetic response of the government, and of many sectors of U.S. society. In this sense there was a dramatic distance between "the establishment," which included members of the older generations and a certain proportion of young people as well and the numerically smaller, but extremely vocal and visible, members of the New Left and the counterculture:

What had begun in the early sixties with civil rights marches, and matured in 1964 as the Free Speech Movement, ended in 1969 with tear gas, shotguns, firebombs, and Molotov cocktails in Berkeley and all over America. The fate of the New Left was in part determined by the behavior of the American state. The administration persisted in a war it could not win unless it employed means that were unacceptable to world opinion, the American people, and finally even to itself. Each step of "escalation" only revealed all the more plainly the pointless and fruitless brutality of the war. When opposition at home became bitter, extreme, and violent, first Johnson and then Nixon moved to repress it, but again with methods that goaded further opposition rather than suppressing it. In the end, as we now know, it was a draw. Both sides collapsed from inner fatigue more than outer defeat. Given the inequality of the forces involved in this David and Goliath encounter, we would have to declare the New Left the undisputed winner, were it not for its near total disarray well before the collapse of its bitterest opponent. (Bellah 1976, 83)

Bellah is writing specifically about Berkeley, but many of his observations apply to the New Left as a whole. He notes that in 1970 "the burned-out activist was almost as common...as the burned-out drug user. For many of them 'getting my head together' became the first priority" (Bellah 1976, 87). This was certainly true for many young people on the East Coast, and in university towns and cities all across the country, although it was probably less visible as a phenomenon in other places.

The founders and early participants in the Sullivan Institute community were part of a marginal "counterculture" that has had a long history in New York City. During the late 1960s and early 1970s, they were able to recast their theory and practice in a direction that enabled them to attract a larger following. They rejected "American" ideals of self-reliance in terms of each individual's need for a "do it yourself" existence, while stressing self-realization on the other hand. They rejected the primacy of interfamilial relationships, believing instead in a community of like-minded others. They sought to establish new cultural forms that would enable the individual to live a more fulfilling life in the face of the restrictive nature of traditional small-town U.S. society and the conformist consumer society that was rapidly replacing it.

CONCLUSION: POLITICAL AND CULTURAL CHANGES—THE NEW AND OLD LEFTS AND THE DEMISE OF THE COUNTERCULTURE

The political upheavals of the 1960s have already been recounted. However, it is important to reiterate here that both the leadership and the membership of the Sullivan Institute/Fourth Wall community had strong ties to various leftist organizations and teachings. Saul Newton viewed the theoretical innovations that he and Jane Pearce set forth in their book as adjuncts to his revolutionary politics. At the same time that he and Pearce were finishing Conditions of Human Growth (1963) and founding a residential community, the civil rights movement—and later the antiwar movement—were in full swing. Many of the therapists and patients in the group were active in one or both of these movements.

At the time there was nothing unusual about these beliefs or practices. If one had interviewed other residents of the Upper West Side of Manhattan who met similar demographic criteria for age, education, socioeconomic status, and ethnicity, it is probable that a similar percentage would have been involved with (or at least interested in) nontraditional therapies, civil rights, and the antiwar movement.

That the Sullivan Institute/Fourth Wall community was in some respects a combination of both the Old and the New Lefts is of special interest, since the relationship between the two in the larger context was characterized by a lack of continuing connection and support (Isserman 1987). In addition, Pearce and Newton's involvement with the CP/USA and later with the psychoanalytic community put them in the unusual position of attempting to combine these two different weltanschauung into one unified project. They embraced the New Left, and in the late 1960s and early 1970s were actively attempting to recruit patients and "trainees" who had activist backgrounds or aspirations.[12]

The decline of the Old and New Lefts is relevant to both the founding and the continuing existence and expansion of the Sullivan Institute/Fourth Wall community. The 20th Communist Party Congress, at which Khrushchev publicly admitted the truth of the Stalinist terror, took place in 1956. The Sullivan Institute was founded in 1957, and the training program was founded in 1970, as the New Left was declining. These might have been coincidences were it not for Pearce's and Newton's political involvement and aspirations.

The transition that the Sullivan Institute/Fourth Wall community made in the 1980s from a "post-millennial" to a "pre-millennial" group was directly related to changes in the political situation in the external world. Conservatism was gaining ascendancy as a popular political position in the United States, and it seemed that the liberatory impulses of the 1960s were ridiculous aspirations. It was not a time to celebrate the birth of a new social order. The leadership of the group mandated a "circling of the wagons," and the membership became increasingly isolated from the mainstream.

NOTES

1. In large measure because the leadership of the institute scrupulously avoided any publicity.

2. Mentioning the names of individuals without prior authorization is tantamount to "outing" them as members of a deviant group. Therefore, only those individuals who are deceased or have publicly acknowledged their membership are mentioned here.

3. The term "mainstream," although problematic, is used here to refer to norms, values, and mores accepted by dominant groups in society.

4. There were cultural factors at work here as well, for example, the Protestant Ethic.

5. Newton often recounted his experiences in Spain to community members. The most notable aspects mentioned by him were his claims that he was good at murder, and that he had killed Trotskyites and other so-called dissidents during his service.

6. During the 1950s many Communist Party members went underground—they retained their membership secretly.

7. It would have still had an impact on the community of psychotherapists composed of the training analysts and the students of the Sullivan Institute.

8. The capitalization of "Communist" is used here to denote Communist Party members.

9. This included a high percentage of Jews, some born in Europe. This is not surprising, given the high percentages of Jews in the Communist Party and in the psychoanalytic profession, especially in New York City.

10. This is in quotes because it was more of outsiders' term, rather than "freaks" or "heads," which were insider terms.

11. These changes are visible, for example, in the changing expectations of the commitment that the individual should make to extended family. The expectation that grandmothers will take care of young grandchildren so that the mothers can work or perform other household tasks is no longer a given for many families. Conversely, the expectation that aging relatives will reside with daughters' or sons' families is no longer to be taken for granted.

12. This was true insofar as these individuals did not seem to be interested in or able to criticize their teachings.

_____

Chapter 3

Theoretical Background and History of the Formation of the Sullivan Institute

THE U.S. PSYCHOANALYTIC MOVEMENT OF THE 1950S

The postwar period was a time of growth and change for the U.S. psychoanalytic profession. There had been an explosive popularization of psychoanalytic theory during World War II for a variety of reasons. The military employed many psychiatrists and psychoanalysts to provide mental health services for its troops and to weed out those recruits who were "unfit to serve." Popular literature and film of this period reflected a fascination with psychoanalytic ideas on the part of writers. The demand for psychoanalytic services was growing so rapidly that the approved training institutes could not produce enough graduates. (Hale 1995, 214)

Whereas the British psychoanalytic profession was able to maintain some unity after the death of Freud by incorporating the different theoretical perspectives of Anna Freud and Melanie Klein in the British Psycho-Analytical Society, there was no such institutional cohesiveness in the United States (Kurzweil 1989, 202). When Freudian psychoanalysts emigrated from Europe during World War II, they found a small psychoanalytic movement in the U.S. that no longer concerned itself with political and social issues as had been the case in Europe (Jacoby 1983, p. 9). Those who chose to remain within the more orthodox Freudian camp quickly became part of the medical profession, which charged high fees to wealthy patients. Any critique of society that may have been found in the work of the first generation of Freudians was lost.

Beginning before the World War II period, and increasing in magnitude during the 1940s and 1950s, some expatriate and American psychoanalysts diverged in specific and significant ways from more orthodox Freudian theory. As early as 1939 various debates within the psychoanalytic community resulted in a "radical break" between the Freudians and those who came to be known as the neo-Freudians (Ghent 1989, 175). Among the most prominent of these theorists were Erich Fromm, Frieda Fromm-Reichman, Clara Thompson, Karen Horney, and Harry Stack Sullivan. Central to their ideas were the rejection of drive theory, and their belief that the conceptual model of the id, ego, and super-ego was an insufficient construct to explain human personality structure. Additionally, and of central importance, they differed with Freud over the causes of psychopathology, believing that interpersonal and social environmental conditions—particularly the quality of the relationship of infants to their caregivers as well as the nature of the communities which the infant "inherits," the socioeconomic status of the immediate family and so forth—were causal variables of personality development. Sullivan's particular focus was on the interpersonal level of human experience, and his expressed goal was the creation of a comprehensive, interpersonally based psychoanalytic theory. His work was influenced by the theory of symbolic interaction put forth by George Herbert Mead, both substantively and methodologically. In terms of methodology, Sullivan based his theory on "observable things that go on between people" (Chapman and Chapman 1980, vii; italics in original). He knew that this notion was problematic because "there are no purely objective data in psychiatry, and there are no valid subjective data, because the material becomes scientifically usable only in the shape of a complex resultant—inference" (Sullivan 1954, 3; italics in original). In terms of theory, Sullivan took up Mead's proposition that individuals can only develop consciousness in an interpersonal context—in relation to other human beings.

Both Clara Thompson and Karen Horney had been members of the New York Psychoanalytic Society and Institute, the U.S. center of "orthodox" Freudian psychoanalytic teaching and practice. Horney's had been one of the more strident voices raised in criticism of certain aspects of Freudian theory. In two books, The Neurotic Personality of Our Time and New Ways in Psychoanalysis, published in 1937 and 1939 respectively, "Horney had increasingly rejected standard psychoanalytic theories" (Hale 1995, 139).

She argued that social and cultural factors, not the presumably uniform 'biological' experiences of infancy and early childhood, such as the Oedipus complex and the other 'stages' of psychosexual development, were crucial to the formation of neuroses. They were caused by a basic insecurity created by the conflict between hostile impulses and the need for affection. She was rejecting precisely the grounds on which Freud had established the criteria of heresy: the primary importance of his sexual theories. And in some passages she seemed to be founding a new school. (Hale 1995, 139)

In 1941 the New York Psychoanalytic Society voted to demote Horney from the status of training analyst to that of lecturer. Horney, Clara Thompson, and three other analysts walked out of the meeting and resigned. They formed the American Association for the Advancement of Psychoanalysis immediately thereafter. Sullivan and Erich Fromm were given the status of honorary members.

Sullivan was living in Bethesda, Maryland, when these events occurred, but was following them closely. He had started the journal Psychiatry with Ernest Hadley and had also been one of the founders of the Washington School of

Psychiatry. In 1943 Clara Thompson and Erich Fromm left Horney's group and together with Sullivan founded the New York City branch of the William Alanson White Psychiatric Foundation (Hale 1995, 218). The Washington-Baltimore Psychoanalytic Institute had already disaffiliated itself from the Foundation due to the political pressures that had arisen in New York between the American Association for the Advancement of Psychoanalysis, who had refused membership to Erich Fromm, and the New York Psychoanalytic Society. In 1946 the New York branch became incorporated separately as the William Alanson White Institute of Psychiatry in order to provide its students benefits under the G.I. Bill (Perry 1982, 391).

Unlike many Freudians, Fromm and his ex-wife, Frieda Fromm-Reichmann, Clara Thompson, and Sullivan worked with schizophrenic patients and believed that there was a chance for limited success with this population. Sullivan especially spent a great deal of his career working with schizophrenic boys. Much of his theoretical work is based on these experiences, and on what he called "the operational approach to the study of communications." (Will 1954, xiv in Sullivan 1954). His work is still considered pioneering and is greatly respected in this subfield. Among his theoretical contributions is an alternative (to Freud's) formulation of developmental stages. Sullivan's seminal work was accomplished at Shepperd Hospital from 1922 to 1930. He was given the freedom to set up his own ward of male adolescent schizophrenics. He banished all women from the ward and trained the attendants himself, making them part of the collaborative process, and stressing his belief that schizophrenia was a human process; that is, that all of us are able to understand schizophrenia and schizophrenics. The result was an environment in which patients and attendants were encouraged to minimize their differences and to make use of their similarities; many relationships, including friendships, were established between staff and patients, and the recovery rate was high (Perry 1982, 194–200) compared with more conventional regimens. Although he experimented with different clinical methods, such as hypnosis, Sullivan rejected most of them except for the use of alcohol with patients. He found that intoxication broke down a certain level of paranoia in his patients, and allowed them to proceed with their recovery. He also advocated the future establishments of camps and communities for recovering schizophrenics:

When...the efficiency of socio-psychiatric treatment has been demonstrated, I surmise that we will be encouraged to develop convalescent camps and communities for those on the way to mental health. In a not too distant time, these socio-psychiatric communities may come to be the great mental hygiene, with a great reduction in the incidence of major mental disorders, at least of the schizophrenic type. (Perry 1982, 196)

As an adjunct to Sullivan's interest in schizophrenic adolescents, and to his interpersonal theory in general, he reconceptualized the therapeutic relationship as one in which there was an active exchange between both individuals, and where the therapist became an advocate for the patient's improved understanding of his/her problems in living. While this description of a patient-therapist relationship may now seem commonplace, this was not so in the early days of the psychoanalytic movement, in which the Freudian orientation prevailed. Freud viewed the analyst as a type of tabula rasa, where the patient's feelings and thoughts about his/her life could be projected. Sullivan, following Ferenczi through his relationship with Clara Thompson,[1] developed the notion of an active patient-therapist relationship, in which he emphasized the role of the therapist as the *validator* of the patient's improved understanding of his/her own past experience and of the continuation of the process of maturation. The notion of validation in Sullivan's theory refers to his belief that the developing infant cannot consciously experience his or her needs unless they are acknowledged by a caregiver. Those needs that are not acknowledged are relegated to the unconscious, and it then becomes the work of the therapist to uncover them and to assist the patient in making them conscious by validating them, as the parent should have done initially.

Unlike other theorists and clinicians, Sullivan downplayed the importance of the analysis of transference as a core structure of the psychoanalytic process. The notion of transference refers to the tendency of patients to *transfer* onto the therapist feelings that they have about significant others in their lives (usually the parents). The therapist can (and usually does) become a larger-than-life figure to his or her patients. Many psychotherapists then consider it to be necessary to discuss these feelings with patients, in an attempt to both gain increased understanding of the relationship that they have or did have with significant others, and to build a more authentic relationship with the therapist. If this does not take place, there is a danger that the patient will continue to view the therapist as an omnipotent figure.

Sullivan utilized the methodology of participant observation—developed by other social scientists—to advocate both participation and a certain distanced perspective on the part of the therapist. He was an acute observer, and believed that there was a great deal to be learned from the nonverbal behavior of his patients. He also postulated that the self of the therapist was the "principal instrument of observation" (Sullivan 1954, 3). By this he means that the shared cultural and human context of the therapist and the patient is the basis for their communication. Beyond this, however, the therapist must never assume that he or she knows exactly what the patient means unless s/he has examined the statements carefully and critically. Convention can often lead people to unintentionally obscure the meaning of their statements if they actually know what they are attempting to say. If the patient does not know exactly what he or she is trying to say, it is the job of the therapist to help him or her clarify this:

A patient tells me the obvious and I wonder what he means, and ask further questions. But after the first half-hour or so, he begins to see that there is a reasonable uncertainty as to what he meant, and that statements which seem obvious to him may be remarkably uncommunicative to the other person. They may be far worse than uncommunicative, for they may permit the inexperienced interviewer to assume that he knows something that is not the case. (Sullivan 1954, 8)

Sullivan makes the point that all verbal communication is inaccurate, because words can never be 100 percent precise in their ability to convey our thoughts and feelings. Therefore, the therapeutic relationship is only a more self-conscious example of any conversation that two people might have. The difference lies primarily in the degree of attention paid to the interaction and to the patient's communications and feelings.

PEARCE AND NEWTON—THEORETICAL FORMULATIONS

As a student of Sullivan's, Jane Pearce, M.D., elaborated on several aspects of his work, both theoretical and clinical. In the theoretical arena, she strove to give more form and substance to the specific developmental stages elaborated by Sullivan. She also attempted to consolidate Sullivan's conception of the different systems composing the personality. At the same time, she, along with her husband, Saul Newton, attempted to take these ideas and his practice in regard to the development of therapeutic communities in the direction of actualization. Their plan was in many ways one possible (and logical) outcome of Sullivan's work, especially his interests at the end of his life when he began to view mental illness as a public health problem caused by adverse social and economic conditions. As Sullivan had come to conclude, Pearce and Newton viewed U.S. culture itself as pathogenic, and therefore it was the so-called "normal" individual who was pathological. Their community was not formed as a haven for "sick" individuals, but rather as a "city on a hill"—an example for the world to follow. For them, it was acceptance of the status quo in society that was insane—they used the phrase "pathology of normality." Insanity for Pearce and Newton is a set of functionally useful mechanisms developed in order to survive an emotionally limited or destructive parent. This defense system outlives its usefulness when a child is no longer dependent on his or her parents for survival, and needs to be analyzed in psychotherapy in order to be overcome, and for the patient to reach his or her full potential. According to Newton, the goal of therapy, and of human growth in general, was the development of the capacity for intimacy with others. This capacity was the hallmark of true maturity (Newton 1979, 10).

According to Newton, Sullivan's death in 1949 was followed by a repudiation of his theories by his students and colleagues, who felt that without him they could not continue to pursue his more progressive ideas. Additionally, the William Alanson White Institute, which had been Sullivan's base in New York, moved to disqualify non-M.D. applicants to their training program. Newton, who himself did not have an M.D., gave these two factors as the impetus for the founding of The Sullivan Institute for Research in Psychoanalysis. The first class of students was formed in 1957 (Newton 1979, 9–10).

Pearce and Newton viewed themselves as disseminators of Sullivan's theories, but they also envisioned their work as a radicalization of his ideas. As far as they were concerned, Sullivan was a liberal who did not take his critique of the family or of modern capitalist society to its logical conclusion. When they wrote Conditions of Human Growth (1963)—their initial and comprehensive theoretical statement—they mention that they plan a contemporary statement of interpersonal theory. While they do not openly criticize Sullivan in the book, statements from those who were involved with them at that time make it clear that they felt he did not take his critique of the family or of U.S. culture far enough. In her 1977 play, In the Beginning, Joan Harvey critiques not only the family, but also the role of the "establishment" mental health professionals in maintaining the attitude that individuals who were depressed or confused by the prevailing social order needed to "adjust." The following excerpt is taken from a speech that the main character, an eighteen-year-old who is in the process of leaving home, delivers to her parents: "Those mother-fucking doctors have sold us out too. They want us to learn adjustment, compromise and understanding. We should learn how to make it with you, just as you are. We have taken on your mottoes—order and consistency—so we'll learn to make it in the world just as you define it (1980b, 76).

By 1980 Joan Harvey was willing to say openly that Sullivan was "an apologist for capitalism and for the status quo" (Harvey 1980, 4).

One of the clearest points of theoretical difference between Sullivan and Pearce and Newton was Pearce and Newton's stipulation that conventional marriage is simply a continuation of the social isolation of the mother-infant dyad, and can be destructive to the individual's further growth. While Sullivan may have believed that this was the case with many marriages, nowhere does he generalize this opinion in regard to all monogamous relationships. Pearce and Newton also viewed parents in general, and mothers more specifically, as "donors of the status quo" (Harvey 1980a, 6). These ideas were put forth in Conditions of Human Growth. They were also actualized within the Sullivan Institute itself, in the sense that marriage was not considered an emotionally satisfying way of life. The leaders of the Sullivan Institute were, in some cases, engaged in sexual relationships with the spouses of each other's patients, and encouraged other analysts and patients to have all types of interpersonal experience in addition to the marital relationship. This included sexual relationships as well. Married couples who entered therapy with a Sullivan Institute psychotherapist were encouraged to "date" outside the marriage. This policy resulted either in the breakup of marriages or in the departure of couples from therapy and the community.[1]

In addition to their differences with Sullivan regarding monogamy and the role of parents in propagating the status quo, Pearce and Newton also diverged theoretically from him in their view of the role of anxiety in personal growth. For Sullivan, anxiety was an unpleasant and potentially dangerous concomitant of growth and insight for the patient. It was dangerous because a person who became too anxious could become unable to function in his or her daily life, and could experience a "psychotic break," commonly defined as a loss of one's sense of reality. For Pearce and Newton, however, anxiety was not necessarily to be avoided:

...Sullivan went by a clear-cut rule of thumb. The therapist if possible should only evoke that level of anxiety that they could work with within the framework of an individual session. It is the therapist's job, however, to search out in the course of a session the forces of anxiety in the patient and move towards them. What's wrong with most therapy is that it is not oriented towards evoking anxiety in the patient. . . .

...You must trust the proposition that growth is more important than anxiety....

In Sullivan's system, the avoidance of anxiety was considered a need on the same level as other needs. This is one of the major divergences from Sullivan's theory that we have developed. We do not believe that the avoidance of anxiety is a need. (Pearce and Newton 1970, 4–5)

This position on the role of anxiety in the maturation process was followed up in practice within the "Sullivanian" community in the sense that unusual behavior was often regarded as a sign of anxiety, which signified that the individual was undergoing a process of "real" growth.

Additionally, Pearce and Newton expanded upon Sullivan's conception of validation. Sullivan defined validation as the recognition by an adult of the infant's needs. The expanded notion not only took into account the recognition of needs, but the mood of the adult as well. In other words, if a parent or caregiver acknowledged and addressed a particular need of the infant's, but was in an agitated or irritable mood while doing so, this would have as negative an impact on the infant as the need not being met at all. The implications of this revision of Sullivan's theory are far-reaching—any adult who has anything other than totally loving feelings for the infant can harm him or her permanently.

Although Pearce and Newton believed they were following Sullivan's "true" intentions in their founding of the Sullivan Institute, their clinical methods diverged from his. While Sullivan had implied in some of his writings that individuals could get "stuck" at a particular developmental stage, he had not used this conception in the same way that Pearce and Newton did. The clinical method that they evolved consisted of diagnosing the patient as "stuck" in one particular developmental stage, and then formulating specific analytic "projects" that the patient needed to complete in order to become "unstuck," that is, to grow. If the therapist concluded that one needed more same-sex friends, the patient would be directed to find some "girlfriends" or "boyfriends" and "hang out." As the community became more established, therapists would encourage their patients to attend specific parties, or to rent a summer house in Amagansett (where Pearce and Newton maintained a summer home) with other patients of "Sullivanian" therapists. If a patient were found to be deficient in sexual experience, he or she would be directed to meet some new partners.[3] While Sullivan may have believed that individuals needed to make up lost childhood experiences, it is doubtful that he would have formulated specific projects for his patients, or that he would have been so directive in his prescriptions as to tell them to have more sex or to join a summer house.

The difference described here between Sullivan and Pearce's and Newton's clinical methods exemplifies how different practitioners can put the same theory to use. This was the result of personality differences between therapists, but also of very different ideological beliefs—progressive liberal versus authoritarian. While Sullivan stressed respect for the patient and a refinement of the communication process between analyst and patient as the critical factors in the therapeutic relationship, Pearce and Newton believed that ends could justify means. For them, the means of personality change in many cases was action first, understanding second. If an individual took certain actions, even if he or she did not want to or believe they would help, the results would show that the actions were warranted. These differences illuminate the importance of distinguishing between theory and practice, and between ideology and the dynamic, process-oriented approach that Sullivan emphasized in his work and teaching. While Sullivan may have adopted a developmental approach, he did not reify the stages of development into requirements or hurdles that a patient had to pass through before moving on to maturity. Nor was the goal of therapy for Sullivan what it finally became within the Sullivan Institute/Fourth Wall community—to create a "revolutionary" individual.

In order to understand the theory of Pearce and Newton, it is necessary to take into account that, like any theoretical formulation, it was constantly in flux. Different elements of the theory were stressed at different periods in their careers, and breaks with past formulations may have also taken place. Particularly because this theory was used to train several classes of therapists within the Sullivan Institute, it was constantly evolving. However, its evolution took place within the confines of an exclusive intellectual community—Pearce and Newton were less and less engaged in a dialogue with the psychoanalytic community at large. It can be said that by the late 1960s, Pearce and Newton were completely isolated from the rest of the profession. After The Conditions of Human Growth was published, their theory became a separate strand in the development of U.S. neo-Freudian theory.

To illustrate the changing nature of their theoretical conceptions, in The Conditions of Human Growth, which was their first and only published theoretical statement, Pearce and Newton mention that they incorporate, through Sullivan, Freud's notions of unconscious motivation and of the active nature of repression. (1963, p. 7) Later, in an unpublished paper written circa 1970, they criticized Freudian theory as "deeply pessimistic" about human nature, and therefore supportive of the "capitalist establishment:" "Given Freud's deeply pessimistic theories about man's nature and development, it is quite logical that his support of the capitalist establishment continued despite the writings of Karl Marx and the revolutions of 1848. His "apolitical" stance withstood the challenge of the Russian revolution and its initial libertarian social legislation such as abolition of laws against divorce and abortion" (Pearce and Newton 1970, 2). This is not something they would have said in 1957, when they still considered themselves part of a larger intellectual community. Additionally, they contrast Freud with Sullivan, who stressed the importance of interpersonal relationships in the formation of the personality, and of the general sociocultural environment. According to Pearce and Newton, Sullivan believed that "hostility between people is rooted...in social frustration" (1970, 3). This belief is a radical departure from Freud's belief in the innate aggressive nature of human beings.

In the opening paragraph of the Foreword to Conditions of Human Growth, they begin by stating that social and cultural changes generated by modernity have made it necessary for human beings to learn to cooperate with each other in ways that were previously unnecessary:

We live in a dangerous world. The technical inventions of the twentieth century have hurled us into the necessity in order to survive, of inventing hitherto unconceived social forms (italics mine). Both the invention and the implementation of such forms depend on a capacity for flexibility, cooperation, and rate of change in human personality never before crucial in the history of civilization. The more we can understand about our potential for individual growth and human interaction, and about the personal illusions and resignation that impede it, the greater the chance that people can meet the challenge for their own survival. (1963, 7)

For Pearce and Newton, the mother[4] is the first agent of repression in life, and the vehicle by which capitalism as a system creates the ideal capitalist citizen/consumer. Only those needs of the infant that she responds to will be met and become conscious; all others will be repressed by the child. This belief in the mother's ability to hamper her child's development extended to the physiological maturation process as well as the psychological. Many patient-members of the SI/FW community were told that their physiological problems were due to early maternal rage, which was directed toward them simply because they were "alive," while the mothers were thought to be generally "depressed" or "dead."[5] Unless other significant adults who would respond to the child's needs are accessible ("alternate validators" in Sullivan's terms), the child's growth will be limited. This ontological "fact" is then elaborated into a theory of personality based on three interacting systems: the self-system, the central paranoia, and the integral personality. While individuals are exposed to a myriad of experiences in early life, not all of these experiences are retained in consciousness. If a specific experience is reacted to with intense anxiety by the parent, it will be repressed by the child. Therefore, an individual's self system is composed of those experiences that are allowed to remain conscious. The self-system is composed of those functions, needs, and abilities that the individual can consciously act on, and that compose his or her self-concept. The other repressed experiences and needs remain part of the personality, but are unconscious:

The creation of the self-system is an inevitable by-product of our culture. The therapist's job is to undo, to destroy, the self-system. The goal is widening the horizons of the productive self-system. Most therapy is not oriented this way. And politically these therapists and their theories are apologies for capitalism. These therapists and their theories are the psychological counterparts of political liberalism...

...We believe in the withering away of the state and the restrictive self-system, a combination of the political and the psychological. (Pearce and Newton 1970, 5)

The central paranoia is composed of a set of "logical fallacies" (Pearce and Newton 1963, 16) that put forth the proposition that the unconscious experiences never took place, and never could. It serves to defend the self-system in the sense that it prevents the individual from experiencing certain aspects of life that would make the parents, and the individual, anxious. The central paranoia prevents one from growing beyond familial expectations. The infant's personality, according to Pearce and Newton, is organized to repudiate those needs that cause the mother to become overly anxious. The infant cannot reconcile the difference between his or her mother when she is loving and responsive, and when she is angry and distant (Pearce and Newton, 1963, p. 82). These two distinct aspects of the same person become (respectively) Good and Bad Mother. Needs that the mother responds to in a positive way are consciously experienced, while needs that she responds to angrily are repressed and become part of the central paranoia. According to Harvey, "If the patient allows a peer to become important past the construction of the self-system, this all of a sudden evokes intense despair and loneliness. A paranoid mood moves in to bring the patient closer to the mother" (Harvey 1974, 4).

The integral personality is referred to by Pearce and Newton as "the guerrilla fighter for growth of the personality" (1963, 14). It incorporates all experiences, whether these cause anxiety in the parents or not. By definition, then, the integral personality is not entirely conscious. Nevertheless, it is constantly pushing us to grow in precisely those directions that were most forbidden by our parents because it is these forbidden areas that are the most stunted. For Pearce and Newton, the integral personality is "who we really are" (1963, 21). It addresses itself to our true needs, rather than only those needs with which our parents can feel comfortable. This conception of the integral personality was an extension of Sullivan's work and was developed by Pearce and Newton in conjunction with other theorists at the Sullivan Institute (see Ghent 1989, 187).

The role of anxiety that is delineated by Pearce and Newton is important for an understanding of future attitudes within the community. Both Sullivan and Pearce and Newton had a double-sided view of anxiety. Anxiety was thought to be counter-productive in terms of acquiring new functions. In other words, an infant whose mother becomes extremely anxious when feeding him could develop digestive problems because her anxiety would interfere with the integration of the digestive functions.[6] However, Pearce and Newton also developed a positive view of anxiety. They believed that anxiety was experienced when people were attempting to do something new, to acquire a new function that would have evoked anxiety in their parent(s). Therefore, evidence of anxiety within the community was seen as a sign that the patient/member was challenging an early restriction and therefore growing beyond the narrow confines of the life that his/her parent would have wished for him/her. This will be discussed in greater detail in later chapters.

Pearce and Newton emphasize the notion that most parents limit the interpersonal growth of their children by limiting interaction with others who are different, either culturally or in terms of economic class. Furthermore, when children become adolescents, they are pressured to choose a career, a religion, and a mate for life before they have a chance to explore alternatives. This process reinforces cultural norms and stereotypes, often resulting in early marriage and acceptance of the interpersonal, cultural, social, and political status quo. In order to grow, the individual needs experiences with others who do not share his or her background and cultural assumptions. Early marriage and childbearing prevent the young adult from having these experiences and therefore limit his or her self-conception.

Later, after the Sullivan Institute became a large community, and during the cultural changes of the 1960s, Pearce and Newton wrote a paper that was never published but was circulated among the trainee therapists and some others in the community, called "Establishment Psychiatry—and a Radical Alternative." In this paper they carry the theory to much more radical conclusions than those they began with in the mid-1950s. They begin by stating that traditional notions of mental health are based on acceptance of the societal status quo: "Inherent in every psychological theory is an attitude about society as a whole. This orientation is expressed in definitions of mental health, insanity, normalcy, deviance, 'adjustment' and 'cure.' Most psychiatry is based on an acceptance of the established social order" (Pearce and Newton 1970, 1). They also emphasize that "the concept of sexual fidelity or even serial monogamy, which is central to the nuclear family, is also central to the restriction of spontaneous interpersonal interaction." They also advocate the discontinuation of pro forma parent-child relationships after adolescence, arguing that it can be destructive to both parties.

Due to the rapidity of social change in postwar society, Pearce and Newton state that notions of personal security are harmful delusions. In order to adapt to a constantly changing world, people must accept the fact that nothing is secure, including relationships. They considered the desire for security a neurotic symptom (1970, p. 6). The individual should live in a state of constant "revolution" in his or her personal (and public) life. Unlike most mainstream psychoanalytic theory, Pearce and Newton put forth the notion of radical personality change for adults. The implications of this belief were carried out in practice in what later became the Sullivanian community. Relationships were considered important inasmuch as they met certain needs for the individual at a specific period in his or her interpersonal development. If and when they ceased to meet these needs, they could become impediments to further growth and should be terminated. Stability was thought to be a false need.

Pearce and Newton use the repressive nature of postwar U.S. society as evidence of the need for a social and cultural revolution. They use a statement that Bobby Seale (a Black Panther Party leader) made—that a man and a woman should be able to enter into a relationship solely on the basis of natural attraction (rather than based on social factors such as race or class)—to lend a contemporary referent to their critique of the repressive nature of interpersonal relationships in capitalist society (Pearce and Newton 1970, 22–23).

Bobby Seale has said that the goal of the Revolution is that a man and a woman can get together on the basis of natural attraction.

He understated his case. The goal is for one person and another person to be able to get together on the basis of natural attraction regardless of sex, and whether or not physical contact is involved. This is not only the goal but also part of the impelling force towards revolution. (Pearce and Newton 1970, 22)

While Seale focuses his criticism on sexual relationships specifically, and on heterosexual relationships only, Pearce and Newton expand this to include all relationships. In other words, they believe that we should not only be advocating a sexual revolution, but an interpersonal revolution as well. Individuals should be able to form friendships with whomever they feel attracted to, regardless of race, class, gender, ethnicity, or any other socially constructed categories. They view the individual in contemporary society as isolated and bereft of love and caring: "The level most lives are led is without friends. Envy is acceptable. Isolation is there, and it may or may not be experienced. Caring is abhorred.

Each individual moves into a state where the exploitation of the other is acceptable. Each person accepts the premises of his own self-system without question" (Harvey, 1980, 6).

Pearce and Newton link their stated goal of revolution to a radical change in the organization of interpersonal life. They believe that the revolutionary process will produce the kind of human being they describe. This change includes the reorganization or elimination of the nuclear family. Pearce and Newton discuss this proposal in their scenario of the revolution that is to come. They point out that during a revolutionary period, traditional family and legal bonds are often superseded by one's membership in a revolutionary community. Once the revolution has succeeded, however, the revolutionaries usually return to the traditional family structures while attempting to change other aspects of society. Pearce and Newton are arguing that unless family structure is also changed, society will not be fundamentally different than it was before. The needs of all human beings depend on the development of a new type of society—one that can quickly adjust to rapid technological change.

For Pearce and Newton, who were loosely associated with various Marxist and anthropological views regarding human cultural evolution, social progress was measured in terms of interpersonal relationships. Their theory concerning the development of the individual, discussed above, is based on a belief that all culture is repressive, but that an evolutionary process is taking place that will eventually result in a nonrepressive world culture (if humans are to survive as a species). The culmination of this evolutionary process is the revolution, in which relationships will be radically changed and provide the basis for a new society.

THE DEVELOPMENTAL SEQUENCE IN PEARCE & NEWTON'S THEORY

In order to understand Pearce and Newton's rationale for the formation of the Sullivan Institute community, an overview of their conception of the process of human development is essential. In The Conditions of Human Growth, they give the reader a structured and sequential picture of the process of psychological maturation:

Infancy is the period between birth and learning to talk, at about two and a half. Childhood is the period between the development of speech and the age when the need for contemporary playmates becomes intense, characteristically from two and a half to four years of age. The juvenile era, which may last from four or five to eight or eighty, is the period during which the individual learns to deal with contemporaries in the group situation, by the political arts of compromise, competition and cooperation. Preadolescence is marked by the experience of chumship, when a contemporary assumes coequal importance with oneself, characteristically between age eight and puberty. Adolescence coincides with the onset of puberty. Adulthood refers not to maturity but to the age at which the parents have outlived their usefulness as the primary source of validation. (Pearce and Newton 1963, 69)

Each state of development is cumulative; therefore, it is not possible to consolidate the skills that need to be learned in the juvenile era before mastering those of infancy (for the most part). It is possible, however, for an individual to master certain tasks of a particular era without mastering others, and then to move on to the next developmental stage. As implied in this statement, certain types of growth must take place in order for an individual to become a mature adult. Pearce and Newton, however, characterize most adults, as "immature adults"—individuals who have reached the chronological age of adulthood and are somewhat independent, but who still retain many deficits from earlier developmental periods. In order to mature, both adults and children need what Pearce and Newton refer to as "tenderness" or "validation."

Pearce and Newton subdivide infancy into early and late periods. Their general conception of human growth is functional in the sense that they define developmental eras on the basis of particular functions that have been mastered by the individual. They define early infancy as the period between birth and learning to walk, and late infancy as the period between learning to walk and learning to talk. The important functions that should be integrated during this period are physiological—respiration, temperature regulation, food intake, mastery of certain physical movements, and an ability to identify the "emotional attitudes of the mothering ones" (Pearce and Newton 1963, 87). As mentioned before, Pearce and Newton believed that severe anxiety on the part of the "mothering one" during this period could result in physiological problems such as asthma and eczema.

Late infancy is conceived of as a time when mobility is of primary concern, and when the infant forms more selective relationships with people than previously. The world of objects is also very important to toddlers, and they spend a great deal of time attempting to master it. Although toddlers know some words, most communication is still carried out through dramatization. Pearce and Newton hypothesize that the ability to produce and enjoy music can be initiated during this period, but if it is not validated, the adult can become tone deaf. Again it is interesting to note the one-to-one correlation between experiences they believe were denied the infant and deficits in the adult. They also postulate that the infant's increasing independence is a threat to the mother. Anything that the child or young adult undertakes that was threatening to the early caretakers can cause severe anxiety and somatic symptoms or phobias (Pearce and Newton 1963, 90).

Pearce and Newton characterize childhood as the period between the development of speech and the conscious need for playmates. It is also viewed by them as the time when the child's experiences become "differentiated into those that are available to consciousness and those that must be denied and repudiated" (Pearce and Newton 1963, 91). Mastery of speech is an important hallmark of this period, and the number of significant adults increases to include others in addition to the parents. Interpersonally, Pearce and Newton characterize the most important development of this era as the integration of the function of parallel play. Parallel play is defined by them as "the positive mutual stimulation and empathy experienced by two children in each other's presence, while each is, at the same time, apparently focused on his separate individual project of physical mastery" (Pearce and Newton 1963, 93). This they consider to be the precursor of real empathy and friendship.

Pearce and Newton refer to the subsequent stage of development as the "juvenile" era. It is defined chronologically as the period between ages four and eight, and developmentally as the period after the child has developed some sense of physical competence in the object world, and has also achieved some competence at parallel play. While the child's world is still controlled by the parents, he or she has the opportunity to experience adults outside of the immediate family circle. This is seen as extremely positive because it allows the child to "validate impulses toward growth besides those sponsored by his family" (Pearce and Newton 1963, 99). Since the family is seen as inherently repressive of the child, the ability to expand one's horizons beyond it is extremely important in Pearce and Newton's theory.

The major projects of the juvenile era are cooperation, competition, and compromise with his or her peers. If the projects of childhood have been successfully integrated, the juvenile will be able to take on different roles with peers than the ones expected of him or her at home. The younger brother can become the lead in a school play, or the older sister can play the baby in a game. The juvenile develops a secure sense of participation in a group, and only on this basis is he or she able to take a position against the group at certain times. Those children who do not experience this security may be subject to following the dictates of the group unquestioningly. An additional concern of the juvenile period may be the search for alternate role models to those in the family— intense identification with fictional or other real people may take place.

If the individual is not able to accomplish these projects, he or she will be beset with problems in relating to groups, and a variety of pathologies can develop. He or she will only be able to participate in groups on the basis of relating to others in the same modalities as he or she relates to family members. Or, alternatively, new types of roles may be taken on, but they may feel unreal. Another type of difficulty can consist in the inability to consider people more interesting or important than objects or personal comfort. Or, if the individual is not able to take the perspective of the other into account, people can be treated as if they were objects. Pearce and Newton believed that a large proportion of society consisted of adults who were "stuck" in the juvenile stage.

The next stage of development, preadolescence, takes place (ideally) between age eight and the onset of puberty. It is characterized primarily by the development of what Pearce and Newton refer to as a "chumship." This is a love relationship with a member of the same sex in which one experiences the other person as very much like oneself, very important to oneself, and with needs that are just as important as one's own. Unlike the relationships of the juvenile era, it is not competitive or manipulative, and takes places independently of the parental frame of reference (Pearce and Newton 1963, 105). The chumship is critical to the development of self-esteem in the preadolescent—through the identification with another person and the cherishing of his or her experiences and needs, one comes to see oneself as also important and lovable. The chum becomes more important than the parents as a "source of validation and affirmation" (Pearce and Newton 1963, 106). Pearce and Newton consider this vitally important to the growth of the individual, because they view this type of friendship as the first significant expansion for the child past the parent's frame of reference. It is also the first experience of love between equals, rather than between a child and his or her parents, to whom the relationship is unequal and dependent. For Pearce and Newton, the chumship is often the height of an individual's life in terms of relationships (Pearce and Newton 1963, 107).

As with the other stages of development, the integration of the projects of preadolescence—namely, the chumship—can be interfered with for a variety of reasons. Pearce and Newton state that most people never reach this stage of development, and if they do, there are many cultural constraints that make it difficult to fully experience this type of relationship. However, they view it as a vital prerequisite to "genuine heterosexual love," which they equate with the search for a life partner, hence the stress within the community they formed on the development of same-sex relationships.

Adolescence, while theoretically following preadolescence, is not actually conceptualized in this way by Pearce and Newton. Since they believe that few individuals ever reach preadolescence, the issues of adolescence are often intermingled with those of childhood, the juvenile era, and preadolescence. They view adolescence as consisting of two primary projects: the capacity to love another individual, and the development of partnerships. In Pearce and Newton's terms, partnerships, while they may be viewed by the culture as marriages or romantic liaisons, do not necessarily imply any particular stage of interpersonal development. Partners may be working out juvenile issues of cooperation and competition within the context of their relationships, or, if they have integrated the experience of a chumship, they may be love relationships. Most adolescent partnerships are not true love relationships, according to Pearce and Newton, but "groups of two," in which the partners work on those deficits that they still retain from the earlier stages of development.

Regardless of whether the adolescent has consolidated these earlier stages, Pearce and Newton stress that once puberty has taken place, all children become immature adults (Pearce and Newton 1963, 111). All growth that could have taken place under the care of the parents has already taken place. The young person needs to move on, and to expand his or her frame of reference. Here they stress that cultural expectations diverge from the individual's real needs. While mainstream cultural norms dictate that adolescents live with their parents, their emotional needs require them to expand their horizons beyond their families. The importance of the family or clan, in Pearce and Newton's view, has diminished in modern society. This belief was one of the primary motivations for the formation of the Sullivan Institute community. They felt very strongly that young people needed to have intimate relationships outside of the family before marriage and childbearing took place. U.S. culture in the late 1950s was overwhelmingly family oriented, and encouraged early marriage and childbearing.

True maturity, for Pearce and Newton, is extremely rare in U.S. culture. They define it as "proportional to one's capacity to relate to his contemporaries, regardless of age, in the context of the process of extending love to include more and more people, and to find the common denominator with oneself in more apparently divergent people" (Pearce and Newton 1963, 116). They stress that mature relationships are not unconditional, because this would be equivalent to the bondage that the culture expects from individuals to state, church, and family. One should be free to continually reaffirm one's commitments voluntarily, but not to feel bound by obligation. The mature person is continually growing, continually making up for past deficits in his experience. He or she is able to expand on the concept of chumship to include identification with intellectual issues, with individuals in other places, and other times.

In the above discussion of the developmental stages delineated by Pearce and Newton, their argument for the formation of a community where patients and therapists would be free to make up the deficits in their interpersonal growth flows naturally from their scathing critique of the culture in which they were living. The overall ethos of U.S. society, with its emphasis on autonomy and individualism, did not lend itself to the development of close friendships outside the family, especially in adulthood. The emphasis of that time on early marriage and childbearing discouraged experimentation in adolescence or early adulthood with different types of relationships. This critique, although formulated in a unique way by Pearce and Newton, was only one of many that excoriated the banality and superficiality of U.S. society in the late 1950s.

THE FORMATION OF THE "SULLIVANIAN" COMMUNITY

Many of Sullivan's writings and his practice foreshadowed the founding of the "Sullivanian" community in the sense that he believed that many patients could be most helped by interacting with others in a controlled group setting. Pearce and Newton believed that he had led the way to a new type of psychotherapeutic practice. If one's problems in living had an interpersonal base, then the provision of a community in which one could form new types of relationships could be the vehicle for the cure. By making a rigid interpretation of Sullivan's developmental stages, they followed what they believed was his lead in terms of same-sex groupings, and encouraged their patients to move into same-sex group apartments. They did not view their encouragement of particular living situations for their patients as unethical. In fact, they believed that in some cases they were preventing these patients from being institutionalized; in others they viewed themselves as helping their patients become less isolated.

The influence of Sandor Ferenczi on Sullivan is also extremely important because it provided the basis in clinical practice for a different type of patient-analyst relationship. As stated above, a nonobjective role was preferred, and one that would actively promote growth in regard to the patient. It is extremely important for any understanding of the patient-analyst relationship within the SI/FW community that this reconceptualization is taken into account. However, while Ferenczi, Thompson, and Sullivan may have had a certain type of relationship in mind, Pearce and Newton evolved a concept that most practitioners today would agree was a great deal more directive than anything these earlier theorists would have intended, and involved the abolition of most professional boundaries.

The fact of Newton's and Pearce's prior Communist activism is also crucially important to the development of the "Sullivanian" psychoanalytic discourse. Although it is not documented in their early statements, the theory itself shows the impact in terms of its emphasis on the importance of external socioeconomic factors in the formation of the individual psyche. The decision by Pearce and Newton to form a community, to be activists in this way rather than to remain psychotherapists, affecting a disparate group of people, also reflects the radical political orientation of both founders. For the present study, this political aspect of the formation of the discourse adds the complex dimension of self-reflexivity to the actors being studied. In other words, they were aware of, and had their own specific notions regarding, the relationship of knowledge and power.

Pearce and Newton decided on the basis of what they called a radical interpretation of Sullivan's ideas to form a separate psychoanalytic institute, which they called "The Sullivan Institute for Research in Psychoanalysis." They viewed themselves as revolutionaries, rather than as reformers, the latter of which they believed Sullivan had been. The radical nature of their ideas centered on their critique of monogamous marriage and of "pro-forma" parent-child relationships. In other words, they believed that monogamy and the nuclear family in general were restrictive institutions that discouraged individual growth. They also argued that the continuation of relations between adults and their parents could only lead to a tendency on the part of the individual to continue to conform to the narrow expectations that the parents had for him or her. In order for their patients to become healthy, they needed to provide alternate experiences to replace the negative childhood experiences. This could only take place within a community of like-minded others, and away from parental influences. In the process of creating the community, they elaborated their ideas into book form and published The Conditions of Human Growth in 1963. While the book is not open about their desire to create a community (or about these other "radical" precepts), it does lay out the specific developmental stages that Pearce had extrapolated from Sullivan. The development of their "discourse" can be seen as taking place as the community evolved into an increasingly insular quasi "total institution" (Goffman 1961).

The new institute was located in Pearce and Newton's brownstone on 77th Street between West End Avenue and Riverside Drive on the upper West Side of Manhattan. The first institute training classes were held there. The new institute also began to take on patients, and to continue to formulate what they considered to be a radical conception of psychoanalysis. Pearce and Newton also attempted to apply Sullivan's methods of treating schizophrenic patients to those patients who had acute psychotic episodes but were not diagnosed as schizophrenic. They used these innovations to suggest the desirability of therapeutic communities.

[Sullivan] did extensive research into conditions that might lead to a positive outcome of an acute psychotic episode. Similar methods are being applied by many people who are trying to organize therapeutic communities. Some of the most effective of these applications can be seen in experiments in communal living. These experiments abide by the admonitions: "Hang together!" "Keep talking!" "Don't worry about eerie experiences!" "Protect against impulsive suicide!" "Maintain adequate manpower!" "Never do it alone!" (Pearce and Newton, 1970, p. 5)

As they accumulated patients in the late 1950s, Pearce and Newton (and their associates in the Sullivan Institute) began to experiment with a more informal approach to psychotherapy. In contradiction to established ethical norms governing the practice of psychotherapy, they socialized with their patients and encouraged them to meet and become intimate with each other and with themselves. Over a period of approximately ten years (1959–69), this resulted in a number of patients of Sullivan Institute therapists living together. At first patients rented summer houses together on Eastern Long Island; eventually some moved together into apartments on the Upper West Side of Manhattan.

Although it was not discussed by Pearce and Newton anywhere in print (at least not publicly), they were in the process of creating a community that would produce the "new individual" that they describe above. Two classes of M.D.s and Ph.D.s were accepted into the Institute's training program. During the late 1950s and early 1960s, a small community formed around Pearce and Newton. At first the community consisted primarily of the two classes of trainees, along with a small group of patients. These individuals, and some of their patients, began to live together and to share summer houses in Amagansett. Patients were encouraged to find living situations with other patients, and therapists to live with other therapists, provided they were of the same sex.

The custom of "dating" was instituted, here used to mean specifically that individuals of either sex would schedule specific times to engage in particular activities together—including anything from studying to having sex.

Many of the new patients and therapists were integrated into an already existing social circle and began to live together in groups, encouraged by Pearce, Newton, and the other psychotherapists who were in the Sullivan Institute. These living arrangements did not take place randomly; they were formed in consultation with the individual therapists and with Pearce and Newton. Men and women were discouraged from living together because it was felt that this would constrict their freedom to enter into relationships with other members of the opposite sex. The assumption on the therapists' part was that people who joined the community needed to have social experiences with a wide range of others. These experiences included sex as well as friendship—ideologically there was no distinction between those people one would have as friends and those with whom one would have sex. If members were allowed to live in mixed gender groups, the leadership believed they would be more likely to form "unhealthy" exclusive attachments to other members in their living groups.

This thinking completely disregarded the existence of homosexuality within the community in spite of the fact that there were gay members, and even two gay psychotherapists. While sexual experimentation was encouraged within the Sullivan Institute community, those who preferred to have sex only with members of their own gender were considered developmentally "stuck." In other words, they were acting immature and should experience the world of heterosexuality as well as that of homosexuality. However, this judgement did not work both ways—heterosexual members were encouraged to experiment, but if they chose not to have homosexual experiences, they were not considered "stuck."

The prohibition against "mixed" living arrangements resulted in some unintentional subversion of the founders' original intentions. By encouraging groups of women and groups of men to live together, they made it easier for homosexual relationships to go unnoticed. In some cases it was possible to maintain a relatively exclusive relationship with a roommate without attracting attention from the leadership. In other cases, roommates who were having romantic relationships were ostracized. Overall, homosexuals were a minority within the community, but a significant minority—probably composing the approximately 10 percent that are thought to exist in U.S. society at large.

Although the community was initially small—consisting of approximately forty to sixty individuals—during the late 1960s and into the 1970s, it began to increase its numbers. The appeal of a community that challenged mainstream notions of sanity, that regarded the "personal as political" in an activist sense, and that encouraged sexual promiscuity will be obvious to any reader who either lived through or has read about the culture of the late 1960s. Pearce and Newton realized that their chance to gain new patients for the institute, and to interact with a whole new generation of patients—the contemporaries of their own children—had come. They began to solicit younger patients, at first through their own and their patients' children. Several of the institute psychotherapists wrote letters to the draft boards requesting that patients and friends of patients be exempted from the draft. When they wrote these letters, they were often soliciting patients at the same time. For example, a young man would see one of the therapists for a consultation with the implicit purpose of getting a letter of exemption from the draft. The Sullivan Institute therapist would agree to write the letter, but would also recommend at the same time that the young man see a therapist. In 1970 the training program was initiated, with its stated goal of providing therapy for those who could not afford to see a licensed M.D. or Ph.D. The training program was the catalyst for the rapid expansion of the community.

THE ROLE OF CHARISMA

Although there is no doubt that the theoretical formulations of Pearce and Newton were one source of their attractiveness to others in their field, and to many prospective patients, it was not theoretical insight alone that motivated individuals to apply to the Sullivan Institute or to choose a particular "Sullivanian" therapist. Jane Pearce was an extremely intelligent and well-educated woman who was reputed to be a good therapist. Socially, however, she was often extremely uncomfortable—not charismatic. Saul Newton, however, was experienced by many people, not only women, as extremely compelling. One ex-member describes his first encounter with Newton:

It was at a group banquet in Amagansett, L.I., on Water's Edge Road. I was the only non-shrink at table, a new recruit. Blanche told me Saul really liked writers, but he seemed chary of me, and I later learned he thought I was out to do a job on his group in the press.

The meal was bluefish baked to a turn. Saul's Corsican chef, an anarchist, doing penance to the Stalinist-Sullivanians, prepared a special ice cream bombe for dessert. People seemed to be unusually mellow; some were holding hands.

The man opposite me had just finished explaining why he'd given up his career as a painter to become one of Saul's therapists.

"I really love Saul," he said.

"You mean you had no talent?"

"I love Saul," he said. "What else matters?"

"Talent, sometimes," I replied.

"I didn't love myself that much," the man said, sheepishly. (Elman 1991, 33)

. . . I can remember watching a celebrated modern painter with a big six-figure income and galleries showing his work around the world cower before a withering summary of his character structure and then try to appease the old devil with a gift of a painting allegedly worth thousands of dollars.

Philistines are more impressed with the jawbone of an ass. Saul couldn't be bought except with money.

"YOU'RE ALL A BUNCH OF DESPERATE FAKERS, LIARS, AND SCAM ARTISTS," he would tell the artists, "AND YOU KNOW IT, WHICH IS WHY WE TALK." (Elman 1991, 34)

While this account is retrospective and clearly influenced by the author's anger at Newton, it is still able to capture others' feelings about him. For many patient-members, Newton was a distant and somewhat frightening patriarch. For others, he was a stern but loving father. For the many women that were involved with him over the years, he was captivating in a variety of ways—perhaps in different ways for different women. Still other women were simply expected to deliver sexual services on demand. In any case, he was an extremely powerful leader who was able to maintain the community in some cohesive form for over thirty years. Without Saul Newton there very probably would not have been a Sullivan Institute or a Sullivan Institute/Fourth Wall community.

Newton's particular attraction for certain artists and certain members of the intelligentsia consisted in his ability to take advantage of the self-deprecation and guilt that in many cases come with the label of "artist" or "intellectual." While such individuals have often been held up to society in certain historical periods as exemplars of the pinnacle of human achievement, there has always been an anti-intellectual and anti-artistic strand running through U.S. culture. For the object of this stereotyping, the results of these mixed responses from the public can be a feeling that one is a fraud and doesn't deserve any special treatment. This is even more likely to be true of those individuals whose political sentiments run from liberal to leftist. Many of the fainter of heart were dazzled by Newton's stories about the Spanish civil war and his military abilities. He was the quintessential working-class hero—albeit a Jewish one.

According to Max Weber, charisma arises to meet extraordinary needs— "those which transcend the sphere of everyday economic routines" (Weber 1978). The birth and expansion of the Sullivan Institute grew out of a need in some segments of U.S. society to go beyond accepted truths about relationships and families, about success and the superiority of the American "way of life." As discussed earlier, the late 1950s and the 1960s were periods of political, social, and cultural upheaval in many parts of the world, including the U.S. Newton's charismatic abilities were able to meet the extraordinary needs of those who were searching for alternatives to more traditional ways of life.

CONCLUSION: THE IMPORTANCE OF CONTEXT—THE MACRO LEVEL

In order to understand the larger context in which this community came about, what enabled it to attract so many adherents, and what caused its demise, it is necessary to examine the milieu in which it came to exist. In historical terms, three predominant strands of U.S. intellectual, political, and cultural life intersected to provide the sources from which the founders of the Sullivan Institute/Fourth Wall community drew both theory and practice. All involved significant shifts or breaks with past traditions, and the challenging of previously accepted sources of authority and wisdom.

Changes in intellectual life that were pertinent involved primarily those related to psychoanalytic theory and the psychoanalytic community. Changes in the political landscape involved the emergence of the New Left, its relation to the Old, and the demise of leftist politics. Changes in cultural life involved the emergence of countercultures and dramatic, rapid shifts in lifestyles and values.

CHANGES IN PSYCHOANALYSIS AND THE PSYCHOANALYTIC COMMUNITY

We have examined the place of the Sullivan Institute for Research in Psychoanalysis within the psychoanalytic movement of the 1950s and 1960s. Many voices were raised during this time period against the elitism and single-mindedness of both the theory and method of the U.S. psychoanalytic movement, and the neo-Freudian critique gained widespread acceptance.

In the 1940s and 1950s, psychoanalytic theory and techniques had been popularized in the United States by magazines, filmmakers, television, novels, and practical books such as Dr. Spock's *Baby and Child Care* (1946). In the 1960s an explosion of popular books and new therapeutic techniques reached the general public. Paul Goodman, Norman O. Brown, Herbert Marcuse, Erich Fromm, and many others published books that were widely read, and that were extremely critical of the degree to which conventional Freudian psychoanalysis accepted U.S. culture.

In addition, R. D. Laing published several books during this period that placed much of the blame for adolescent schizophrenia on repressive societal and family conditions. He founded treatment centers where disturbed teenagers lived together with therapists, and advocated psychotherapy that focused on the family as a system that could be responsible for mental illness. Esalen Institute in Big Sur, California, was also founded during this period, and became a national center for innovative and radical therapies. In this context the Sullivan Institute was part of an international movement that challenged received wisdom in almost every field of human endeavor. While this movement could simply be seen as part of the process of modernizing Western Europe and the United States, I think it is more accurate to regard it as a disjuncture with previous periods, and as a challenge to aspects of enlightenment rationality *and* traditional religiosity.

NOTES

1. Sullivan and Thompson were both colleagues (Sullivan was Thompson's mentor) and friends, and at Sullivan's suggestion, Thompson went to Europe to be analyzed by Ferenczi for a few consecutive summers, and then returned and imparted what she had learned to Sullivan.

2. This was common knowledge among members of the community, including myself.

3. I both observed and participated in these practices during my adult membership in the community (1974–85).

4. The word "mother" is used almost exclusively in the class notes to refer to the primary caregiver. This is reflective of the predominance of mothers as sole caregivers in this historical period, and therefore of the antipathy toward mothers that was common in the psychoanalytic community at the time.

5. These are terms that were actually used by the therapists who were in the Sullivan Institute.

6. This is also an example of a somewhat determinist approach to psychopathology.

The "Halcyon" Years: 1969–78: Expansion and Consolidation of the Community

While the Sullivan Institute community may have begun as a trickle that was part of the small stream of political and cultural critique of the 1950s, it was soon caught up in the flood tide of social, political, and cultural activism of the 1960s. While the founders of the institute itself did nothing intentionally to initiate this sea change in U.S. values and behavior, it certainly affected them profoundly, and they also used it to their advantage. Some members of the community had participated in the antiwar and civil rights movements, but most only did so peripherally. Some had participated in the counterculture—living in communes and rejecting mainstream sexual, religious, and economic values. In terms of the more cultural aspects of the 1960s—the "sexual revolution," and the human potential movement—the Sullivan Institute theories and practices dovetailed perfectly with these more popular aspects of the cultural milieu of that period. E. C. discusses his move into a "Sullivanian" group apartment:

There was nothing outstanding about the whole thing. I moved through a number of different groups of people. There was the whole hippie scene in downtown Newark, and then, and then there was this separate hippie scene that was in Orange, so this was another hippie scene. At that point it wasn't all that different. The biggest difference that I remember was that because M.V. was in the [training] program we couldn't have grass in the apartment. At that point people still smoked in other places, but we couldn't. But some other guys had an apartment on the tenth floor, so we went there. (E. C. 4/5/88, 9)

At this point in the history of the community, it was just one of many "alternative lifestyles" proliferating around the U. S. and in many other parts of the world. While the "Sullivanians" may have been somewhat notorious in the psychoanalytic community in New York City, in terms of the counterculture they did not stand out. In later years, as the country grew increasingly conservative, the community became more authoritarian in its practices and more noticeably different from the mainstream. This contributed to a feeling amongst insiders of being separate and special—both "above" the general public and persecuted by it.

THE ETHOS OF THE PERIOD

During this period in the history of the Sullivan Institute community, the emphasis was on individual growth and expression. Patients (and therapists) were encouraged to express their feelings openly, even if that might result in confrontation, or in screaming at others in anger, or regression to some infantile state. The term "catatonic" was used often to describe individuals who "were getting in touch with their feelings." So an individual community member might come home from seeing his or her therapist and say

I had a very difficult session, I just need to space out tonight and watch a movie because I'm digesting all this heavy material. . . .

So this meant something good was happening, if you had a lot of anxiety or you were catatonic. Later on, as functioning became totally valuable in regard to keeping the theater operating, etc., etc. these things became bad. (Ofshe 1988b, 22)

As discussed in greater detail below, the overarching conception of the community that was held by the leadership at this time was that it would provide a safe and nurturing environment in which both patients and therapists could integrate those experiences they had failed to have in earlier periods of their lives. The Amagansett experience was thought of as a summer camp for adults, and the group lifestyle in the city as an extension of life in a college dormitory.

THE SULLIVAN INSTITUTE TRAINING PROGRAM

The community grew slowly throughout the 1960s, until the initiation of a new type of training program at the institute in 1970. This program took as students young people who had little or no previous formal training in psychology and put them into private practice immediately. A bachelor's degree was not required, nor was any prior training in psychology or counseling. The "trainees"[1] became the third class of students at the institute[2]. They were required to be in therapy with one of the "training analysts," to be closely supervised on all their patients, and to attend Sullivan Institute classes and seminars. These younger therapists (most in their early twenties) charged a nominal fee for their services, thus attracting many people who could not have afforded psychotherapy with a licensed therapist. The result was an exponential increase in the membership of the community from approximately fifty to sixty people to over 400.[3] This number includes people who, as David Black put it, were not members of the inner circle who lived and socialized exclusively with each other (Black 1975, 37). During the 1970s it was possible to be somewhat involved with the community, in therapy, and so on, and to live alone and maintain relationships with outsiders. Later this became impossible, as the number of members declined and "mainstream" society became increasingly hostile to "deviant" lifestyles.

The young therapists or "trainees," as they were called, lacked any prior formal training in psychology or counseling, a factor that made it extremely difficult for them to question or critically examine any of the teachings of the Sullivan Institute faculty, thereby concentrating even greater power in the hands of the training analysts. At the same time that the trainees were becoming the intermediary strata between the leadership and the patient-members, several of the older therapists, who had for years enjoyed a great deal of power and prestige, were essentially cast out of these positions. They were thought to have been less innovative than the trainees because they had all been through formal clinical training before coming to the Sullivan Institute. Therefore, according to Pearce and Newton's reasoning, they were less able to learn or practice this "revolutionary" kind of psychotherapy. Many of these older therapists discontinued their practices and found other types of work.

Behind the formation of the training program was an elaborate theoretical conception. Pearce and Newton envisioned the program as making possible the provision of therapy to individuals who could not have otherwise afforded it. They were specifically interested in taking on patients who had been involved with the New Left as a means of creating future political leadership. E. C. discusses the political goals that the Sullivan Institute leadership incorporated into the formation of the training program:

What I was told to say when I went for my consultation . . . there was a whole thing about how much you were going to have to pay to be in therapy and M.V. coached me that I should say that one of my things was that I wanted to do more politically. Then it was more likely that I wouldn't have to pay a lot. That one of the reasons that I wanted to get into therapy was that I was unhappy with what I was doing politically. (E. C. 4/5/88, 22)

FORMAL AND INFORMAL INSTITUTIONAL STRUCTURES

Several informal institutional structures developed within the Sullivan Institute community during this period. The formal structure consisted of the Institute itself and its programs. The informal structures guided the daily life of each individual member, including therapists as well as patients. Before discussing these structures, it is important to describe the hierarchy that promulgated them.

As he or she was integrated into the community, the patient-member became aware of a more or less clearly delineated hierarchy within the community. Status was granted for different reasons depending on the period in the evolution of the community. In the 1970–79 period, the leadership consisted of four "training analysts" who supervised all other therapists. The next level down was that of the students or "trainee" therapists, and then of patient-members. One gained prestige in several ways: by "dating" (having an ongoing relationship with) one of the leaders or the therapists, by moving into a living situation with leaders or therapists, by becoming a therapist, or by transferring from a trainee therapist to one of the "training analysts" for therapy. In 1978, when the Fourth Wall Repertory Company started to become the main locus of member activity, the prestige system was affected in that it became extremely prestigious to be chosen for a leading role in any of the theater productions. A new avenue of status attainment was added.

The social hierarchy in the "Sullivanian" community can be described visually as a pyramid. At the top of the pyramid was the leadership; composed in the early years of Saul Newton and Jane Pearce, it gradually changed. Newton and Pearce divorced in the early 1970s, and it was Pearce who was somehow demoted from a leadership position. Newton married Joan Harvey, but also had been in a long-term relationship with Helen Moses, whom he married after he and Harvey divorced. Harvey then married Ralph Klein. By the early 1970s, the leadership of the community consisted of Newton, Harvey, Moses, and Klein, all of whom bought a building where they lived as couples[4] with their children and three other roommates. These four held the positions of training analysts in the Sullivan Institute, and in order to be accepted as a trainee, one had to be in therapy with one of them.

At the next level down on the pyramid were the trainees. This category included any therapist who was not a member of the leadership, and had patients in the community. In the 1960s the first two classes of students at the Sullivan Institute were from traditional psychoanalytic backgrounds—they all had either M.D.s or PhDs. in clinical psychology. The third class (which could also be broken down further into the different years they joined the program) had almost no members with advanced degrees. Both these groups formed the second level of the hierarchy within the community, although there were significant differences in the degree of power they wielded. Although the first two classes of students had been fairly high up in the power structure in the 1960s, their status declined with the advent of the new training program in 1970.

It is important to understand how and why this took place, because it was part of an anti-intellectual movement[5] within the Sullivan Institute community that took different forms in later periods. This type of anti-intellectual movement became more predominant in the late 1960s and early 1970s as part of a counter-cultural critique of functional rationality, and was also adopted by parts of the New Left (e.g., Weathermen, Yippies, etc.). This was the period when SDS split up into several factions, some of which advocated revolutionary violence, rather than "empty talk and theorizing" (Gitlin 1987, 392). Nor was it solely confined to the United States. The 1960s were a time of international questioning of certain aspects of the traditional social order, as discussed in chapter 1. The cultural revolution in China moved intellectuals to the countryside to become farmers because they were thought to be inhibiting change. It is not surprising, therefore, that Newton (who had not been trained as a clinician) was able to convince the other members of the leadership that the new young trainees, who lacked any formal educational background in psychotherapy, were somehow superior because they hadn't yet been "fucked up by the system." The older students were often passed over for new referrals, and were no longer looked upon with the same degree of respect than had previously been the case. In a conversation reported in an article by a member at that time, Newton mentioned that his heroes were "Harry Stack Sullivan and Chairman Mao" (Elman 1991, 34).

Later, when the Fourth Wall Repertory Company was founded in 1977, the leaderships' notions of democracy became much clearer. The issue of democratic process, or of how decisions were made in the Sullivan Institute/Fourth Wall community, is extremely important to any attempt to understand the experience of those inside it. Newton had said many times over the years that democratic political process was not a viable form of governance for states or for smaller entities. He proclaimed himself a communist and made it quite clear that he preferred the examples of Stalin and Mao to those of Trotsky or any Euro communist model. He believed strongly in the notion of a vanguard party, and saw himself and the other members of the community leadership (whom he had chosen) as that vanguard.

With regard to power and hierarchical relationships within the group, the lowest level of the pyramid was the patient-members of the Sullivan Institute community. Since each therapist often had approximately twenty patients, there were considerably more patients than there were therapists, so this level was also the largest component of the group. Within this group there was a great deal of differentiation in terms of prestige between newcomers and individuals who had been "around for a while," and also between patients who were seeing members of the leadership (either for psychotherapy or socially) and patients who were seeing trainees, although this was somewhat variable.

It is important to note that in spite of this three-tiered structure, with the possible addition of other, more refined differentiation between individuals, every member of the community was a patient, except for Saul Newton. He was the only individual who was not formally in treatment. This means that while the middle level of therapists was in a more privileged position vis-à-vis the patients, all members were subject to Newton's authority in one way or another.

"Dating"

The attempt to actualize the theory discussed in the previous section resulted in the "construction of hitherto unconceived social forms," which became institutionalized over the years. One of the most important of these was the "date." The notion behind this was that in order to grow, each individual needs to be exposed to a variety of people and experiences. As mentioned previously, monogamy was considered an outmoded cultural construct, which constricted the individual's growth and well-being by severely limiting his or her intimacy with many people. Whereas in mainstream culture, the term "date" was most commonly used to refer to individuals who were seeing each other with romantic intentions, the "Sullivanian" usage was quite different.

The social lives of community members were, to a great extent, directed and regulated by the therapists and the leadership. The organization of members' social lives revolved around the "date," a block of time that could take place in either day or nighttime, during which people spent time together engaged in various activities. During this period of the group's evolution, the "date" was the basic unit of all social activity." Dates" were categorized in various ways: as "drink" dates, "dinner" dates, "study" dates, "sleepover" dates, and even "fuck" dates (the purposes of these being obvious from their descriptions). It should be noted that the "sleepover" date entailed sharing a bed with someone of either sex for the night, and did not necessarily include sex. However, it was generally assumed that if one agreed to a date with a member of the opposite sex, sexual activity would be part of the date. Group members who primarily identified themselves as lesbians or gay men were expected to engage in heterosexual sex. Heterosexuals were encouraged to "try out" gay or lesbian sex, but were not expected to do so.

The therapists advised their patients to have as many dates as possible with different people, and to pursue any activity that might interest them. They were also encouraged to have sex with any other member that they felt attracted to. Although it was up to individuals to seek out sex partners, it was not acceptable to choose only one person, nor was it considered desirable to spend much, if any, time alone. The interpersonal emphasis of Sullivan was interpreted to mean that no psychological growth could take place without direct interaction with other people. This included reading, which could easily be viewed as an interpersonal activity, even when engaged in alone, since one is reading the words that another person has written, and presumably being affected by him or her, even if he or she is not physically present at the time:

If you were alone, you were made to feel guilty about it. . . . They'd ask, "Why are you avoiding the experience of sharing your time with someone else? . . ."

Being alone is dangerous. Being alone may allow one to find strength that is not dependent upon the group. . . .

It is possible for a Sullivanian to have a walking-on-the-beach date for an hour, a play date for two hours, a lunch date, a work date in the afternoon for four hours, a women's group or a men's group, a house meeting, a dinner date, a class in *The Conditions of Human Growth*, a late date, and a sleep-over date. Dates are made weeks in advance. (Black 1975, 55)

CLASSES

During this period in the history of the Sullivan Institute community, a "renaissance" spirit prevailed. Each member was encouraged to fulfill his or her creative potential in all areas of life. At this point many different classes were taught within the community—painting, writing, dance, poetry, and so forth. Members were encouraged to join these classes and to fully explore their personal potential for artistic and intellectual expression. All classes were taught by members of the community, and in order to teach, one had to obtain the permission of one's therapist, who had to check with the leadership. Not every member was considered mature enough to teach, but the individual who was interested in teaching would not be told this in so many words; the individual would be told that he or she either lacked the necessary experience, or that he or she was not "nice" enough to teach.

Those who were selected to teach the classes were usually professionals in these fields, and the community had a high percentage of members in creative fields, as well as in academia. In this respect, the demographic makeup of the community reflected that of a segment of the Upper West Side during that period. The basic ideas behind the pedagogy used in the classes were those of progressive education at the time—students were encouraged to enjoy the act of creation or participation in the class rather than to focus on the finished product, or on performing better than the other class members. There were no expectations that any student needed to learn a certain amount, or achieve any particular level of proficiency in order to be successful. Success was defined in terms of enjoyment of the process, and of the interaction with other students.

GROUP APARTMENTS AND SUMMER HOUSES

. . . What I ended up doing was getting the thrill of the beginning of many relationships and I took that to an extreme. There were a few times where I was dating fifteen different women, especially coming out of the summers, those wonderful summers! It would be like, you know, having four dates a day. (E. C. 1988, 10)

The quintessential "Sullivanian" experience of this period in the life of the Sullivan Institute/Fourth Wall community was that of group living in general, and particularly the "Amagansett" experience. Amagansett is a small town on the eastern tip of Long Island on the Southern shore; it is the last town before Montauk, which is the tip of Long Island. Pearce and Newton owned a house there as early as 1955, and when the Sullivan Institute was first formed, students and other training analysts were invited there for weekends. Later, as the community grew, other analysts and patients began to rent summer houses in Amagansett to be near each other on vacation. In the 1970s, this trend exploded into a situation where there were as many as twenty houses rented and six houses owned by group members. Although it was not required that patients summer there, it was expected. One had to have a very good excuse not to be involved, or else risk being labeled a recluse or simply a person who was "too scared" of contact with other human beings. This type of label had serious repercussions within the community—since all positive human experience was thought to reside in relationships, a person who was "too scared" to get involved with other people was seriously risking his or her mental well-being.

In the 1970s the patient summer houses could have as many as twenty members or shareholders. Some people rented half-shares, which usually meant they were entitled to come to the house every other weekend and for some vacation period during the summer. In this respect, the social structure of the Sullivan Institute community was no different from that of many young New York City residents who rented houses together on Fire Island or in the Hamptons (of which Amagansett is considered part). However, there were several significant differences. One of these differences was the "dorm room"/"date room" configuration adopted in many of the patient summer houses. This was an arrangement in which house members did not have specific rooms assigned to them. Instead, depending on whether they had a date with someone they intended to have sex with, they were assigned a "date room," which consisted of a private room with a double bed, or a "dorm room," which usually consisted of three or four mattresses, often on the floor, where house members and their same-sex dates slept.

In terms of social activities, the Sullivan Institute community summer houses were structured quite differently than other summer share houses. They were for the most part limited to patients of "Sullivanian" analysts, although occasionally a friend of a group member was allowed to join. Houses were limited to same-sex members, just as group apartments in the city were. Most members came to the house on weekends, and those who could get time off from jobs would often come for anywhere from one week to one month. During the summer weekends, the average day was a whirlwind of activity compared with the average summer weekend for someone who was not in the community. The morning might consist of a writing or art class, or a group trip to the beach. Some members might see their therapists on the weekends, if a session had been canceled during the week, or if they were in any type of crisis. Afternoons could also consist of classes, trips, or dates. Most weekend evenings consisted of a group social activity— specific houses would make "dinner dates," in which the members of one house would visit the other and participate in barbecuing, cooking, and often heavy drinking. After dinner one or two houses would usually sponsor an evening party to which the houses in that social circle would be invited.[6] The parties usually lasted until two or three in the morning with more drinking, dancing in the common areas, and some couples going off to private rooms to have sex. People who didn't have overnight dates would often go to the parties to "pick someone up." Sleeping alone on a weekend night in Amagansett was regarded as somewhat of an interpersonal failure.

The personnel in the summer houses were determined in several different ways. During the 1960s through the mid-1970s, the therapists' offices were also used as part of a communication network for the community. Signs were posted advertising summer house meetings for people who were interested in renting a house with other patients in Amagansett. Other signs announced parties, some publicized classes that were accepting students, still others mentioned guitars or beds for sale, or people who could type or edit student papers. S.B. described the experience of going to the summer house meetings:

. . . Then I started to go to summer house meetings, to try and find people I would be in a summer house with. And that became like another kind of women's group, in a way. It helped to have been in a women's consciousness-raising group, because then I could go into these group meetings in the cult that felt a little like that, and the people kind of looked like that, too. There was kind of a way that people looked, like kind of like hippies, you know, it felt like a familiar group somehow. (S. B. 1988, 4)

S. B.'s description illustrates a few aspects of the group structure. One is that in creating its social forms, the community adopted both styles and contents from existing frameworks in the New Left and the counterculture. Another is that the summer house groups, like all groups within the Sullivan Institute community, served a dual function. First, they served their stated function as a means whereby individual patients could find summer house roommates, and second, they served as informal social groups where patients could meet each other, form friendships, and possibly find roommates for their city apartments.

The summer houses for patients, as opposed to those for therapists, which were much more carefully put together, were composed of individuals who either knew each other prior to their involvement with the community, or who attended the meetings, or who met each other in some other way, such as at a "Sullivanian party," or even in their therapist's office, where, as opposed to most offices of this type, patients were encouraged to talk to each other.

The Amagansett experience had more significance for group members than that of summer recreation. It attained a kind of mythical status in the minds of many members because it was the birthplace of many of the utopian, almost ecstatic aspects of group experience. Although the "Sullivanians" were known for their "wild" parties in New York City, the parties in Amagansett could be even wilder because there was more space, fewer neighbors, and often more attendees. For example, in the summer of 1974, a few houses in East Hampton were rented by group members, one of which was a mansion with a swimming pool. One party held at this house had over 100 people, half of whom were in the pool at the same time! The "wildness" consisted of heavy drinking, couples (and larger groups at times) departing for various bedrooms to have sex, dancing, which was often done in circles, loud rock music, jumping, splashing, and other games in the pool. A useful analogy in today's cultural scene might be the fraternity party, although even these may be much tamer now than the parties of the 1970s.

Amagansett, because of its relative isolation, was the scene of some of the more unconventional aspects of the "Sullivanian" experience: "Sullivanians who feel they were weaned improperly wander around sucking on pacifiers. Sullivanians who feel they missed out on the experience of hanging around with pals go out and cultivate adolescent-type friendships" (Black 1975, 55). It was not unusual to see group members with stuffed animals, or drinking "screwdrivers" (vodka and orange juice) out of baby bottles. In certain respects, the community mirrored the activities of the Esalen Institute in California, and other trendy therapies of that time that purported to allow participants to relive and "work through" infantile or early childhood traumas.

A large number of the new patients (and some nonpatients) who came to Amagansett for the first time were integrated into an already existing social circle and began to live together in New York City. Group apartments in the city usually consisted of fewer roommates than was the case in the summer houses. Most members had their own rooms—some shared with one other person, except in extreme cases.[7] These apartments usually consisted of anywhere from three to eight roommates, each of whom had his or her own room. The organizational framework of these apartments was specific and unique—each group met once or twice a week for "house-meetings," which covered both the physical organization and the interpersonal aspects of group living.

The physical organization of the group apartments in the earlier years consisted of each member paying a certain amount of money per month into a joint "house" account. One member would be chosen as the treasurer, and would collect and disburse the money. Almost every apartment hired a cleaning person who would come once a week and would clean the kitchen, bathrooms, and common living areas. Individuals were responsible for cleaning their rooms to some extent. Many houses rotated cooking, dishwashing, and shopping chores on a weekly basis. In other words, a different roommate would do the weekly shopping each week, a different member would cook dinner each night, and another member would clean up after dinner. Later, more complex arrangements were devised to free members from housework. Many apartments hired someone to shop weekly, and many also hired cooks for at least a few nights a week. These arrangements varied somewhat from apartment to apartment and depended in large measure on the income of house members. Sometimes two apartments that were in the same building, or in adjacent buildings, would hire a cook who would set out dinner in one apartment, and the residents of both apartments would eat together. The cooks, cleaners, and shoppers were almost exclusively members of the community, so this was one way that members supported each other. However, this lifestyle became increasingly expensive with the addition of each new service.[8]

House meetings were used to discuss both relationships between roommates and to help each house member with his or her personal problems. Most apartments at some time or another would decide to "do history." This meant that each person would attempt to give the others an account of his or her life, beginning with the parent's backgrounds as well. These accounts would usually mirror those that were given to the therapist in the early stages of therapy, and recapitulated at various points along the way. Histories included the interpretations of the therapist as well as the patient's recounting of his or her life story. They were often taped by the individual giving the history, for possible use in therapy. Other house members were expected to give their comments—to use their own insights to help the presenter understand his or her history more thoroughly. Disagreement with the interpretations of the therapist would not have been welcome. It would usually take a few months for a house to get through every member's history—each person would usually take a few weeks.

Other "interpersonal" issues that were dealt with in house meetings included intragroup and extragroup relationships. Members could be criticized for failing to perform household responsibilities reliably, for staying alone in their rooms too much (being "isolated"), for being too involved with any one other house member (or nonmember) to the exclusion of others, or for being generally "angry" or "depressed." They could also be praised for improving their attitudes, their relationships, or their performance of house responsibilities. Since the group apartment was the site of the day-to-day practice of the "new social forms" that the community was attempting to implement, it was considered extremely important to monitor each house member's participation.

There were many occasions where members were asked to leave a particular apartment. This was never done without the knowledge of, and was often at the instigation of, a therapist. Although the rationales for these actions were always psychological, there were often motives of politics and prestige behind them:

One Sullivanian who questioned the authority of Saul Newton in a men's group was given a matter of hours to vacate his room in a group apartment. He wasn't even allowed time to find another apartment. . . .

Another Sullivanian, whom Saul Newton overheard making a slighting remark about a girl in the group, was told by his therapist not to come back. Newton had immediately called the therapist and passed down the word that the patient was to be ostracized. (Black 1975, 56)

On other occasions, group members would be asked to leave a particular apartment, but not "kicked out" of therapy or of the community at large. In these cases they would be given time to find a new living situation, and would be treated with some degree of concern as well as disdain. S.F. described a roommate of hers who had "fallen from grace" in a more prestigious group of members, and was "exiled" to S.F.'s apartment, which was clearly a step down in the hierarchy of the group.

She talked about this disgraceful thing that she had done which made her fall from grace, which was part of her falling from grace, which was that she had been in a consciousness-raising group with all the therapists in the group and all the women from the training program and E.O. E.O. had been doing her history and C.G. fell asleep while E.O. was doing her history, and that was like a capital crime. This was considered the worst thing that a person could do, and she used to talk about it as through she was like a felon. (S.B., 1988, p. 10)

Another instance of a member who was asked to leave his or her apartment was described by L.C., and took place in the first few years of his membership in the community and the training program. He was living in a group apartment with several other therapists, and Saul Newton and Ralph Klein (two of the four leaders of the community) became honorary house members because they wanted to participate in an all-male house situation even though they were living with Joan Harvey, Helen Moses, and two female trainees at the time. During this period, L.C. turned down an invitation to spend a weekend with Newton, Moses, and one of the female trainees, who he was dating at the time. He reported that his refusal was taken as evidence of his immaturity, and therefore he was asked to leave his apartment and to live with other men who were lower down in the group hierarchy.

CHILD-BEARING AND CHILD-REARING

Child rearing and childbearing were restricted in the community to only those members who were deemed mature enough by the leadership. In the early to mid-1970s, only therapists were allowed to have children, with the exception of one woman, an anthropologist who was very close with the leadership. Even those members who were approved to have children were restricted in their choice of a parenting partner. It was not possible to simply select a mate and decide to have children together. One had to have one's choice approved by his or her therapist, who was mandated to consult with the leadership before granting approval. In the early years of the community's existence, most members either did not have children, or entered after having already become parents. The handful of women and men who did become pregnant or adopt babies during this period were either therapists who were students at the Sullivan Institute, or patients of the leadership.

Since monogamy was not an acceptable arrangement, individuals who wished to have children might or might not choose to do so with another person. In the 1960s four male therapists chose to have children without partners, and adopted babies from South America. Three other couples in which both partners were therapists were given permission to have children during the 1960s. In the early 1970s three female patients also decided to become single parents, and bore children who had no acknowledged fathers. The leadership decided that one of these women was experiencing post-partum depression. Saul Newton and Joan Harvey (who had replaced Jane Pearce by this time) decided that she was "too angry" to be a parent and the baby was adopted by another woman in the community who was in favor with the leadership at the time.

Pearce and Newton incorporated the concept of a Leninist political vanguard into their practice in the Sullivanian community. Pearce and Newton, and, later, Harvey, Klein, and Moses, who were the other training analysts in the Sullivan Institute, were considered the most emotionally mature, and therefore the political and interpersonal vanguard of the community. During this period Saul Newton married Helen Moses and Joan Harvey married Ralph Klein. The two couples bought a building together where they lived on separate floors as couples, but with separate rooms. Joan Harvey and Helen Moses were Newton's fifth and sixth wives respectively, and Ralph Klein married Harvey after her divorce from Newton in the mid-1970s. Although the leadership were the only married couples in the community permitted to practice cohabitation, it is important to note that these were not monogamous marriages; both spouses were free to have sexual relationships with other members, and did so.[9] The other therapists were considered to be directly below the leadership, and the patients were thought to be below the therapists in regard to their level of interpersonal growth. This belief system resulted in the elaborate and rigid hierarchy of political, social, and sexual power within the community.

The couples who were permitted to have children did not live together—the children usually lived with the mothers on a regular basis and spent one or two nights a week with their fathers. Due to the belief system that was based on *The Conditions of Human Growth,* neither parent was expected to spend what would be considered an optimal amount of time with their children in mainstream terms. Full-time child care was hired for all children of group members, based partially on the belief that no parent should have to take care of their child on a full-time basis, and partially on the notion that mothers usually behaved in an envious and hateful manner toward their children.

Beginning in approximately 1970, nonleadership parents were instructed to send their children to boarding schools. For some of the children this began as early as three years of age. The rationale was the same as that for full-time child care—the less exposure to one's parents, the better one's mental health would be. Conversely, it was considered that parents needed to "get on with their lives," meaning that they would be mentally healthier if they developed interests and activities separate from their children. Pearce, Newton, and the other members of the leadership believed that one of the primary causes of maternal envy, and therefore of neurosis in general, was a lack on the part of mothers of activities and interests that would excite them and stimulate their creativity as their children grew less dependent on them and finally left home. Therefore, it was believed that as long as a parent provided his or her children with good child care, education, clothing, and enough money to buy or do anything they wished, it was preferable that they spend as little time with them as possible.

In 1976 one of the patients who had sent her son to boarding school was sued for custody by her ex-husband (the father of the child), who was not a member of the community. He claimed that W. E. was an unfit mother because she had sent her son away to summer camp at age three, and to boarding school at age five, which is generally considered to be quite young for camp and boarding school in this culture. W. E.'s therapist was called to testify in the case, and he affirmed that she was not fit to raise the child, and testified that she had been advised to send her son away "for his own good." On this basis the judge awarded custody of the child to the father. A section of the court's judgment is quoted below:

Concededly, because of her heavy work and school schedules and psychiatric analysis plaintiff did not visit Jim very often. In fact rarely. When Jim visited her in New York City, he was usually left in the care of baby-sitters, due to plaintiff's busy schedule...

Based on her actions and conduct, the court must conclude that plaintiff is unable to accept the role of a mother and duties of motherhood. She continually defers parental responsibilities to others through schools and camps. . . .

. . . Plaintiff is still more concerned with herself, her school and her career. Undoubtedly plaintiff loves her son but spends more time with her therapist than she does with her son. She has been in therapy since 1971. (Law Journal 1976, Bollinger v. Bollinger 6–7)

This decision effectively ended the practice of sending children away to school—but it did not prevent several situations in which children suffered the psychic pain of separation from their parents. Some of these children experienced debilitating psychological problems at the time of separation or later in life. One committed suicide later, one attempted suicide, several became heavy drug users, and one became a repeat felon. Others became successful, highly functioning adults. Following is an excerpt written by the stepmother of a child who was sent to boarding school and attempted to return to live with her father, rather than her mother, who was a group member.

Nine years ago, Virginia sabotaged our plan to have Katherine live with Steven and me. Katherine was fourteen, and it had been more than ten years since she had lived in a family. I expected some passive disapproval from Virginia and the commune, little else. Our plan, after all, demanded almost nothing from Virginia, who knew that Katherine was unhappy to be so far away in New Mexico where the commune always sent their children to school. I thought, with Steven and I taking care of Katherine's day-to-day needs, Virginia might play the part traditionally reserved for divorced fathers. She could visit with her daughter now and then, and reap the benefits of having a teenage daughter who was eager to admire her mother's accomplishments. . . .

"She cries and says that she's miserable," Steven explained. "She wants to live with us. That's all she keeps saying."

The headmaster told Steven that Katherine was rebellious and refusing authority. Our home represented far more than escape from school, he reassured us. It was a chance to live with a parent, a chance for Katherine to make a long-held fantasy a reality. "It would be very good for her," he said. Legally, Virginia was the custodial parent, and Steven also feared reprisals from the commune, but the headmaster was willing to take the risk of releasing Katherine in our custody.

"What did Virginia say?" we asked Katherine as soon as she hung up the phone that first day home.

'She didn't say much of anything,' Katherine said. As the day, unfolded, I grew confident that Virginia would do little to interfere with her daughter's new life. We relaxed. I helped Katherine unpack, and we discussed how we'd make small alterations in her bedroom. . . .

Suddenly, the dog scrambled to his feet and barked angrily; the brass door knocker resounded throughout the house.

"Who the hell is that?" Steven said loudly, and then, without opening the front door: "Who is it?"

"Katherine! Katherine!" A shrill female voice: "Give me Katherine! I want my baby. My Baby!"

"Oh my god, it's Mom," Katherine said. From the kitchen I saw the beams of flashlights. There were two people at the front door alone with Virginia. A third beam of light moved from the driveway toward the porch.

"She's not alone," I said.

"This is a commune scare tactic," Steven said. 'Lock the kitchen door and the porch door. Hurry.'

. . . "Come back in the morning, Virginia." Steven opened the door a crack, positioning his weight behind it so that he could shut it quickly again if he needed to.

. . . Two weeks went by with no word from Virginia. Katherine broke the silence to telephone her mother and announce that she'd begun to menstruate: "So what do you want me to do about it?" Virginia responded. Katherine lay crying on my bed: "A girl wants her mother at a time like this."

. . . For most of Katherine's life, Virginia had been a mother by long distance. Twice a year she saw Katherine for one day when she bought Katherine clothes and took her to the dentist and doctor for checkups. Katherine blamed the commune for coming between them. . . .

After the third week, Virginia telephoned: "You have two weeks to return to boarding school. If you don't, I will wash my hands of you entirely. I will never speak to you again or have anything to do with you."

. . . "If you ignore the threat, Virginia will give in," we told Katherine, but she was not prepared to take the risk. We did not blame her. (Neufeld 1989, 80–81)

Community members commonly used the tactics employed by Virginia to deal with threatening outsiders. They were almost always masterminded by Saul Newton and carried out by trusted members. Two additional group members accompanied Virginia in order to intimidate Steven, Alice, and Katherine. In most of these cases, the dialogue was scripted by Newton and the person's therapist, and Virginia would have been following specific orders regarding both her statements and her actions.

Child-rearing and childbearing practices within the community changed somewhat in later years. These changes will be discussed in the following chapters. The basic premise, however, remained the same—that the less time children spend with their parents, the better their mental health will be.

COERCION AND VIOLENCE

Newton was known within the Sullivanian community for his penchant for threatening members with violence, and, at times, striking them. He often boasted of his involvement in the Spanish Civil War and in World War II—he claimed to have a talent for murder. In approximately 1970, a baby-sitter told one informant that Newton was physically abusive to Joan Harvey, his wife at that time, on a regular basis. Others have reported that on several occasions Newton struck other members, or ordered others to do so, arguing that this was a constructive means of expressing justified anger. On one occasion, when something was stolen from a communal rehearsal space, he ordered a forced search of every apartment in the community. On another occasion he and Joan Harvey ordered the violent takeover and occupation of a theater that the community had leased, including physical violence and property damage. Later he organized an armed security force to protect himself and other members of the leadership.

Most important in terms of its impact on the community was the fact that Newton approved of the use of violence under certain circumstances. This usually meant that he needed to approve any violence that might take place either within the community, or by members of the community. He orchestrated most of the incidents that took place—L. D. describes one of these:

I personally was very afraid of Saul. He hit me a couple of times. He once had G. T. beat me up, visibly. That's not even that long ago. I was living at Joan's and I had waked G.T. up. He was sleeping upstairs in Helen's room and he was supposed to be baby-sitting for one of the kids on Joan's floor. And it was 9:30 on a Sunday morning and I called

Helen's number because I knew George was up there. M.W. and me were baby-sitting and she said to call George and wake him up. . . . And the next day George followed me into the elevator and hit me twice and slapped me right across the face. I had two really black-and-blue marks here. And he said "That's for waking me up." And he said, "This is from Saul and this is from me. And don't ever do that again." (L. D. 1993, 27)

Later, several incidents of violence took place toward both outsiders and ex-members of the community. These will be discussed in the following chapters.

The issue of coercion in the context of the Sullivan Institute community is a complex one. In terms of the threat of physical violence, Saul Newton did threaten violence on a regular basis, and was capable of physically and verbally attacking individuals he felt were challenging his authority or that of his wives or lovers in some way. It was not uncommon for individuals to be asked to leave the community and given no time to find another place to live—these people were hardly mentioned by members, the stigma was so great. The effect of these actions was to intimidate the remaining members so that they would be extremely unlikely to do anything to arouse Saul's anger. In other words, it was not necessary to threaten every member of the community in order to achieve compliance—one or two "examples" a year sufficed.

In addition to the threat of physical violence, then, the threat of sudden expulsion from the community was always present. The effect of this threat on the membership was pervasive—inasmuch as the group served as an alternate family *and* social support system, as well as a source of employment for many of its members, the idea of any member suddenly losing his or her living situation, friends, lovers, therapist, and possibly even his/her source of income as well, was terrifying. Regardless of whether or not this fact can be defined as coercion, it was a powerful force, which effectively silenced most dissent.

The community was also notorious for using orchestrated acts of intimidation and feigned hysteria as a means of silencing any individual or group who attempted to act against its perceived interests. In the discussion of child-rearing above, one of those incidents is described with regard to the child of a group member who attempted to live with her father, who had left the community. Many others occurred during the history of the community. Some of these will be described in later chapters.

THE ECONOMY OF THE SULLIVAN INSTITUTE COMMUNITY

In the 1969–78 period, with the inception of the training program and the expansion of the community, the cost of therapy with a trainee was quite low relative to the amount charged by most psychotherapists at that time. Trainees began working for as little as $5.00 an hour thereby making it possible for college students and other young people with very little money to afford therapy. Group apartment living was also relatively cheap, since the average apartment had approximately five members who split the rent of an inexpensive (at that time) apartment on the upper West Side of Manhattan. Initially, many new members of the community were students or other individuals who did not have steady sources of income. Summer house membership was an additional expense, but most members could afford to split the rental with ten or fifteen other people. In addition to all this, almost every group apartment hired a cleaner as a matter of course, and later most hired cooks and shoppers as well.

The amount of money required for membership in the community rose continually from 1970 on. Whereas it had initially been possible for students, artists, and free-lance workers of various types to live without working full-time, the cost of therapy and of group living went up each year. The combination of these factors with the overall economic downturn in the United States in the late 1970s eventually resulted in a situation in which many individuals decided to leave the group for economic reasons[10] Others took full-time jobs as typesetters (a relatively highly paid skill that had recently been de-unionized), waiters and waitresses, taxi drivers, or any other work that could provide enough money to pay for therapy and apartment expenses. Graduate students used government loan money to pay their living expenses, thereby accruing large debts. Other members went to their families for money, saying that they needed help with their education, or that their therapy was helping them and that they needed additional funds to pay for it.

Many members worked double shifts or held down two jobs in order to maintain their community membership. Members who were also parents had even greater demands placed on them. While this is true of all parents in most cultures, it was much more expensive to have children in the Sullivan Institute community because the definition of a decent life for one's child usually included private school, sleep-away camp, and often therapy as well. Many members were heavily in debt—some borrowed from richer members, others evaded their taxes, and still others declared bankruptcy. These situations were rarely addressed in therapy or by the leadership, and if they were, they were usually considered the patient's individual problem. In a group that professed to have a communal orientation, each individual was held responsible for raising the funds necessary to pay the expenses of life inside the community.

Each apartment had a house account with a designated treasurer who collected a predetermined amount of money that varied house to house depending on rent, the cost of a cleaner, and the shopping and cooking situation. In the early days of group living in the Sullivan Institute community, certain tasks were divided up among the residents of each apartment, such as cooking and shopping. Later, most apartments hired cooks and shoppers as well as cleaners. The expense of these services added a great deal to the monthly amount that each individual was required to pay. Life within the community became increasingly expensive.

While group living was certainly a defining characteristic of "Sullivanian" life, the financial aspect of members' lives remained individual throughout the life of the community. Each person's living situation was based on the amount of money he or she possessed—whether through earnings or trust funds or other sources of income. Individuals who entered the community with large sums of money or with high earning power were able to live more comfortably, and in some cases were also able to move up the social ladder by "donating" money to help the leadership in various ways. This was not always the case—some wealthier members were held in contempt by the leadership in spite of the fact that they may have "donated" large sums of money. On the other hand, some members who had gained the favor of the leadership were given jobs in various capacities—baby-sitting was the most common, but also cleaning and cooking—that enabled them to support themselves and remain in the group.

While the economic relationship of members to the Sullivan Institute therapists and the Fourth Wall Repertory Company was individual in the sense that each person was required to pay for his or her therapy and living situation, there were also communal aspects to the economic life in the sense that members were given a great deal of professional guidance and concrete help, and often borrowed large sums of money from each other. It was common for members to borrow money from each other. Some members had money in the bank, but others might take out loans or use credit cards to borrow money for friends who had asked for help. This was encouraged, and in some cases strongly suggested, by therapists.

In the early 1970s, many "Sullivanians" became computer typesetters because these jobs were available and also often had flexible hours. They paid a much higher hourly rate than an individual could expect to make as a typist or a secretary, although many of the same skills were employed. If an individual in the community needed work, his or her therapist might suggest typesetting, and would then give him or her the names of some of the other people in the community who were already employed as typesetters. Those individuals would be expected to help the neophyte to get training and to find a job, even if that meant lying to employers about their credentials or giving false references. Later, in the 1980s, this function of the group became much more highly developed.

CONCLUSION

The 1969–78 period within the Sullivan Institute community was a crucial one in which the group was able to establish itself and to develop the organizational structure that would carry it through the next twelve years until its final dissolution in approximately 1991. The development of the training program, and the concomitant influx of younger people that would carry the community forward, was crucial to this process. Additionally, the ethos of this period, in which the emphasis was on self-exploration and self-discovery, on "doing what felt good," and celebrating life, attracted many new members. Historical factors, such as the demise of the New Left and the mainstreaming (in some senses) of the counterculture, also contributed to this influx.

The economic structure of the community was especially interesting when compared with the changing economic relationships in mainstream society. Due to the ideology, which viewed the mainstream U.S. nuclear family as repressive, traditional marriage between members was prohibited, as was cross-gender cohabitation. Even when members decided to have children together, the mother and father continued to live separately (no same-sex couples had children together). Mothers continued to work as they had before they bore their children, and child-care, cooking and household tasks were performed by paid labor.

Traditional male and female roles within the family did not exist.

An anthropological perspective on the practices of Sullivan Institute community members leads to a discussion of the relationship of these practices to U.S. mainstream society of that time period (1960s–80s). Middle-class women moved into the professional workforce during this period, and used paid child-care and housekeeping as a means by which to free themselves of their traditional responsibilities. In some ways the Sullivan Institute practices simply foreshadowed practices that would become common among middle-class urban professionals.

As we will see in the next and later chapters, the 1969–78 period saw the largest influx of members in the history of the Sullivan Institute community. Without this expansion the community would have remained a tiny group of professionals and would not have impacted the lives of close to one thousand individuals (many more if their families are included). Although this expansion might have been possible during other historical periods, it is clear that the political and cultural movements of the 1960s were a critical factor in the growth and consolidation of the group.

NOTES

1. This was the common way of referring to these individuals within the community.

2. The first two classes, as mentioned earlier, consisted of M.D.s and Ph.D.s.

3. In 1975 David Black's article in New York Magazine reported estimates of anywhere from 350 to 600 members. These estimates were based on the number of therapists in the community, and the average number of patients that each therapist saw (Black 1975, 37).

4. The four leaders were the only individuals in the community who lived as couples, although they also maintained multiple sexual partners, and therefore had separate rooms from each other.

5. Although it was in some senses anti-intellectual, this movement was also part of a critique of traditional education that had become popular among segments of mainstream culture as well.

6. The social circles usually followed the structure of the hierarchy described earlier in this chapter, although there were exceptions.

7. Later, in 1983–84 when the new building was being renovated, some members had sold apartments in order to pay for those renovations and were forced to live doubled up until the building was ready.

8. The economics of life in the Sullivan Institute community will be discussed in greater detail below.

9. The marriages of the leadership were similar in some ways to the "open marriage" concept advocated in the book of the same name by Nena O'Neill and George O'Neill (Open Marriage: A New Lifestyle for Couples, New York: M. Evans, 1972). Pearce and Newton explicitly referred to this book.

10. For example, one individual who was studying dance left the community because he would have been unable to pursue his career if he had stayed because the financial requirements had become too great.

_____

Chapter 5

The Therapeutic Relationship

The patient-therapist relationship was the basic unit of the Sullivan Institute/Fourth Wall community. It was the primary vehicle for the transmission of Pearce and Newton's (and later, Harvey's) psychoanalytic theory, and the primary site of identity transformation and social control. Through the psychotherapy, entirely new identities, or self-conceptions, were fashioned for the patients. This process was crucial to the formation of a successful community. Individuals came to see themselves in terms of the theory, which comprised the foundational belief system. The issue of coercion in the context of this relationship is an extremely complex one with no definitive answer; nevertheless, it is possible to conclude on the basis of the experience of numerous ex-patients of psychotherapists that unethical practices[1] were common within the community, and that individuals were pressured to take certain actions that they came to believe were not in their best interest.

For most practitioners of psychotherapy, and for most patients, the therapeutic relationship is an extremely delicate and important one. First this is true because in any relationship where a trained "expert" is paid for a particular service, he or she is in a position of power over the client or patient. This is recognized in the case of medical doctors by the Hippocratic oath, in the case of lawyers by the requirements for admission to the bar in the United States, and in the case of psychotherapists by the American Psychological Association's Code of Ethics. These legal and ethical devices were devised precisely to protect clients from irresponsible behavior on the part of the providers of these services. Nevertheless, the APA codes are not enforceable unless a patient comes forward and brings charges against his or her medical doctor or therapist. This can be an extremely difficult action for a patient to take, even if he or she feels that the practitioner has acted in a questionable manner.

In the context of the psychotherapeutic relationship, the issue of the emotional attachment that can and must develop in order for therapy to be successful is the subject of an enormous amount of attention within the discipline. The notion of transference is central to most clinical theories, and although the various schools of psychoanalytic thought define transference somewhat differently, there is a great deal of agreement regarding the nature of this phenomenon. Briefly, transference is defined as the transferring by the patient onto the therapist those feelings he or she had for significant others in his early years, usually the parents. Freud characterized it as the development of a fascination by the patient with the personal life of the therapist, and analyzed it as resistance to an understanding of the patient's own problems (Freud 1966). Later theorists (Racker 1968; Guntrip 1973) have given transference an even more central place in the analytic process, as the process of the patient involving the therapist in the "inner world" of his or her psyche. Through an understanding of how the patient does this, a great deal of insight can be gained regarding the basic functioning of his or her personality, and it may be possible that the problems that originally led him or her to seek help may be addressed. Some psychoanalysts consider the analysis of the transference phenomenon to be the central task of therapy (Racker 1968, 50).

In any patient-therapist relationship, the danger of abuse exists, and while the American Psychological Association may have defined abuse in a particular way, not all practitioners agree with these definitions. Additionally, while there are guidelines for psychotherapeutic practice, many practitioners may not follow them, but will not necessarily be in violation of any ethical codes. For example, it is commonly accepted that the job of the therapist is to help the patient to resolve whatever difficulties he or she may have come to therapy for, not necessarily to show the patient how to live a "perfect," or more fulfilling, life. However, the line between interpretation and admonition is often a difficult one to draw. For example, a patient comes to psychotherapy because he or she is having problems with a marital relationship. The biases of the therapist can easily enter into this situation. In the context of the Sullivan Institute, "traditional" marriage was considered unhealthy and unsatisfactory. Therefore, a psychotherapist would attempt to demonstrate to the patient that he or she would be much happier if the marriage ended. There would be almost no interest on the therapist's part in helping the patient resolve certain problems within the marriage.

Most mainstream therapists would view their job in terms of helping the patient clarify what the sources of the difficulties were and then helping him or her decide what to do about them. Even if a particular therapist felt that a patient should end a marriage, he or she would not necessarily consider it proper to state that opinion to the patient. However, even therapists who attempt to keep their opinions to themselves can often communicate them in various ways, some of them nonverbal. This is especially true in the context of a patient-therapist relationship that can become extremely intimate over a number of years— nuances of expression and intonation can easily communicate approval or disapproval to the patient.[2]

In addition to the differences discussed above, there were other differences between psychotherapy and more traditional therapies. The most noticeable of these was the abrogation of the professional boundaries that are usually mandated between patient and therapist, particularly in the form of extramural relationships. This practice had many interesting ramifications. Therapists received information about their patients from many sources within the community: personal contact at parties, "dates" with the patient's roommates or friends, community meetings, theater productions, communications from other therapists in the community whose patients would give them information, and so forth. It was not unusual for the four training analysts of the Sullivan Institute to have sexual and romantic relationships with their patients:

I had two women patients come to me, transferred from Saul because they couldn't afford to see him anymore. One was brave enough to complain how much she hated having to give him . . . a blow job every single session. This was something a lot of us knew, but you wouldn't really talk about this. . . . And Harvey slept with all of her male patients. Took me to bed twice but we never fucked. (L. C. 5/15/88, 19)

In addition to the existence of extramural relationships between therapists and patients, there was also an extensive surveillance network that developed within the community on the basis of the intensive supervision required of the students in the training program:

Certainly no major issue of a patient's life, of any patient I saw in the first five or six years that I was there, would have happened without my having talked to a supervisor or Harvey as therapist, about it. . . . there was so much supervision of therapy, I'm talking about six private hours[3] a week plus classes. . . . There was really ample time given to turning over information about patients. Completely under the guise of getting psychoanalytic supervision once again. I didn't think of it as control in those days. (Ofshe/L. C. 1988, 4)

This network made it possible for information about individual's thoughts and feelings to reach the leadership quickly and discreetly. Additionally, almost every decision that a patient made about his or her life, including where to live, who to live with, what career path to pursue, medical decisions, to name just a few examples, was subject to approval or disapproval by the leadership. L. C. states:

. . . if you were moving from Brooklyn to Manhattan and you wanted to live on the lower east side in some crummy apartment to save some bread rather than move to the upper west side with some roommates—because you wanted to save some money because you wanted to go to graduate school next year—this would get interpreted and analyzed as this is your penchant for self-deprivation and self-destruction and your refusal to move on, and your compliance to your mother's wishes.[4] (Ofshe/L .C. 1988, 5)

Another unusual characteristic of the therapy was the degree to which therapists directed their patients' lives. Patients were often "ordered" by their therapists to pursue a particular career, to enter into or terminate a relationship with a particular individual, to move into a particular group apartment, or to make other critical life decisions. These "orders" may have been couched in the form of advice, but if the advice was not taken, the patient could be threatened with expulsion from therapy, and from the entire community. Although some other novel therapies are equally as directive, this degree of directiveness is definitely out of the mainstream. L. C. describes this process in the context of supervision:

In supervision there were three kinds of things that would happen. There would be . . . some psychoanalytic interpretation of the patient's life, their personality. There would be direction as to what the therapist should do with the patient, crazy or not. Two—what you should do. Literally verbatim, often, what you should say to the patient. And three— what the patient should do in their life. . . . And I can't stress enough how directive it was . . . it was just an intrinsic, inherent part of the therapy that you told people what to do. . .

S. H. was a brilliant guy who is now on the faculty of a medical school. I was told, and I did, to tell him that he could not practice medicine with patients. And if he wanted to he could go into research, but he was too "inhuman" to work directly with people.

J. C. was very wealthy and I was given explicit instructions to make myself executor of his will. When J. C. was entering a hospital for tests, Newton gave me directions to have him change his will before this procedure, to leave money directly to the Fourth Wall. (Ofshe/L. C. 1988, 6)

In addition to the particular examples mentioned above, there were other general areas of patients lives that would be dictated by their therapists. These included relationships between parents and children within the community. L. C. reports that he was routinely told by his supervisors to: "tell these parents that they were shits, murderers, no different than Nazis—that if their kids stayed with them they would end up dead or in a mental hospital. . . . And the only saving possibility for the kids would be to send them off to boarding school. And to literally dictate when they could go visit, how often, how often the kid could come back" (Ofshe/L. C. 1988, 8).

For all patients who joined the community, the process of distancing them from their families of origin was the first task of the therapist. As described below, eventually all members were required to terminate or to severely curtail their relationships with parents and siblings.

The issue of transference, a particularly difficult one in any therapeutic relationship, was also dealt with in an unconventional manner. Whereas more traditional psychotherapies attempt to analyze the transference and to help the patient learn from it, the Sullivanian therapists allowed and encouraged their patients to view them as powerful, larger than life figures who had the power to give or take away happiness. In fact, this was true in the sense that any individual who alienated his or her therapist could be expelled from the community. L. C. describes his feelings about his therapist:

I think right from the beginning I would have followed this woman anywhere on earth, you know. And this went on simultaneously with all these other thoughts I was having. I thought that this woman was literally god's gift to humankind. . . . I think there is a feeling at the beginning of therapy, particularly with my type of personality and the type of transference I was in, where in feeling at all understood about anything, you feel like "my god, this woman is unbelievably empathic and wonderful and understanding" and if I voiced that she would basically say 'that's true, I am empathic." She told me she didn't experience envy, she was all these things that I was projecting onto her, which I think is the key to how one got sucked into later being brutalized. This was the first form of brutality in the therapy, was that the idealized transference is analyzed as true, because the analyst really is that ideal (L. C. 5/15/88, 15).

Additionally, the therapeutic process was significantly impacted by the fact that many (if not most) patients of Sullivan Institute psychoanalysts were members of the Sullivanian community. This meant that not only were they being exposed to a particular interpretation of their experiences and problems in the therapeutic context, but that this interpretation was reinforced by their living situation and most of their social experience as well. Not only did the community reinforce the therapy, but it also provided a surveillance system, that would notify the therapist if the patient did not act on his or her directives.

For many members, the primary initiation into the community began with seeking a therapist. They were referred by friends and colleagues to Sullivanian therapists. Other members became involved with the social activities of the Sullivan Institute community first, and were then encouraged to enter into therapy. In either case, it became necessary for any member of the community to be in therapy with one of the Sullivan Institute therapists. It should be noted that not all patients of psychotherapists were invited to join the community—only those who were thought to be potential assets in the sense that they would be able to pay for their therapy and would not require institutionalization or a great deal of care and attention.

The process of identity transformation in Sullivanian psychotherapy took place over several years. Every aspect of the patient's life was recounted, examined, and interpreted in the light of Pearce and Newton's theory. For analytic purposes, I have conceptualized the therapeutic process in terms of four stages: the initiatory, the novice, the participant, and the adept. Although the conception of these stages is useful for discussion of the particular type of patient-therapist relationship that developed in the Sullivanian community, I must add that they are also somewhat ahistorical. The community was in a state of constant flux, and the nature of therapeutic relationships changed over time (they were different in the 1960s than they were in the 1980s). Therefore some of the stages incorporate aspects of the community life and organization that may not have been contemporaneous. These stages are not necessarily formulated in the ways in which the patients and therapists themselves would have conceptualized them. Additionally, the stages are ideal categories in the sense that not all patients experienced all of them in exactly the same way—they are based on a generalization of individual experiences.

In the "initiatory" or beginning stage, the first task of the therapist was to convince the patient that he or she was in psychic pain and that the therapist both empathized with that pain, and could help the patient understand and overcome it. According to L. C.,

You dig up pain, you would create pain, you would construct pain. . . . It's quite possible to take anybody's life and dig up that which is naturally painful and present it back to them as a deeper problem rather than it's part of the normal course of living. Like my parents died when I was growing up—this is naturally painful. Does this mean that I'm necessarily psychotic over this? No. And maybe some grieving process did or didn't go on, but this is not an indication of psychosis. They are either really in pain (and people can be really in serious pain) or if they weren't, you would take the natural painful events of their life and make it. You'd make them, you'd give them a sense through a kind of emotional response to them, that they were in more serious—that if they were in serious trouble, you understood that. If they weren't in serious trouble, that they were in more serious trouble than they believed, and that was their serious trouble. (Ofshe/L. C., 1988, 20)[5]

After the patient was assured of the serious nature of his or her problems, and of the need for therapy, the major task became the taking of the patient's history. The patient was to start with the earliest memory and proceed to tell his or her life story in terms of familial and emotional life. In the context of therapy, a great deal of emphasis was placed on the potential harmful effects of certain actions of parents on their children. Pearce and Newton's theory stipulated that babies were not conceived with certain personality traits, but that the entire emotional, physical, and intellectual development of a baby depended on the parents' (and caregivers') actions before and after birth. This was an extreme perspective—most psychoanalytic theory gives weight to other factors such as genetic predisposition, environmental conditions unrelated to the specific personalities of the parents, and innate characteristics of all humans. As Harvey asserts,

History as remembered has some of the quality of dreams. History has many interpersonal meanings in the here and now. A patient has to remember it that way for certain reasons. I think the simplest statement of the way each of us remembers our history and forgets our past is that it is originally structured, in the main, to protect the relationship with the mother.

To institutionalize in your memory of your mother the acceptance of the parental dictate as to who you are, or could become. To cast for oneself the memories that would engage one intimately with the manifestation of the mother that would maintain the connection, and to cast out those memories that would break the connection with the mother and therefore threaten one's life and existence. . . .

Some of the kinds of things we get, some of the kinds of data you're likely to get, may facilitate and will have to do with what functions the mother prohibited—and will give indication of these areas. History data will also tell you roughly where the person got stuck in interpersonal development. History will tell you what the patient over and over is trying to work on in a half-assed way.

Some event that a patient recalls and relates and has always been the proof of something, if you move the prism around and see it in a different light, some set of facts suddenly is seen as the mother's death wish to the patient. (Harvey 1980)

While Freudian theory places a great deal of emphasis on the innate drives of the human species, arguing that every human must internalize his or her culture through the relationship to a libidinal object, namely, a parent. Pearce and Newton argued that individuals were no more or less than the products of the families and societies they had grown up in. They did not believe that infants were born with certain inherited traits, or innate characteristics.

In Sullivanian psychotherapy, any problems or traumatic experiences that the patient experienced while under the parent's care were viewed as caused by parental hatred or envy of the child. For example, if a photograph that a patient brought in showed her parent holding her, the expression on the parent's face was often interpreted to indicate anger or discomfort, thus showing the patient that her parent was not "happy" about caring for her. The death of a parent was often viewed by the therapists in the Sullivan Institute as a suicide, even if the cause was cancer or an automobile accident. Memories and dreams were also interpreted as relating to one's parents; almost all menacing figures in dreams turned out to be the patient's father or mother (usually mother), and in memories, any negative feeling was attributed to some action or inaction by the parent. In the case of married patients, aspects of the patient's relationship with the parent that were found to be destructive were often compared to the relationship of the patient to his or her spouse. Many patients were encouraged to have affairs while they were married, and even to end their marriages. Several married couples joined the community, but none remained married if they continued to be members.

In the early stages, the goals of therapy were to demonstrate to the patient that he or she was in urgent need of psychotherapy, and that this need was caused by parental inadequacies and hostilities. Additionally, the Sullivanian psychotherapist would also be extremely supportive of any aspirations that the patient might have that were considered productive. L. C. discusses the process of cultivating dependency in the patient.

Yeah, you're a very intelligent guy, have you ever thought to go ahead and go to medical school? You've always wanted to be an artist—why don't you do that? Or you want to sleep with a bunch of people, why don't you? You kind of lend them a more liberal super-ego. And you be very, very supportive at the beginning. So all of a sudden they've opened up and they're with someone who is saying go for the moon. I mean, you could have it, you really could—whatever you want you could have. And you give some accurate pieces of directive shit that work. Right? I don't know how to get in to graduate school. Well, next session why don't you stay an extra hour—I won't charge you. This happens all the time. And we'll do the application together. . . . You write a brilliant essay for them, they get accepted to the department of bla bla and you've really helped them out. You've been supportive, you've given practical directives. I trust you. A month goes by. Not only do I trust you, you're like the greatest thing that's happened since white bread. I mean, you are wonderful. And at that moment—this is what I think is the crucial moment—basically you say back to them in one way or another, you are right, I really am wonderful. As a matter of fact, you are so troubled that without me to guide you, you couldn't do this. (Ofshe/L. C. 12/31/88, 25)

This fostering of dependency was achieved through misuse of the transference phenomena that was discussed above.

Depending on the patient's reaction, this first stage of the therapeutic relationship may have lasted for a longer or shorter period of time. It was usually a minimum of six months to a year. In it, the patient had to come to accept the parents' malevolence, and the therapist's ability to help improve his or her life. If this did not take place, the therapist told him or her that this behavior was simply a refusal to confront the truth. In addition to interpreting the parent's actions, the therapist also focused his attention on the patient's relationships with peers. These relationships were thought to be the key to the productive aspects of the patient's childhood. Although the parents were believed to be able to limit the type of peer interaction in which their child engaged, they could not do this in all the spheres of a child's life. Experiences at school, with cousins, siblings, and best friends were all interpreted as having contributed to the individual's growth.

M. J. described her experience of starting to see a Sullivanian therapist:

M. R. made these kind of pronouncements, like saying that my husband had been violent ... the most Mark would say about it was that Sam had been a violent guy and my father had been a violent guy, although I had no reason to think my father was violent and M.R. kind of put things together like 1 + 2 = 5.

He articulated the problem, I accepted his definition of the problem, and began to see it everywhere, but I felt totally powerless to do anything about it. I felt like eventually, over time, this guy will help me get over this fixation I have with these violent men, which comes from my father. . . . So he kind of gave me a problem I didn't have by talking about the current problem and enlarging it to contain my husband as well as my father as well as the South as well as the military vis-à-vis the rest of the world. It just got huge, it was so big. And here I had this incredible problem that I couldn't understand, but maybe someday I would get better.

He said I didn't have the experience of liking women and in order to get in touch with myself, who was a woman, I really needed to be around women and make friends with them. I had had girlfriends before, close girlfriends, but he said that I didn't really know how to relate to women. . . . I thought I had friends, but he said I didn't really. So somehow I came to accept this pronouncement also, that I had this other problem that I hadn't realized I had. (M .J. 5/1/88, 4–5)

In many cases the struggle between the patient and the therapist over the role of the parents in his or her upbringing continued for a long period of time (1–2 years), with the patient agreeing with the therapist's interpretation sporadically, and then disagreeing again. On some level it can be argued that this conflict was never resolved completely, because the patient would always maintain some hidden belief that the parent's influence in his or her life was not completely negative. In terms of the initiation into the community, however, the critical factor was for the initiate to say that he or she believed certain things. Backsliding into "romanticization" of the parents did not result in expulsion; however, it was dealt with harshly by therapists (and other members as well). L. C. says, "You then take every little event and you kind of like pump it up 5,000 times more. . . People would begin to cry. And I think the crying was probably a combination of fear of the therapist and . . . fear of loss of the therapist, fear of rejection.... There are some ties you have to me [as therapist] and if you don't really come all the way I'll reject you. So the threat of the therapist rejecting the patient was always there and always used" (L. C./Ofshe 1988, 14).

L. C. uses the example of his therapist to illustrate the method of exerting control over patients:

My mother died when I was 19, my father died when I was four. My only familial—the only family I ever had was my sister, who is living in Israel. I was having a hard time. I was getting letters from her. [My therapist, Joan Harvey, would say] . . . why don't you bring in these letters that you're talking about, I'd like to see them. I bring in the letters. This woman is sick. Your sister. Sick. These are violent letters to you. Next—this goes on a couple of sessions. You know, I've been thinking about this, a lot, and—this is a quote—every time you open one of her letters it's equivalent to your living one year less. The risk of dying of a heart attack like your father, who had his first heart attack in his 30s and died in his 40s. Being under attack from this kind of violence from this woman is literally—literally, we're not even talking psychologically or metaphorically—literally lessening the possibility that you're going to live a full life. And I think you better break off contact with her immediately. Now she's got me between a rock and a hard place. What's my biggest fear? That I'm going to die like my father did. What's my other biggest fear? That I'm going to break off the last contact I have. Which way do I go? My sister is troubled, is she offering me any security in that moment? No, really. I'm in no position, psychologically, to be of much help to her. And I'm being told by a woman who has now helped me out for a year, and I have this idealized transference, that staying in touch with her is literally going to do the very thing I've always been afraid of—shortening my life. (Ofshe/L. C. 1988, 17)

In the "novice" stage, the patient was introduced to the Sullivanian community and became a member. The introduction could happen in a variety of ways; the patient could join a summer house with other Sullivanians (1970–79), a women's or men's group, or be invited to a party by the therapist, or by another patient in the waiting room. In these contexts newcomers were exposed to group life and evaluated as to whether they were ready for it.

In terms of the patient-therapist relationship, the therapist arriving at a diagnosis characterized this stage. In conformity with the stages of growth set out in The Conditions of Human Growth, the therapist would pronounce the patient to be developmentally arrested at a certain stage of development, for example, the juvenile stage (ideally ages 4–8). In addition to the other modes of subjugation of the patient-members in the community, the act of deciding that one's mental age (in terms of interpersonal development) is eight years old encouraged the patient to think of him/herself as a person who could not make decisions without guidance. The diagnosis was sometimes vague; a specific developmental stage was not always specified; the patient was referred to simply as an "immature adult." An additional type of diagnosis that could be made was to label the patient as "psychotic," "paranoid," "schizophrenic," "psychopathic," or "depressed." Although these terms are commonly used in the practice of clinical psychology, they were not used in the same way by the therapists as by the mainstream psychoanalytic community. Sullivanians were much more likely to use these terms to describe patients with much milder symptomatology than the more commonly accepted definitions of these terms. A patient would be told that he/she was "depressed" or "psychotic," when another psychoanalyst might have called him or her "anxious" or "neurotic." L. D. relates her first experience with Joan Harvey:

I don't remember anything about the consultation, except she said to me this line, and I'll never forget it for the rest of my life. She said "If you don't move to New York within 24 hours you're going to die." And I believed her, and I went home and packed that night! . . .

. . . All I know is that I was very scared and freaked out that I was going to die, so I moved. I packed up my stuff in a van, called M. and asked him if he could find me a place to stay. He found me a place to stay at 465 West End Ave. with Q. and P., two therapists on the 6th floor of 465 [West End Avenue], and that's where I moved for the summer. So they were going to be away and Joan gave me the job of taking care of all her animals for the summer while she went out to Amagansett and she paid me some exorbitant amount. Don't ask me how much, all I know is that at the time I was being completely overpaid, but she couldn't find anyone else to watch the animals. She put me on 60 mg. of valium a day, I'm not lying to you, 60 mg. of valium a day, and four times a day I took 15 mg. of valium. (L. D. 6/1/93, 1–2)

The development of same-sex relationships was stressed by the Sullivanian therapists as the most important component of "growing up." All patients who became members of the community lived in apartments (most of them in group apartments) with other members of the same sex. At the same time the practice of what could be called casual sex was encouraged; members were encouraged (by their therapists and friends) to seek out other members they wanted to have sex with, but not to form any exclusive and/or romantic attachments.[6] This attitude toward sexuality shared a great deal with certain trends in the mainstream culture of the late 1950s and 1960s.[7] Additionally, members were encouraged to be heterosexual or bisexual—the emphasis was on the casual nature that was mandated of sexual relationships. Gay members were strongly pressured to engage in heterosexual liaisons as well as homosexual ones—this would also prevent romantic involvement.

During the novice period the patient-therapist relationship became much stronger. The patient had acceded to the conception of the parents as the primary repressive force in his/her life, and in many cases told the parents that he or she would no longer have any relationship with them. The emotional impact of this decision was extremely powerful; the community began to be seen as the "rational" substitute for the family, and the therapist played the role of house parent or counselor. The emphasis of therapy shifted from the focus on the destructive role of the parents to a concern with the ways in which the patient demonstrated the same characteristics that presented themselves in the behavior of the parents. L. C. describes this dynamic:

I think a long time was spent with any patient on getting them to hate their parents and to create a picture of the parents as really violent, terrible. . . . Then there was a switch. . . . You spend the first year getting the person to learn how violent their parents were. And then you hit them with how they are exactly like their parents. So after this period of breaking them down, but you're compassionate and you're helpful and you've gotten them into graduate school or art school. . . .Or out of a bad marriage, or out of a good marriage. And after you've identified how violent the parents were, then you say you know what? You are really not that much different. Now the next part of our job is the painful part—now it's to identify how you are exactly like the parents. How you treat people exactly the way your parents treated you—how you treat your kid that way, how you treat your spouse that way, your lover that way, your friends that way. And then, from there on in, you are the psychopath—you are the vicious son-of-a-bitch, etc., etc. That is very powerful. It wouldn't work if it came right at the beginning. It really does work after there's been a year of this is what your parents did to you and it only makes sense that this is who you are. (Ofshe/L. C. 1988, 20)

It is extremely important to understand the sequence of events described by L. C. The power of Sullivanian psychotherapy lay in its ability to "hook" the patient. This was accomplished by exposing vulnerabilities that most humans have, then by offering a great deal of compassion and support in response to these vulnerabilities (i.e., trauma over the death of parents, childhood illness, verbal or physical abuse, and so on). Next, the therapist attempted to demonstrate that all the negative experiences in the patient's past were the result of the destructive impulses of his or her parents, and, finally, after the patient had broken off contact with his or her family, he or she would be confronted with evidence that in fact he or she had exactly the same destructive traits that the parents demonstrated. The only way to overcome these traits was to engage in the "radical personality change" that was recommended by the Sullivan Institute therapists. The patient was constantly compared to an ideal that had been constructed by the leadership (Pearce, Newton, Harvey and so on) and found lacking. The only way to make progress was to continually strive toward achieving this ideal personality. Richard Ofshe puts this in terms of "negative" and "positive" identities that are constructed for the patient.

. . . What is offered is an idealized version of who you could be if you would only totally conform to the demands of the community as a whole and me in particular. . . . I'm constructing here what I would typically describe as a negative identity. And that negative identity becomes very well developed. And as long as the person is conforming, that negative identity is allowed to remain dormant. At the same time there is a positive identity, and that identity is defined by the norms of the group, the expectations of the group—the therapist in particular, as part of the group. The positive identity defined in that way—the person is reinforced for displaying—and is constantly criticized for failing to do it sufficiently—and then over the course of time emphasis shifts so that the criticism is criticism of the difference between who you should be if you were 100 percent conforming and how you have fucked up and only gotten 80 or 90 percent of the way. (Ofshe/L. C. 1988, 25)

W. K. describes the process of learning the community "rules," which included breaking with his family:

And then I started learning the rules, which, I was given the reasons for them, but I wasn't really sure. Some of the rules were that you shouldn't have a girlfriend because it's bad for you. You shouldn't have anything to do with your family and you should trust the people who were in the group. I remember S. R. (W. K.'s therapist) said one time, "it's like being in a large boat with other people having paddles, and it's much easier to paddle upstream with people who are going the same way". And then there was the stuff about dating, and for some reason it would be terrible to sleep alone. It just was the worst, so every night that you didn't have a date with a woman, you had to sleep with someone else. And there would be telephone calls that came into the house: "this is Mary Jones or Tom Smith, anyone in your house that doesn't have a date?" (W. K. 5/9/88, 8)

In the "participant" stage, the patient became a full-fledged member of the Sullivanian community.[8] He or she adopted the therapist's interpretations of her history as valid, and formed a self-image that was consonant with them. The patient-member usually moved into one of the communal living situations (he or she had to apply and be invited by the other residents), and became fully integrated into community life. As noted above, the content of this life was constantly changing; in the late 1960s and early 1970s, for example, it consisted of constant social interaction in the form of "dates." After 1979 the community's theater and political projects dominated group social life.

The interpersonal situation in the communal residences was the member's first exposure to the power of other people (other than the therapist) in the formation of a sense of self. All roommates were in therapy and were expected to discuss "what was going on" in the living situation with their therapists. Every house member became a source of possible "feedback" to the other members. In other words, all of the residents would see their respective therapists, tell them what their perceptions of the occurrences in the house were, and be directed by the therapists on how to speak or not to speak to the other members.

In later years (the 1980s), political education became mandatory for each apartment. The leadership formed a "Politics Committee" that was responsible for choosing and ordering each week's assignment. Members of the committee would then circulate around the community to each apartment's house-meeting in order to monitor the discussions and to teach members about the topic chosen for that week. House meetings ceased to be centered on individuals and their psychological problems, and became political discussion groups.

The relationship between patient and therapist during the participant stage became more complex than in the previous two stages, in which there was one major focus of the therapy. One project in therapy became the increasing integration of the patient into the community. Relationships with other members, especially those of the same sex as the patients, were also an important focus. The therapist became the arbiter of all important decisions in the patient's life. This included professional decisions, choice of lovers, the decision to have or not have children and with whom, living situations, and even in some cases medical decisions.

At this point, the patient's identity became completely enmeshed with the community, to the extent that isolation from it was seen as equivalent to psychological death. The therapist stressed that the only way that the patient-member could stay mentally healthy was to stay in the community. If one were to leave, they cautioned that suicide or psychological deterioration would follow. These cautions are exacerbated by the fact that the general attitude in the community toward outsiders was that they are primitive and unhappy people, and the outside world a cold and forbidding place. L. C. comments on this aspect of life in the group:

And I think the final threat always was you're out. But out has to be understood as—out means I'm going to go insane. . . . I mean, I was told over and over if you ever leave this community you will either end up dead on the street, a drug addict, in jail or in a mental hospital. So the fear of leaving—I don't even know how to begin to put into words the level of terror that people go through as to whether they can construct a life for themselves out. . . . I really didn't think I was going to make it. (Ofshe/L.C. 1988, 22)

Not all members attained the adept stage, and for those who did attain it, there were varying degrees to which they became "adepts." An adept was a member who had taken on (either internally or not) all the values and goals of the community, including its statements about who he or she was. He or she took on the responsibility to move the communal life forward. In the earlier stages of the group, adepts were the leaders in their households; they confronted other members with their "problems," sometimes demanded that those who were not "changing fast enough" leave living situations, policed sexual relationships that had become too intimate, and did not tolerate any discussion that smacked of "anti-group" sentiments.

When the Fourth Wall Repertory Company became the main activity of the Sullivanian community, adepts were given high positions in the theater hierarchy, such as stage manager, director, key acting roles, costume design, and so on. These people were responsible for managing other members in the same way that any stage manager would be. The difference was that if there were problems with a subordinate's performance of a job, they would be reported to the leadership, either directly or through one of the therapists. This could result in problems for the member outside of the theater environment—in the living situation or the therapeutic relationship.

The relationship between the adept and the therapist was usually one of "working very hard in therapy." This means that the patient was consistently concerned with "dealing with his or her problems," which could include additional discussion of historical data, possibly even a visit to the parents for the patient to "interview" them about his or her childhood. Adepts were the only members allowed to have children, although for the most part they did not choose who the other parent would be. This decision was recommended by the therapist, but in fact was made by the leadership. Some adepts were asked to become therapists themselves, others took on what were considered important responsibilities within the organizational structure of the group.

The therapeutic relationship decreased in importance during the evolution of the Sullivanian community. As the Fourth Wall Repertory Company became the focal point of community activities, the power associated with high positions in the theater company came to equal and in some cases exceed the authority of the therapists. Additionally, the goal of therapy changed during this period. In the early years, the goal was to help the individual to develop his or her "full human potential." Later, when the focus of the community turned outward and centered around a vision of nuclear apocalypse, the therapy functioned to create and maintain "good soldiers" who would give all of their time and money to the cause. Individual needs and wants were to be subsumed to these goals. W. D. describes her therapy during this period.

. . . B. P. as a therapist was really to keep you in one piece after these other people had torn you to bits. You'd go to B. P. and she'd like patch you up again, and then you'd go back into the lion's den. I don't know how she did it, but—I swear to god—that was her skill. She would spend a lot of time with me. The sessions would go way over in order for me to get combobulated enough for me to go back and work my butt off, because I worked incredibly hard. And then when I ended up being assistant editor on the film, that was working 16 hours a day for over a year. (W. D. 7/22/89, 15)

The transference that had previously existed for the patient between himself or herself and the therapist came to exist between the patient-member and the leadership. The leadership in this later period consisted of the top therapists (Newton, Harvey, Klein, and Moses), and of those in high positions in the theater and film productions. The experience of the member was often that of being in therapy with the entire group. The therapy retained its importance, however, as one of the main modes of surveillance of the membership by the leadership.

In this later stage of the community's development, the production of identity was tied increasingly to one's social position within the hierarchy. This hierarchy became increasingly rigid, albeit with constant changes of personnel, as the group stopped adding new members to its ranks. Social mobility was still possible, but there were fewer routes to the top. Some members remained in lower positions. Identities became frozen; one was who the community saw them as, and it was very difficult (if not impossible) to change this image.

The question of image raises an important issue in the context of the production of identity in the Sullivanian community. To what extent was the self that was produced via the therapeutic relationship, the self that was seen by the therapist and the other members, real to the patient-member? As Goffman (1959) and others have demonstrated, in the course of social interaction, we sometimes act in specific ways in situations to achieve a certain result. This question cannot be answered objectively, since the only person who knows to what extent he/she believed in the "Sullivanian self" was the patient-member. However, some data on this subject was obtained by speaking with people who had undergone this experience.

The interviews I conducted indicate that it varied greatly from person to person. Some people describe a constant awareness of a "false self" that they created simply to "get by" in the community because they wanted to stay there for various reasons. (In connection with this notion of the "false self," it should be noted that in the case of patient-members this self had to be presented in almost every arena of their lives.) Others describe themselves as vacillating between feeling as if they were "being themselves," and presenting a false self. Still others maintain that they were "true believers," and there are a few of this type who still remain connected with the remnants of the community. However, there is no indication that "true believers" were the only members that remained in the community.

The therapeutic relationship in the Sullivan Institute/Fourth Wall community was the primary site of integration of individuals into the group, and of transmission of the ideology from the leaders to the members. The four stages delineated in this chapter are an attempt to illustrate the process by which new patients became integrated into the community through their relationship with their therapists. For those patients who became community members, the process that they underwent in therapy was reinforced in their living situations and by their friends in the group. Additionally, this chapter has discussed the process from the point of view of the use by the therapist of certain techniques for "breaking down" the defenses of the patient against interpretations that urge him or her to cut off contact with family and former friends. The use of psychic pain and of specific fears and problems that the patient brings to therapy were crucial to the process of creating dependency on both the therapist and the community. Once formed, this dependency was quite difficult to counteract, and could be used as a threat by the leadership.

NOTES

1. The practices can be deemed unethical as set forth in the American Psychological Association Code of Ethics. Additionally, the New York State Office of Professional Discipline reached this conclusion in the cases of Helen Moses and Marc Rice. In the cases of Ralph Klein and Joan Harvey, defendants voluntarily gave up their professional licenses rather than subject themselves to the judgment of the state OPD.

2. Just as Sullivan (1954, 6) points out that the therapist learns as much from tonal variations and other nonverbal forms of communication about the patient, so may the patient get information in the same way about the therapist's thoughts, feelings, and opinions.

3. This entailed three hours of therapy, three hours of supervision.

4. The leadership of the Sullivan Institute community considered the upper west side of Manhattan to be the "only" part of New York City worth living in because the community was located there. A member who lived in another neighborhood was simply resistant to increased interpersonal contact, and therefore, to personal growth.

5. In this interview, L. C. was looking back over his experience as a therapist in the Sullivan Institute community and feeling a great deal of guilt about his actions in this capacity. His description of the method he used could lead the reader to conclude that he was intentionally manipulating his patients' perceptions of their experiences. At the time, L. C. believed that he was helping his patients "get in touch" with various painful experiences in their lives in order to help them understand their cause and to move beyond them.

6. I had this experience when I reentered the community as an adult at age twenty, but anyone who was associated with the Sullivan Institute community at this time would have had the same experience.

7. These trends were the beat and "hippie" counter or sub-cultures.

8. Not all patients of Sullivanian therapists joined the community—as noted above, some were not considered suitable and others refused to get involved.

Chapter 6

The "Revolutionary" Period: 1979–83

INTRODUCTION

The transition from the "hedonistic" or "halcyon" period can be understood from the point of view of both the internal dynamics of the community and in terms of its relationship with the outside world. Internally, the nature of the shift consisted of increased centralization of authority and increased surveillance both by therapists of their patients and of members by other members. It was also a theoretical shift, which, although not articulated openly by the leadership, expressed itself in a total change of focus within the group from concern with individual enlightenment and fulfillment to concern with "saving the world" from nuclear holocaust and environmental catastrophe. It was no longer considered therapeutic to dedicate one's life to the pursuit of intimacy, pleasure, and creative fulfillment. Now it was necessary to devote oneself to the hard work of proselytizing the noninitiated—not to recruit them into the community, but to motivate them to stop the forces of reaction.

The drastic change in the political and cultural climate of the United States during the late 1970s and 1980s was undoubtedly a contributing factor to this transition. The Sullivan Institute community became an anomaly—a group of cultural and political radicals in a reactionary society. The symbiosis between the Sullivanians and the progressive community on the upper west side of Manhattan was severed. The gentrification of the upper west side began, pushing out students and other intellectuals of modest means. It could be argued that in order for the SI/FW community to survive as an entity, it was necessary to "circle the wagons"—to provide an even stronger cohesive force in order to maintain the allegiance of the membership.

It can also be said that for purely economic reasons alone, it was necessary to shift the mission of the community from consumption to production—from its concern with helping members to lead more fulfilling lives to a self-image as an elite group that would show the rest of the world the importance of finding a better way to live through hard work and dedication. An ethic of self-denial, couched in terms of therapeutic and political efficacy, replaced the ethic of hedonistic pleasure. Whereas in the 1960s and 1970s group members had been able to support themselves and their therapists by working as academics, psychoanalysts, painters, dancers, writers, and musicians, this lifestyle became increasingly difficult to support in the late 1970s and 1980s. The leadership began to encourage members to change careers from creative and academic fields to careers in television, filmmaking, and computer technology.

A large-scale activity of this type took place in the early and mid-1980s. This time period was one of rapid growth in high technology fields. There were several computer programmers in the Sullivan Institute/Fourth Wall community. Based on the need within the community for members to bring in higher salaries, some of the most experienced people started a training institute for programmers. A facility in a private apartment was set up with computer terminals and printers. The classes were only open to group members, and individuals enrolled in intensive six-month courses where they would learn the basics of business-oriented programming. At the end of the course, each graduate would be required to take an examination called a technical interview which simulated the types of interviews that employers would conduct in order to establish whether a person had the necessary expertise. Once the student had passed this interview, the teachers would provide assistance with resume writing, and members who already had jobs were expected to attempt to procure jobs for the newly trained members.[1]

This venture was extremely successful—most graduates of this program were able to get jobs, even with minimal programming skills, because they had been told what to say in interviews and also because they often received phone help with problems they were having difficulty with from the more experienced members. Tutoring at night was also available for particularly difficult problems, and more advanced level courses were also offered.

The beginnings of this dramatic change in the life of the community can be seen much earlier, however, in the founding and eventual takeover of the Fourth Wall Repertory Company.

The question arises as to whether the leadership consciously planned the transition, or whether it was the result of a combination of external forces and personal agendas. For example, ex-patients and ex-members commonly observed that Joan Harvey was extremely competitive and jealous of members who exhibited creative talent in music, acting, or direction. When she assumed the leadership of the Fourth Wall, Newton and the other leaders publicly stated that this was an act of concern and self-sacrifice—dedicated to the education and well-being of the membership, as well as to the democratization of the theater company itself. No longer were individuals who were recognized as having theatrical or other performing arts talents considered to be deserving of any respect or priority in terms of writing or acting. The process was to be opened up to the membership, and anyone, no matter how conventionally lacking in talent they were, was to be allowed to sing, act, or write for the stage. Harvey and the other three leaders—Newton, Klein, and Moses—had the same attitude toward these skills as they had exhibited in 1970 toward the trainee analysts who had formal psychoanalytic training. They believed that traditional notions of talent combined with education and experience were not respectable qualifications for the creative fields. As far as they were concerned, these notions were elitist and often prohibited individuals who had not received early training and recognition from performing or writing for the stage.

This attitude resulted in two contradictory trends within the Fourth Wall. On the one hand, members who had been performing either professionally or semiprofessionally were often denigrated and made to feel that their confidence in their own talents and skills was simply the result of parental expectations combined with access to "elitist" forms of training. On the other hand, those who had no experience and no obvious signs of talent were encouraged to learn and to try out their new skills on "Writer's Nights," which were events that took place every few months where company members presented their new material to Harvey and the rest of the Fourth Wall. This resulted in some people having very different experiences from others. For example, a man and a woman who had been involved with the Music Loft in the mid-1970s before it merged with the Fourth Wall were trained and talented musicians who had studied classically. When the Fourth Wall merged with the Music Loft, Joan Harvey them from positions of responsibility for musical production, an act that had serious implications for both professional careers.

THE FOUNDING AND EXPANSION OF THE FOURTH WALL REPERTORY COMPANY

Until the inception of the Comedy Group in 1974 (which later become The Fourth Wall Repertory Company), the Sullivan Institute community had no formal institutionalized structure other than that of the classes, the training analysts and the training program. The comedy group was originally formed by a few members of the community who were interested in comedic theater. Partially inspired by "Saturday Night Live," a television comedy show that used a great deal of structured improvisation, the group met once a week at different members' homes and read and performed each other's material. They also improvised and wrote some skits together—chiefly for their own enjoyment.[2] Later, they selected a director—Luba Elman, one of the therapists who had been involved with the Sullivan Institute since the late 1960s. Elman was not particularly close to the leadership when she participated in the formation of the Fourth Wall—she was one of the "older" therapists (in relation to the trainees) who had a doctorate in clinical psychology. While she almost definitely consulted with her therapist before she participated in the improvisational group, the group was not initially related to any of the activities of the leadership. She had formal training in acting and had worked professionally in California before she came to New York. W. K. was an older member who contributed his observations of the Fourth Wall:

. . . A woman therapist, Luba Elman, started some group called the Fourth Wall, and it was just an acting company so I was a lawyer and I incorporated it. . . . It was something called the Comedy Group, I don't know, they were just going to put on plays. Then the first summer they put on something called "The Skin of Our Teeth." Oh, previously they used to have summer world festivals of art out there. Every summer everybody would put paintings or skits or little things. I was in a writing group, and I did a lot of writing and I wrote a novel while I was in the group, a terrible novel now that I read it. . . .

I guess it was the summer of 1976 was the last summer when everyone came out to Amagansett. The Fourth Wall stayed in some kind of motel complex in Southampton and everyone else was in Amagansett. At that point there was just a very slight social superiority in being in the Fourth Wall. Then the next summer, the Fourth Wall took something up in the Berkshires and there were only about four or five houses in Amagansett, one of which I was in, and at that point, that was the summer when it became clear that if you were going to be an 'in' member of this group, then you had to be in the Fourth Wall. (W. K. 5/9/88, 10–11)

Soon after its inception, the group performed at some parties during the Thanksgiving holidays of 1974. At some point during 1975 the group was named the "Fourth Wall," after the classic theatrical conception of the audience as forming the missing wall of the proscenium stage. During the summer of 1975, members of the Fourth Wall mounted a production of Thornton Wilder's *Skin of Our Teeth* in a rented church in East Hampton with the assistance of many other members of the community. Participation in this production was experienced as an extremely positive experience for many of the nonmembers of the theater group itself, as well as for those who had already been members. Many nonmembers worked in the stage crew, and as ushers and other support staff for the productions. This provided a welcome formalization of relationships and responsibilities between participants that enabled them to mobilize their energies and to participate in a collective endeavor.

In the summer of 1976, members of the Fourth Wall rented a summer house and theater in Southampton, apart from the rest of the Sullivan Institute community, which either owned or rented houses in Amagansett or East Hampton. During the previous year, many people who were in the Sullivanian community had joined the theater group. Several productions were mounted during this summer, with most of the community and other local residents as audience. Some of these were original material, others included Ionesco's *The Bald Soprano,* and *The Great Inspector Hound.* It began to be considered prestigious within the community to be a member of the Fourth Wall. Some members worked around the clock to produce sets and costumes in time for the openings. This devotion to a collective endeavor began to be valued above the initial goals of a summer in Amagansett, which had been to "have fun," "make friends," and to "find oneself." S. B. reports,

The one thing I was going to tell you about was the thing about the esprit de corps. The thing that really epitomized that summer—the story that really epitomizes the sense of togetherness and putting effort into doing. . . is we moved the stage. . . . The performance space itself was this big, sort of cavernous room. I don't know what it had been when it was an animal shelter, but it had to be kind of constructed to make it a theater space. A stage was built. It was a theater in the round or a theater in the semi-round. It had to be moved from one location to another location in the space. . . .

It was only done once because it was a huge effort. I think maybe it was after it was built—after it was constructed. It was moved from one place six feet over to another place in the room. It was huge. It seems to me that it was round. It was all round. I could be remembering it wrong. Maybe it was semi-circle. . . . The thing that I remember was that we were directed almost military fashion. Somebody was calling out the instructions. I don't know if it was Luba or if it was Gary but it was humorous. It was funny. "Take your place, we will now bend down." We all bent down. "Slip your hands under." Everybody slipped their hands under. "And now we will lift." We were talked through it all before, and then we were talked through it to actually do it. It was potentially unbelievably dangerous. We actually lifted this thing which was god knows how many pounds. It could have been a ton, who knows? We carried it over to the new location, and we set it down, and got our fingers out from under it without anybody getting hurt.

. . . It was emblematic. There was something about it that was emblematic of the summer. It was referred to a lot later. It was like, "remember when we moved the stage?' We could do anything. That was all together. All for one—one for all. It was really extremely good-tempered and good-humored. In many ways, people had a very good time. (S.B. 5/5/88, 1213)

Simultaneously with the growth of The Fourth Wall, a group of amateur and professional musicians had been meeting informally for the purpose of making music together. Some community members formed music groups that performed at various group parties, and that met to practice once a week. Others were taking lessons from professionals either in the community or outside. There was a substantial number of professional musicians who had joined the community—some were working in the music business, others were trying to get started.[3] Many members who had no prior musical training began to study—either with the musicians in the group or with outside teachers. Prior to the leadership's takeover of the Fourth Wall, many of the musicians in the group decided to collectively rent a practice space, to be called the Music Loft. Before this space was rented, the leadership decided to expand the takeover of the Fourth Wall to include the Music Loft as well. The groups were to be joined—all members of either group would automatically become members of the other. A theater *and* a practice space were to be rented by the membership and paid for with monthly dues. Newton and Harvey decided, perhaps with the participation of Klein and Moses, that Joan Harvey would assume the directorship of this newly reconfigured organization. This consolidation of community creative activity under the auspices of the leadership took place in the Autumn of 1977. A meeting of all Fourth Wall members and all Music Loft members was held in which they were informed by a spokesman for the leadership that the two groups had merged, and that those who were members of one group were now automatically members of the new organization. There was a considerable amount of dissatisfaction with the new arrangement among the membership, but it was quickly silenced via individual's encounters with their therapists. According to E. C.,

I was in the Fourth Wall, but that wasn't a big deal. The big deal was being part of that band with Mike and Trudy and Rika and Marice. There was a whole thing that happened when we played at a party one night at the therapists' house, and there was a whole struggle because Luba had wanted to schedule a party the same night Joan and Saul had wanted to schedule a party. But [I was] feeling really part of the whole thing at that point. I think shortly thereafter I started to lose it, when the Fourth Wall went to a huge bureaucracy and apparatus at that point, and I joined the Fourth Wall because people I was dating were in it. I didn't have any interest in the acting. (E. C. 4/30/88, 5)

The Fourth Wall was redefined as a political theater company, and membership became almost mandatory for any community member. L. D. describes her reaction to this new requirement for membership:

See, I knew I wasn't totally with it when Joan tried to join the theater with the music and I didn't want to, when everybody was living in those tents. . . . I was very upset when those two groups joined. And I had to decide. I was told by a friend, "You have to decide to either be in the Fourth Wall or you're not going to be in it, because the music is going to join with the theater company." I felt forced to and decided to do it because that was my only social life. I had no idea that I could live any other way. Plus, all my friends joined. Not one didn't join. So here I was in a situation where of my twenty friends, nineteen of them had joined except for me. . . . To me, that was more of a crisis in terms of deciding what to do than any other because I really had to decide if I was going to be in this group or not. And I was being told and Alice was like "Are you crazy? You should do it. You're nuts. Why would you not do it? You're self-destructive." I was being told that I was suicidal and "You might as well hang yourself." (L. D. 6/1/93, 39)

Along with the takeover, the structure of the Fourth Wall became increasingly authoritarian. The community, which numbered approximately 300 at that time, demonstrated this to both the membership and the outside world by its takeover of the Truck and Warehouse Theater (noted above). Although the Fourth Wall had rented this theater, the previous tenants refused to vacate the premises. Rather than going through legal channels, the order went out from Saul Newton to "take over" the theater by occupying it and by threatening the current tenants with violence if they did not leave. A quasi-military operation was organized, with an initial force of approximately twenty members, and a back-up force of approximately fifty. The back-up force was ordered to circle the theater in cars, and to wait for the signal to enter the theater. The initial force entered the theater, destroyed the existing tenant's stage sets, and physically attacked and removed the tenants. Then the back-up force was signaled to enter and to "occupy" the theater. Later that evening the police came and two Fourth Wall members were arrested. The rest of the membership was ordered to stay in the theater for the next week, leaving only to work and to stop at their homes for clothes and food. A hundred or so people slept in the theater for several nights. The experience fostered a mentality of almost military camaraderie among the membership, which served to strengthen ties between participants and increase commitment to the theater company. Newton was overheard during this period discussing the "operation" as practice for future confrontations with political enemies.

W. K. describes his experience of the theater takeover:

That fall they had this period of open membership. They decided that they were going to merge with a music group and then allow strangers to come in, so I got into the Fourth Wall. I was never very active in the theater, I was just in it. I remember the first thing that I did as a member of the Fourth Wall is take over a theater, they had seemingly signed a lease for the Truck and Warehouse Theater and then there was a group that was playing there. It was some gay acting company, they were supposed to be killers as well as perverts, it was crazy. I slept under a seat for three nights, they had hundreds of us at the theater with barricades. It was like the Spanish revolution. (W. K. 5/9/88, 10–11)

During the first six months (approximately) after the takeover of the Fourth Wall, membership in the company, which was redefined as a "political theater company," became mandatory for members of the community. This change represented a dramatic departure from the earlier social structure of the Sullivan Institute community. Previously, membership had been informal in the sense that it depended on whether one was first a patient and second a resident of a group apartment or "dating" other patient-residents. In practice, this meant that individuals who were not in therapy, but who were friends of patients, could move into group apartments under the assumption that they would soon enter therapy with a member of the Sullivan Institute. Conversely, individuals who were not living in a group, but who were already in therapy, could "date" other patient-members, attend parties, and visit summer houses in Amagansett, under the assumption that they would eventually move into a group apartment. The boundaries of the community were more porous in the days before the Fourth Wall takeover. After the takeover any individual who was living in a group apartment or who had been in therapy for a while was expected to join the theater company. Those who did not do so were eventually asked to leave their apartments, and either "dropped out" or were "kicked out" of therapy. The reasons given by therapists for these actions were that those individuals who did not wish to join The Fourth Wall (which had been renamed the Fourth Wall Repertory Company) were not truly concerned with growing and developing as human beings. E. C. describes his experiences as a musician in the Fourth Wall:

I was encouraged to learn music, to do it and develop it. There was no time for anything else. There was no time for any relationships with people. . . . The only thing I was allowed to give time to was music because I was constantly rehearsing for the damn Music Live, or leading a rehearsal, so a lot of energy got channeled into that stuff. . . . I think somewhere early on, when I first joined the group, the focus was on doing whatever people felt like doing—hobbies, everyone had their million and one hobbies and was doing everything. Later on, all of a sudden that got squelched and I think that part of that stuff stuck, so I wanted to go out. . . . certainly by 1980 it was like, either you spend every free moment that you're not working or being in therapy doing something relating to the Fourth Wall, or something's wrong. (E. C. 4/30/88, 8–9)

Creative activity within the Fourth Wall was strictly circumscribed. In the early days of the comedy group and the Southampton summer, the agenda had been both to produce entertaining and insightful material for the enjoyment of the participants and other members of the community, and also to develop ideas that might eventually get produced professionally. In 1978, when Harvey had just taken control of the Fourth Wall, some of the founding members were asked to do a pilot television show for NBC. They performed a group of original skits which were received with interest. When Harvey was told that this had taken place, she threatened to sue the writers and actors for using Fourth Wall material to advance their own career goals. None of the skits had ever been produced by the theater company, but Harvey succeeded in putting an end to the preliminary negotiations, thereby impeding or destroying some individuals' chances for television careers. Then she began to write plays that were meant to be pedagogical tools, both for the members and for an outside audience.

In 1978, during the same period of time that Newton and Harvey engineered the takeover of the Fourth Wall, a property in the Catskill mountains was purchased as a vacation retreat and summer residence of the Fourth Wall Repertory Company. The property, formerly a hotel and bungalow colony that catered to members of the Communist party (and has since become a Jewish Renewal Retreat), was situated on a large piece of land that included a barn, a swimming pool, a main building with a dining hall, and a motel-like structure that contained approximately twenty-four rooms. There were other structures on the property—wooden houses that had probably been used as summer bungalows by the former owners. Each Fourth Wall member contributed $900 toward the purchase of the property. Work began immediately to prepare the property for the coming summer, much of it performed by work crews composed of company members.

During the first summer at the Workshop,[4] the hierarchical structure of the community was concretized with regard to the organization of accommodations for the leadership and the membership. The four leaders and their children occupied "the main house," the most modern and comfortable of all the structures on the property. The rest of the membership had rooms in an old motel called the "Laurels." One room would be assigned to up to eight individuals (usually a city group apartment); mattresses were laid out on the floor, and all occupants shared one bathroom. Some nights there were more than eight people sleeping in one moderately sized room. The "Laurels" building was run down— rugs were stained with water damage and toilets frequently overflowed. There was a barn on the property that was converted into a rehearsal and performance space, and other small wooden houses which were used as "date rooms." The "date rooms" usually consisted of a double-bed or double bed mattress and a lamp. They were barely furnished as they were only meant to be used at night by members and their dates. Each apartment was assigned a "date room," and usually rotated the use of the room among its members. There were additional "date rooms" that could be signed up for each day. These were distributed on a first come, first served basis.

After the Workshop was purchased in 1978, the community stopped going to Amagansett in the summers and all members were expected to spend most of their vacation time and summer weekends in the Catskills. There was a swimming pool and two tennis courts on the grounds which were maintained by members, as were the grounds and the buildings. One of the wooden houses was used as office space for members who needed to work while they were at the Workshop. Parties with music provided by Fourth Wall bands were held every

Saturday night in the barn. Rehearsals for all productions (plays, "Music Live," and the "Comedy Revue") usually began in August.

While the transition from the predominantly hedonistic and individualistic ethos of the "halcyon" days of the community to the self-denial and communitarian ethos of the "revolutionary" period was a slow one,[5] it was nevertheless quite dramatic. Many members left the group at this point because it no longer provided the type of experience that had motivated them to join. On the other hand, some people (albeit fewer) joined at this time because they were specifically interested in acting, and later, in political activism.

The average member of the Fourth Wall was required to pay monthly dues and to contribute his or her labor towards the myriad projects that were being developed. Once again, the cost of living in the Sullivan Institute/Fourth Wall community increased. Not only the cost in money, but the cost of membership in terms of the number of hours donated to community projects also rose. Whereas the earlier ideal lifestyle for community members included a relatively high percentage of private recreational time, the new ethos dictated hard work—at first for the sake of developing interpersonal skills and, after 1979, for a "good cause" as well.

THE THREE MILE ISLAND ACCIDENT

The next pivotal incident in the life of the community was the near meltdown of the Three Mile Island reactor in March of 1979. The leadership concluded that there was a possible danger to themselves if the wind blew radioactive emissions from the plant over the New York City area. They decided that some members, notably those who were pregnant, would flee to Florida to escape this eventuality. While no formal command was issued, when the membership heard this decision, they almost unanimously decided to accompany the leaders to Florida, or to leave New York City for other locations. E. G. talks about this:

I had a date with R. P. that night and we went to a club to see a band that J. H. and J. A. were playing in. I remember before that I was at my night job listening to the radio and hearing about the situation in Harrisburg. It sounded pretty scary, but I didn't really think there was much to do about it. Then I forgot about the whole thing when we went dancing. When we returned to R. P.'s house, which was the residence of several guys who were close to Newton, Harvey, Moses and Klein, many of them were getting ready to leave for Florida. I panicked when I realized that they were leaving, along with the entire leadership of the Fourth Wall community. If they were leaving, then shouldn't we be leaving? If pregnant women could be adversely affected, what about women who wanted to get pregnant someday?

I went home at 4:00 a.m. in the morning—I think I woke the people in my apartment up. I called Trudy (my therapist) and asked her what she thought we should do. She was planning to leave herself, and I remember saying aloud for the first time "I want to have kids someday." She said "why not?" as if it wasn't a big deal for anyone in the group to have children. She said it was our decision, but she was leaving, so I said "then we should leave too," and I guess my other roommates had talked to their therapists too, because we all decided to leave.

We decided to go to Florida because Joan, Ralph, Helen, Saul, B. P., and all the other people who lived at 91st street were going there because of Disney World. We didn't have enough money to fly so we rented a car and drove. Somehow we all ended up staying in this one Howard Johnson's motel—about 150 of us. (E. G. 6/30/94, 14)

While in Florida the leadership appointed a scientific committee composed of two physicists who were group members and Pearce and Newton's oldest son, who was a graduate student in mathematics at the time, to discover exactly what was taking place at Three Mile Island. A committee was also appointed to assist members in concocting stories to tell their employers to justify their unplanned absences from work. No one outside the community was to know that the exodus had taken place. In order to avoid focusing attention upon the group, members of the community returned after one week and attempted to cover up their departure. One member, who subsequently overdosed on valium upon his return, revealed the story to a doctor, and was expelled from the community along with his friends who had accompanied him to the emergency room. W. K. was one of these people:

. . . On a Friday night, one of my roommates, J. A., who was a musician, was performing at some club downtown and there were about 20 or 25 people who went there to see them performing, and there was all kinds of buzzing at 12 or 1 o'clock, "are you going down to Florida?" It seems as though something snowballed, some original suggestion that pregnant wives of therapists leave New York snowballed so that everybody went down to Florida in the next day. That night I came home and everybody had reservations made for them on planes to Orlando and we were avoiding nuclear holocaust. One of the things that disturbed me happened in the cab. We hired a limousine to get to Kennedy the next morning and we were this public service organization who cared for and loved everybody, but I remember telling, starting to say to the cab driver 'do you realize how dangerous it is in New York, we're leaving,' and then one of my roommates, his name was M.J., got furious at me for telling this to the cab driver, even suggesting it. Then we got down to Florida and somehow we all connected and found ourselves in this Howard Johnson's motel, there must have been 300 people.

And it all started getting very crazy down there. Part of the reason it was crazy was that they were telling us everybody's going to die and nobody seemed to die in New York. And then they had one person who said that if there are rays emanating from the current weather patterns, it would direct everything down to Orlando, Florida and not to New York. And then they started coming up with all kinds of food rules. We weren't supposed to eat anything that was growing within a certain range, any grasses or plants that grew. Then this extended itself to cows that ate the grass within this range. This was all going down there, and then I remember that Joan Harvey was always crying. She would sit and cry and people would comfort her, and I guess she was very moved by it all.

I remember I had a case in court, and I came up to try my case in court and I got these weird instructions about wearing things like masks on my face when I came back to New York and going back, and I took the plane up, went to court, and went right back to Florida. Then I remember some other things on that trip were, some people had left animals in their apartments, then there were other people who were expecting checks in the mail, either from unemployment insurance or from their work, and they needed money. It started being very expensive, everybody gave up a week's worth of salary and I think I figured it out that it cost everybody, there were 300 people and it cost each person

$500, it was something like a quarter of a million dollars—pretty expensive. (W. K. 5/9/88, 12)

The emotional climate of Sullivan Institute/Fourth Wall community members during this period in Orlando can be described as a kind of pre-apocalyptic bacchanalian hysteria. It was not clear from the outset when or if members would be returning to New York at all, or would be forced to move elsewhere in order to avoid radioactive contamination. Many members risked jobs to travel to Florida and were concerned about the repercussions of their sudden departures. A great deal of drinking and tranquilizer use ensued—groups of friends would go out together or meet in their respective hotel rooms. E. G. was one of those members:

I had never been one of the people in the group who was into group sex or orgies or anything like that, but when we got to Orlando things were so crazy. It felt like we were in the middle of a war and had been evacuated from our homes, possibly not to return again. I seem to remember the whole week through a drunken stupor. One day—or night (I can't remember which), four of us ended up in a hotel room—me and P. S. and G. T. and S. L., who I knew pretty well, and we all just started having sex. Actually it was me and P. S. together on one bed and G. T. and S. L. on the other and we didn't switch off, but that was pretty radical for me, just to have sex with other people in the room. It wasn't really for pleasure, I don't think—it was almost as if we didn't know what else to do with ourselves. Maybe it was just a way to forget about the whole thing for a while. (E. G. 6/30/94, 16)

Toward the end of the week, the leadership decided that it would be safe to return to New York City, but only if certain precautions were observed. No agricultural produce could be consumed that came from the area around Harrisburg. The science committee was still in the process of researching various types of danger. A food cooperative was formed by the leadership so that they and the membership could be sure that the food they were consuming was not from these areas. When the members returned, it was to a community that took a much more fearful stance toward the world outside its boundaries:

Then finally, we got down there Saturday morning, finally on Friday we were told we could come back, and I think I was on the first plane coming back, and I remember I was on a plane. I came in with my roommates, it was B. G. and S. A., and then also on the plane were P. W., and S. S. and L. S., and I made a date for the next night with S. S. or P. W., I 'm not sure which one, they lived together. I came home that night and S. A., my roommate, was pretty upset, I remember he had lost his suitcase in the airport and he got furious when he lost his suitcase and kicked another suitcase. . . . He came home and then Saturday morning I went to work and B. G. called me and said that S. A. had overdosed on valium and booze and would I come, take him to the hospital. It was April 14th, could I take him to the hospital because he had to get to the accountant by that night. So I remember, you didn't do anything alone, so I called my friend J. P. and said "would you come with me to the hospital" so we drive S. A. to the hospital and then J. P. left, but before he left, there was something called "coverage,"—one was never to be alone, so S. A. was taken in and they started pumping his stomach. It seemed like a perfectly normal thing to do, so then I called either P. W. or S. S. who I had a date with and told them that I'm keeping a vigil in the hospital for S. A. and then three of them came over: P. W., S. S., and L. S. And at that time S. S. said she was quitting the group, she didn't think the therapy worked, and this thing down in Florida was too crazy for her, she couldn't deal with it. But we tried to persuade her otherwise, we thought, well she's a lost soul, she's going to disappear from the face of the earth. And here we had just complimented her because she had gotten her kid brother into therapy.

So then we're sitting there for a while and waiting for S. A. to come out and they kept coming out and saying he was better. Then finally a therapist came out to us and said "we're ready to discharge him, he seems okay, but he's telling this very bizarre story. He said that he was just down in Florida with an acting company of 300 people, who were there to avoid nuclear holocaust." He said "I would ordinarily release him, but this seems like a very weird story." And I'm pretty smart, because I knew what I was supposed to say and what I wasn't supposed to say. I said "well, will you discharge him even with the story?" and then P. W., who is, maybe not as smart as I am or whatever, said "oh, no, no it's all right, it's a true story." And at once I knew that something was, you know, you shouldn't say this. Why you shouldn't say it wasn't clear, but I knew you shouldn't say it. So I stupidly telephoned Joan Harvey to report this. And I told Joan Harvey and she said "I'm going to kill you." And this was on Sunday. Monday night there was a rehearsal, and I went to it, and I noticed that people were looking at me, and then Tuesday I heard that there's going to be a special meeting at 11 or 12 o'clock at night at the theater, which is down in the East Village, and everybody must attend. So I attended this meeting and at this meeting I was drummed out of the group. My roommates were told to get rid of me by the next morning. I left the next morning and what happened is that these 200–300 people completely cut me out of their lives. It was impossible to have anything to do with them, and nobody talked to me, people would avoid me on the street. I took busses with them, they would stand up if I sat down next to them. I remember getting off a bus with A.P. where he was going to my corner, but he pretended to go around the block and then I met him at my corner. You know, crazy things like that went on. And later on some people tried to break into my apartment. That was when Luba left and they thought that I had the secret to where Luba had stolen a kiln or something. (W. K. 5/9/88, 13–16)

The events that W. K. describes above were pivotal in the transformation of the Sullivan Institute/Fourth Wall community. They marked the beginning of an era of increasing regimentation and separation from mainstream society and catapulted the group into the antinuclear movement. The political concerns of the community became increasingly important at the expense of the earlier emphasis on personal growth and pleasure. Sacrifice of one's time, money, and personal preferences was increasingly required. Additionally, the public expulsion of five long-time members of the group had the effect of creating a climate of fear within the community. Any member who did not follow to the letter the rules set forth by the leadership could be expelled without notice, and lose his or her living situation, therapist, and all contacts within the group in a matter of hours.

THE EMERGENCY COMMUNICATION SYSTEM (ECS)

After the return from Florida, every member of the community was required to fill out a schedule form detailing his or her whereabouts and activities for twenty-four hours a day every day. An emergency communication system was devised that kept copies of all members' schedules and kept a twenty-four hour phone tree in operation.[6] The rationale for this practice was that since the Three Mile Island or Indian Point reactors might melt down at any moment, the members had to be ready to make their escape and therefore be available by phone or beeper at all times. Plans for disaster preparedness included the purchase of a fleet of .Z. for evacuating the entire community. Furthermore, a food co-op staffed entirely by community members was opened because the leadership decided that no food from contaminated areas in the country should be consumed.

As stated, at this point the Sullivan Institute/Fourth Wall community became involved in the antinuclear movement that had become widespread in the United States. Joan Harvey, who had become the "artistic director" of the Fourth Wall, began making a documentary about Three Mile Island that required the financial support of the entire community. In addition to their regular monthly dues, members were assessed varying amounts of "contributions" depending on their incomes as reported to their therapists. The therapeutic aspects of the group began to become less important as the political component grew. Emphasis was now placed on the impact the group could have on the outside world, most notably the antinuclear movement, but the general public as well. The leadership began to view themselves as serving a propaganda function in society at large, rather than simply concerning themselves with the creation of the "new man" within the confines of the community. Members were expected to sacrifice both their money and their free time to the cause. Those that refused to cooperate were either berated, threatened (often physically), or expelled.

While the ECS was originally intended for use in emergencies, it became the leadership's way of communicating with the membership. If a general meeting was called, the ECS "phone tree" was used to inform all members. If a work crew was needed at the theater or the Workshop, or for any particular purpose, a message would be sent out. One of the two heads of the ECS saved one of these periodic (and quite frequent) messages:

THIS IS THE ECS—THIS IS NOT AN EMERGENCY

The Workshop is in need of all our efforts to help ready it for the summer. Each member is expected to free up at least one weekend day between now and Memorial Day. Give your ECS rep all the possible weekend days that you could work, indicating your first, 2nd, or 3rd choices and The Work Committee will schedule you and arrange for your transportation. This information is due by midnight Thursday, April 4 to G. F.

All members who do radio watch between 9:00 AM and midnight must call in any changes in their scheduled radio times to The Work Committee answering machine before 8:00 PM the day before their watch. (M. B. undated, handwritten)

THE PLAYS OF JOAN HARVEY

Beginning in the Fall of 1978 through 1985, Joan Harvey wrote a play each year which was produced by the theater company as the serious dramatic work in its repertory. Other productions included a children's play,[7] "Music Live," a performance of original and other songs by company members, and a comedy revue composed of short satirical skits. Harvey's plays were meant to make serious political, social, and psychological statements about the problems of U.S. society, the global economy, the environment, the military-industrial complex, and other current issues. The earlier plays focus more on family conflict, but these themes were continued throughout the later plays as well.

When the Fourth Wall became the main project of the Sullivan Institute community, the role of psychotherapy in the formation of the self-conceptions of members diminished to some extent as status in the theater company assumed greater importance. If Harvey chose a member to play a major role in one of her plays, that member's status in the hierarchy of the group rose immediately. Conversely, it was necessary to have a "special" relationship with Harvey (or Newton, in some cases) in order to be chosen for one of these roles.

Due to the leadership's fear of media coverage, and to their increasing involvement with the theater company, there were no documented statements of theory made either in Institute classes or in print after 1979. The plays written by Harvey are the major theoretical and political statements of the community after this date. Each play bears her name, and the community printed copies to be distributed to the general public. Since the plays were written as propaganda, in the sense that they were meant to teach the audience something about the pathology of U.S. family life and about politics, love and friendship as well, they provide a rich source of information concerning the changing beliefs, ideas, and interests of Harvey and the other three leaders. It was commonly known that Harvey consulted with Saul Newton, and probably also with Klein and Moses to a lesser extent, so the ideas expressed in the plays can be said to reflect those of the leadership.

"In the Beginning," Harvey's first play, which was written in 1977 before the Three Mile Island Accident, was an autobiographical work (as were many of her plays) based upon her experience of leaving her parents' home at age eighteen. It was aimed at a middle-class audience, and focused primarily on the malevolence of a mother who does not want her children to leave home, become successful, or have important relationships outside the family. To a nonmember reading the play, the mother seems like a very extreme case of maternal possessiveness and envy.[8] This is not to argue that the character of the mother in the play is unrealistic, but that she is hyper-real. Additionally, Harvey attempts to connect the parents in the play to larger-scale social problems, such as nuclear proliferation, militarism, environmental problems, and political complacency.

The portrayal of the mother, and the speeches that the daughter gives—which are meant to unveil the "truth" about the family dynamics—give the reader a very clear conception of how the leadership thought about these issues:

You know yourself I don't ask a whole lot, even dad says I'm too liberal . . . and compared with the other parents, well forget it! . . . But *I* believe you guys have to have room to spread your wings, try the ways of the other kids. With moderation everything works out better. Good families make good friends. (Putting her hand to his chin in motherly jest.) But I have to know where my children are for just as long as they choose to stay close to the nest. (Harvey 1980b, 3)

This line is meant to convey the manipulativeness of the mother—she portrays herself as more liberal than the other parents, yet at the same time she is demanding to know the whereabouts of her eighteen-year-old son as long as he lives at home. This speech takes place on the day of both her children's graduations from high school. She begins to cry when thinking about the fact that they are growing up and will soon leave home; this is portrayed as manipulative, and as an attempt to evoke guilt and fear in the children (1980, 8). She is shown deliberately interfering with her daughter's relationship with her best friend, who is asking her to move into an apartment with her. For Harvey, Newton, Klein, and Moses, this is simply typical maternal behavior. They are justifying their belief that adolescents and young adults need to get away from their parents' control, and that in order to achieve this goal, it may be necessary to sever contact with parents. Inasmuch as the play can be read as autobiographical, we can also surmise that Harvey is generalizing her own experience to include almost all others.

The play is also an analysis of family dynamics—in this case the dynamics of a family in which the wife and mother is the dominant force. This was not an accidental occurrence in Harvey's play, and is very much in keeping with the beliefs of the Sullivanians, and the beliefs of other clinicians and theorists of the 1950s and early 1960s period, that frustrated and hysterical mothers were the primary cause of psychopathology in middle-class U.S. society of this time period. The time frame for the play is unclear. While Harvey alludes to drug use and the social movements of the 1960s, the father in her play says that he worked with the W.P.A. Then the daughter's friend estimates the father's age as forty-five. Since the W.P.A. ended in the 1940s, the father would have been a great deal older than forty-five in the late 1970s. The role of the mother and the dialogue bears a much stronger resemblance to the 1950s—the time of Joan Harvey's youth. The fact that this is left unclear to the viewer is an indication of her intention to make a universal statement—nothing has changed in U.S. culture since then, nor was it different before that time.

The centerpiece of this play is the speech Jane makes to her parents before she is led off to a mental institution. This speech (excerpted below) contains not only the views of Harvey and others on the dynamics of interpersonal growth and the family,[9] but their analysis and critique of the entire society as well:

When *is* the right time—when it is easy to do something you never tried, Dad? Give me a chance, nothing important happens when it's convenient. I'm . . . I don't feel good . . . What comes easy? Or plops itself nicely, nicely on the dining room to be sampled like a salmon loaf. Sometimes it's upsetting. And in this house, if you're the least upset, it's a sign that you're wrong, your judgment's off balance, coo-coo, and "we" have to figure it out. (39–40)

This first paragraph is a critique of what Pearce, Newton, Harvey, and others referred to as "the pathology of normality."[10] This is a reference to the private/public split in the context of the family, and to expectations that family members present a "united front" of normality to both the community at large, and in some cases, to each other. It is also a reference to the antipathy toward change that Harvey perceived in U.S. culture in general, and to the norms and expectations that downplay conflict and change, while foregrounding continuity and cohesiveness. When Jane tells her parents that she is planning to leave home, the response of shock and reproach that she expects from her parents is simply the classic Sullivanian statement that parents never want their children to leave home in search of their own identities or of a better life for themselves. This may have been true for Joan Harvey, and for some others in the community, but was certainly not the only possible response of families to their offspring's' desire to go out in the world. Before college education became as widespread as it did in the 1960s, many families could not afford to send all their children to college. Those who could often saved money by sending their children to a school near enough to home so that they didn't have to pay housing costs as well.[11] For Harvey and Newton, this was indicative of the underlying hostility of parents toward their children. If the money had not been saved for college, this simply meant that the parents wanted their children to stay home, and not to become socially or economically mobile.

Next, in a speech meant to show us that Jane is getting increasingly agitated and in need of medical (psychiatric) intervention, Harvey gives us her diagnosis of societal ills, with pollution and environmental degradation heading the list. She also accuses her mother and brother of having a symbiotic (i.e., unhealthy) relationship. In the play Jane doesn't believe her children will live past twenty because the environment will be too polluted.[12] This is a call to political action. Newton and Harvey regarded the peace movement (the antiwar movement of the 1960s and early 1970s) as a waste of talent that could have been used to make a revolution in the United States. For them the counterculture was simply a distraction from the work at hand. This position is consonant with that of the CP/USA of that time. The educational system is lambasted for deadening minds and failing to teach important truths, and at the same time it is connected to the know-nothing attitude of Jane's family. Modern society becomes a conspiracy to depoliticize and to generally disempower all citizens—especially the young. Some of the points made in this play are almost identical to those made far more eloquently by Mike Nichols approximately ten years earlier in *The Graduate,* regarding the corruption of the older generation, their materialism, and their hypocrisy.

For Harvey, one generation passes on inaction and despair to the next. The references explicit in her plays are to the 1960s, but the indictment of the family is the same for all generations in the sense that Harvey believes that the family has remained static since the birth of capitalism. She argues that the widespread use of drugs in the 1960s and 1970s contributed to political and social ennui among young people. This analysis is questionable, although it may contain some valid points, in the sense that drugs were used by many different segments of the population during the 1960s and early 1970s, including both political and countercultural activists. While there were certainly many drug casualties during that period, there were many more casual users than addicts or abusers.

The message of this play, which is conveyed in a style that could be labeled socialist realism, modeled after some of the plays of Clifford Odets and Bertolt Brecht, is that not only should parents allow their children to become intellectually and economically independent, but that we all need to become activists if the world is to be saved. The play contains a quasi-apocalyptic view of the environmental crisis, along with an indictment of maternal envy. Although many of the statements that it makes ring true in some aspects, they both tend toward conspiracy theory interpretations of the motivations of mothers and the causes of environmental crisis.

Harvey's next play, written in 1978 and entitled *Ride a Red Horse,* shifts its focus from her adolescence to the adolescence of her teenage daughter. This play is clearly set in the present, and contains no problematic historical references. The two main characters of this play are Lee Ann, a middle-aged woman who is a full-time activist for an "anti-nuclear woman's group," and her seventeen-year-old daughter Muffy, who is involved in one of the civil disobedience groups that participated in the antinuclear movement of the late 1970s. The action is centered on Muffy and her group's planning for the occupation of a nuclear plant—an act of civil disobedience engaged in by man activists during this period. The ancillary characters in the play include Lee Ann's crotchety old communist father, and her oldest child, Chris, who is twenty-nine years old and a self-described revolutionary.

Ride a Red Horse is a departure and a new development from *In the Beginning* in several aspects. Rather than focusing on mainstream society and critiquing its problems, Harvey chooses to depict a family of left-wing activists. This play is meant to be exemplary in a way that *In the Beginning* was not—to demonstrate to the audience a superior life of social and political engagement. It is also much more explicitly political than *Beginning* in that it goes beyond a diagnosis of the planet's ills to enter into the debate within the left over internal democracy—that is, how activist groups should be led. It also presents a political economic analysis of the world situation that is explicitly socialist, a diagnosis of the problems of the Old and New Left movements in the United States, as well as an insider's view of the problems of the antinuclear movement. At the same time, Harvey is attempting to show her audience how conflicts between parents and children can be resolved. The language of the play, as in all of Harvey's plays, is designed to be as down-to-earth and nonintellectual as possible in an attempt to reach an audience that included college students and residents of halfway houses such as Phoenix House and others.[13]

In reference to the SI/FW's position vis-à-vis the antinuclear movement of the late 1970s, Harvey makes several statements throughout the play. One of her concerns is the tendency of some activist groups to uncouple the issue of nuclear power plants and their unsuitability as a power source from the military's production and use of nuclear materials. One of the other issues is the conflict between Lee Ann and her daughter over tactics in the upcoming march on Washington in which they are both involved.

Through a conflict that emerges between Lee Ann and her daughter (which is again autobiographical),[14] Harvey attempts to teach the younger members of the antinuclear movement why and how some of their tactics are misguided. It was common practice in the late 1970s and early 1980s for small groups of activists to occupy the land on which nuclear plants were built. They were inevitably arrested, and some resisted arrest using the classic civil disobedience tactic of "going limp" when the police tried to lead them away. The play tries to demonstrate that these tactics are divisive and dangerous. Many of these groups were run by consensus—every member had to agree on an action before it could go forward.

It should be noted that Harvey's assessment of the danger of the situation her daughter was putting herself in was extreme. Throughout the duration of the antinuclear movement, few (if any) activists lost their lives through violence, or were assaulted by police during civil disobedience. The result of the action at Shoreham was anticlimactic—the affinity groups that went over the fences to occupy the plant grounds were led off the premises by the police, taken to the local police station, given $50 tickets and released. After this event, Harvey's daughter discontinued her involvement with the antinuclear movement.

While the issues of strategy and mother/daughter conflict remain the central theme of the play, the appearance of Lee Ann's older child—her twenty-nine-year-old son who is referred to as a revolutionary—is also important, and he provides yet another viewpoint on both the world political economic situation and on Muffy's plans. The son, Chris, is engaged in organizing an "international" of some sort—although it is not specified in the play what type of organization this is. He has come from South America, where he has been "organizing," and is waiting to meet a Chicano friend who is in hiding because he was framed for doing political work. They enter into political debate:

Lee: This time, we're in a funny war—you don't know this one. No real support from any large political party, and no major country—capitalist, socialist—it doesn't matter, they're not with us this time. The United States is committed to the arms race and Russia has to live with us. So Russia's forced into the arms race, and corrupted by it too. . . . As usual, the right is unified by its international conspiracy and the left helps the right with its splintering, separatism, and the tactics and theory of the Trotskyites.

Chris: Mom, I worked in the sixties, it was filled with the kids moving away from all old leadership ideas. . . . Stick to her organization for a minute. You're really calling it reactionary. How?

Lee: It's against all centralized decision-making. It stops action by using consensus procedures. You know, a consensus can be blocked by a single goddamn objection. A single objection? Necessary radical actions are delayed, avoided and destroyed by any apparently well-meaning, naive, or just hateful, good-looking jerk. (Harvey 1979, 16–18)

This is the clearest statement of the political position of Newton, Harvey, Klein, and Moses made in any public forum at that time. Their analysis of the global political situation of the late 1970s was that the Soviet Union had been pulled into the arms race by the need to maintain military parity with the United States, and that it was therefore up to the "grass roots" organizations, unaffiliated with any political parties, to push for global disarmament. Newton had been a

Stalinist since the Spanish civil war or before—his and Harvey's distaste for Trotskyites and for those who challenged notions of democratic centralist leadership is obvious in the speech. They viewed the challenge to established power relations within the leftist organizations that took place in the late 1960s and early 1970s as counterrevolutionary and debilitating to progress. Given the fact that they viewed the left organizations of the 1960s period as lacking in good structures of leadership, it could be hypothesized that through the plays, and through their participation in the antinuclear movement, the SI/FW leadership meant their community to become a sort of vanguard, which would show other groups how they could be effective, and that would possibly provide leadership for the larger movement.

Ride a Red Horse is a play about three generations of radicals. Through it we learn that Harvey and Newton believe that the CP/USA took a wrong turn in the 1950s—away from the notion of a Popular Front and toward left sectarianism. Although it is not verifiable, it is possible to guess that Newton may have left the Party over the Foster/Browder split right after World War II. This schism was centered on the CP/USA's policy of the Popular Front, adopted during the war, which was a successful attempt to ally itself with other antifascist organizations. In 1946 a letter was sent by Jacques Duclos, one of the members of the Central Committee of the Third International (the international communist organization), criticizing the Popular Front policy and urging the Party to become more militant and therefore more sectarian. This led to the expulsion of Earl Browder, who had been the head of the U.S. Party. From that time on, the Party became increasingly divorced from the concerns of the majority of Americans, and more concerned with maintaining the "correct line." When the McCarthy era began in the early 1950s, the CP/USA leadership felt it was necessary to send most of its leadership and some of its membership underground. Harvey is criticizing them for these actions, accusing them of cowardice and of incorrectly evaluating the political situation at that time. Additionally, she is criticizing the CP's actions during the mass movements of the 1960s—they failed to ally themselves with the New Left because most New Left groups did not adhere strictly to the Party's political economic analysis. Nor did they agree on tactics—many of the newer groups had much more flamboyant, confrontational styles than that of the CP/USA. The resulting schism between the Old and New Left, and the New Left's tendency to reject the lessons of the past as having any relevance for the present, resulted in a movement that did not view itself historically, and did not have much long-term perspective or guidance from the previous generation of leftists. The understanding of global politics that Harvey presents in her plays is based on an oversimplified Marxist analysis.

Harvey and the other leaders believed at this time that "fascism" or military dictatorship could be just around the corner in the U.S. This fear was communicated to the membership of the SI/FW community through the skits in the comedy revue, and in the politics classes that had already started in the summer of 1979. One of the interesting contradictions regarding the political research and teaching that was being carried out within the group during this period was between the production of some extremely well thought-out and researched projects, such as "The Zirconium Connection,"[15] an article published by two physicists in the community who had analyzed the Three Mile Island disaster and come up with a valid scientific explanation of what had actually taken place, and some almost shockingly poor research, such as the distribution of a manuscript called "Iron Mountain" to the membership, which purported to be a government and corporate plan for the safekeeping of important people and records in the event of a nuclear war. Harvey and some of her researchers had discovered this book, which upon further examination turned out to be a fictional piece, and represented it to the membership as an actual corporate document. When it was discovered that the manuscript was fictional, it was pulled from distribution in the community without any comment. It was only those who made an effort to discover the truth that found out what had happened, and even then the whole affair was treated as if it had been a minor error.

Ride a Red Horse was the first play in which Harvey attempted to come up with a psychology of activism. Although this had been alluded to in some of the community's theoretical writings and classes, the link between the acceptance of the status quo learned in the home and the difficulty of acting politically had been explicitly made.

The language of *Ride a Red Horse* borders on the religious in the sense that it is about faith—about pushing back despair in the belief that the good can overcome the bad. Whereas it claims to have a rational foundation, the language of light and darkness, even of creation, lends a metaphysical slant to it. The thinking and language move easily into the domain of millennialism.

Harvey's next play, *Death Watch?*, written in 1980, takes place in a communal living situation in which some members of the commune (or collective) work to support other members who are full-time political organizers. While the structure of the Sullivan Institute/Fourth Wall community was different from that of the commune in the play, the membership of the Fourth Wall paid both monthly dues and frequent "assessments" to support various projects. These projects included the production of three feature-length documentary films, the operation of the Truck and Warehouse theater, and the purchase and maintenance of a vacation property in the Catskill Mountains. Although the leaders worked as therapists and supervisors for patients and trainees within the community, their income and working hours did not match their lifestyle. They owned a large building on the upper West Side of Manhattan, and had eighteen children among the four of them (Newton fathered 10, Klein, 8—with several mothers). All the children were sent to private elementary schools and colleges. Before they were old enough to stay home or travel alone, each child had a full-time baby-sitter. Additionally, the leaders maintained a household staff that included a cook, a cleaner, and someone who did their grocery shopping for them. Few other members of the community could afford to live in this manner, and those who could were often asked to lend or give money to the leadership.[16]

The message of *Death Watch?* operates on several levels. It is meant to educate the public about the dangers of nuclear waste and nuclear power by giving specific information about nuclear plants, chemical waste, and arms stockpiling. It attempts to tie those issues in with what Harvey refers to as "international finance capital" and the supposed threat of a military coup in the United States. It is also meant to address the issue of lifestyle in an exemplary fashion—namely, by showing the audience a better way to live than the traditional nuclear family. And for the membership of the Sullivan Institute/Fourth Wall community, the play was intended to convince them that the money that they paid the leadership—in therapy fees and in dues and assessments to the Fourth Wall—was worth the sacrifices they were making in terms of time spent and general quality of life.[17]

With the production of *Death Watch?* (or possibly before), a new perspective regarding relationships began to be put forth by the leadership. The priority for people was supposed to be "the struggle," rather than spending time with people one enjoyed. Therefore, it wasn't important whether one was liked by her/his housemates, only that he or she be an active participant in the political task at hand. One was thought to "grow up" or "become human" by engaging in the political work that needed to be done—not by "dating" or "working on your relationships," as had been the case in earlier years.

The message of the play regarding sexual relationships was intended by Harvey to be both libertarian and pragmatic. In the first act Kate (the protagonist) is seen sleeping with Jim; in the second she is shown in bed with Joe. When teased about her "loose morals," she declares that she is an atheist and a Communist. This is done in what is intended to be a humorous fashion, and then Joe and Kate engage in some light-hearted banter on the subject. Harvey's intention is to link the personal with the political:

Kate: Screw, but don't screw around! You are mine, baby, and don't you forget it. Private property (She salutes.) is the cornerstone of democracy.

Joe: Only one to a customer.

Kate: Oh, then you'd better take care of me, I'm all that you're allowed. (She rolls on top of him, thinking.) But watch out, I'm needy, hungry—gotta be fed; take care of me, put a roof over my head, make me happy. Put a ring on my finger, what am I?

Joe: You are oppressive! (Pushes her off of him.)

Kate: For 100,00 dollars, you guessed, I am private property! (Harvey 1980c, 52)

This argument is a fairly long-standing (Marxian or bohemian) one: marriage as private property, and monogamy as restrictive and therefore unhealthy. For the outside audience, this dialogue was meant to teach—for the members, it was meant to model the desired behavior.

As compared with *Ride a Red Horse,* with its predictions of nuclear catastrophe and claims regarding infiltration of the antinuclear movement by the intelligence community, *Death Watch?* puts forth a more foreboding message. It argues that the individuals who control the large international banks control the world, and that because military build-up and war are profitable for these corporations, a military coup is likely to take place in the United States. A political scientist is one of the characters in the play, and Harvey uses this character to preach mistrust and contempt for academia by having him working on a secret international project on the viability of world peace. The conclusion that "war . . . is essential to the very existence of separate nations or states . . . [that it] stabilizes the internal structure of a state" (62) is reached by the scientists working on this project. They also conclude that nuclear war could be more beneficial than conventional warfare because, while conventional warfare weakens the species by killing off the strongest individuals, "nuclear warfare has the residual effect of killing the weaker of the species." (Harvey 1980c, 66)

Harvey also wants to make her position regarding the Soviet Union clear. This is a very important matter for her as both the daughter and the wife of men who were CP/USA members.[18] She and Newton believed that the conditions that existed when the USSR came into being made it imperative for them to participate in the arms race, if only out of a need for self-defense. She illustrates this in *Death Watch?*:

Jim: No, damn it, you take a new socialist nation, set it plunk in a world, a *world* of finance capital, and against the allied war machine. . . . You can't tell me the Russian leaders and generals had a choice but to build a military machine and arms stockpile equal to the west. . . .

Look. . . terrible things happened in the Soviet push for power. They took a backward people, and conventional generals and erected a gigantic, war power. Maybe some of them got to like power. Sure . . . some of the leaders got consumed by power . . .

Kate: (Lost in thought.) I just wonder, existing in a capitalist world, just how much corruption for money could get going among leaders in socialist countries. (Stopping Jim from arguing.) Not the people, not the philosophy, but individual men. They could be bought. (Pause.) You know what worries me. There's a weakness in the communist bloc . . . gives them a wedge. a place to put pressure. The hatred between China and Russia is such a weakness in the unity of socialist nations, it's got to give us a wedge . . . pushing on the hatred. It's a place to put pressure. (Harvey 1980, 71–72)

The need for an analysis of the Soviet Union—and the need to explain to the public (and to the membership of the Fourth Wall) why the USSR would participate in the arms race—does not simply arise from a sense of obligation to family or history. In order to make the case for a socialist United States, it was necessary to explain what seemed to be an obvious failure of socialism in the USSR. If the "capitalist" world could be blamed, then there was still hope for a world revolution. This type of explanation (sometimes referred to as apologism) was by no means the exclusive domain of the Fourth Wall leadership. Many other left groups shared this opinion as well.

As in *Red Horse*, the issue of leadership is also addressed in *Death Watch?* Harvey once again alludes to the factions and ethic of antileadership that she believes destroyed the social movements of the 1960s. The communal living situation depicted in the play is meant to be the model for the social structure Harvey and the other leaders believe will enable a new socialist movement to be built. For example, when a female character who is married to a right-wing political scientist decides to leave her husband, she is given what was known in the jargon of the community as a "summary." A summary was a speech—sometimes given by an analyst to a patient, but also given by friends to each other—that confronted an individual about some basic aspect of his or her personality that was considered to be "unproductive" and demanded that he or she change. Jessica is scared about living without her husband, and Kate is pushing her to give up her old "security operations."[19] The speech is also significant with regard to the Sullivan Institute theories about the importance of living one's personal life in a radical fashion. In this belief the group is closer to the New Left and countercultural beliefs of the 1960s and 1970s that "the personal is political," as opposed to the CPUSA and other Old Leftists who lived relatively conventional personal lives while advocating radical political and economic change.

The plays are also full of examples of certain types of interactions that occurred commonly within the community. The "summary" above is one, and immediately following it, Harvey gives us an example of another confrontational technique that was commonly used by the leadership to embarrass and intimidate the member-patients. This technique consisted of reacting to an individual's discomfort in a particular social situation by calling attention to it and labeling it as an intentional behavior, which could be discontinued at will. In *Death Watch?* Kate does this to Alice, who has entered while Jessica and Kate are still "having words." Whereas in conventional middle-class U.S. society, it is considered to be quite normal for a stranger who intrudes on a screaming match between two friends to experience discomfort and to wish to leave the situation in order to allow the friends to "have it out," in the Sullivan Institute/Fourth Wall community, this was considered a priggish and outmoded attitude:

Alice: I think I should just go. (She starts to pick up the papers.)

Kate: (Still preoccupied and irritated with Jessy.) (She speaks to the two guys.) Don't do that to people. Damn it, not everybody is as glib as you—give her room. (To Alice.) You cut it out, too. Not everybody in the world is uncomfortable because Alice is here. You are uncomfortable with everyone else. See, I'm mad at her (She points at Jessy.) and she's mad at me. Hell, we wouldn't even notice you if you weren't so self-centered. (Harvey 1980c, 104)

The effect of this type of treatment of individuals who were uncomfortable to begin with was that, because they felt that their discomfort was a hostile act that they could control, they felt even more uncomfortable but sometimes felt compelled to act as if they were not. The rationale for this was that it contributed to the breakdown of the isolation that is fostered by the capitalist social system.

The only way to end this kind of alienated existence, according to Harvey, is to become a revolutionary. In order to do this, one must abandon interest in self-preservation and accept the likelihood of being killed by the defenders of capitalism—the military and the police. The play ends with Jessica and Alice—the uncomfortable researcher who is "told off" by Kate (Harvey)—moving into the commune and becoming political activists.

Freedom Ain't No Bowl of Cherries, Harvey's next play, opened in

September of 1981. This play was the first to have musical numbers and dance incorporated into a dramatic plot. Harvey wrote it specifically for the purpose of having it tour the world as part of the Fourth Wall's organizing efforts. This was one of the most outwardly-directed periods in the history of the community. The play was written without the long didactic speeches that appear in the others—the music and light banter is presumably meant to "lighten the load" of the heavy message. The characters seem to be purposely one-dimensional—created to convey a message rather than to show any character conflict or development.

Freedom shares with the other plays the mixture of psychological and political message. The play opens with a patter about the connections between the weapons industry and the U.S. government, with a brief mention of the erosion of civil rights that is discussed in *Death Watch?*, and with a song called "Excuses for Authority" that attempts to connect rejection by one's parents with the existence of the military-industrial complex.

As mentioned previously, all members who become mothers were expected to work full-time almost immediately after they had given birth. The rationale is clearly laid out in the song—most mothers have very little excitement in their lives other than their children, and are envious and resentful of the time and work they must devote to childcare. They expect their children to fill the gaps in their lives by becoming the people they wish them to be. Therefore, neither mothers nor fathers should be engaged in full-time childcare—it could only harm the child.

Freedom Ain't No Bowl of Cherries was the first of Harvey's plays to deal with the issue of male homosexuality. Again the parallel with Harvey's life is quite literal. The role of Bruce is played by her lover at that time, who was a gay man. The relationship that Barbara (Harvey's part) and Bruce have in the play is taken directly from this experience, with very little embellishment or substitution. Bruce doesn't want to have sex with Barbara in the play because he is "phobic," the diagnosis that Newton and Harvey arrived at for both gay men and lesbians in the community. Since a phobia is a pathological phenomenon, the expectation was that these individuals needed to become bisexual in order to develop fully as human beings. Interestingly enough, this expectation did not work identically for heterosexual individuals. Although heterosexuals were encouraged to experiment with gay and lesbian sex if they were so inclined, this was not a requirement. In the case of gay and lesbian members, heterosexual sex was "strongly encouraged," if not required. Sex was viewed as a "need"—mostly for physical contact and support rather than for erotic pleasure.

Bruce: Why am I phobic?

Barbara: Wait till I put my thinking cap on. Okay.

Bruce: You know, why is my taste . . .

Barbara: Up your ass? Oops. (They both laugh together.) I meant you have no taste.

Bruce: (Thinks for a second.) Mean turns me on. You're right, I have no taste.

Barbara: Actually, you are very self-centered. . . . And selfish. Oh, I forgot, arrogant.

Bruce: Come on.

Barbara: No, you asked. In two years of traveling, you get drunk once and turned on. We fuck. You get turned off once, and scared. We talk. That's not a lot of intimate contact for a needy person like myself.

Bruce: Come on, you know how I feel.

Barbara: Yeah, I know. And that's supposed to be enough? I'll try to remember how you feel in the middle of the night when I feel disgusting and rotten, or lusting after your stony body, or just plain scared. . . .

Bruce: . . . But what is it you really want from me? I can never figure it out. . . .

Barbara: Let's just say I have an affinity for pricks. . . . God, do I have to have a reason? Listen, we keep the world from blowing up, I got what I want. (Pause.) Of course, it's not much in bed, mind you.

Bruce: I'm sorry . . .

Barbara: Think, if people lived their personal lives with the integrity of their politics. (Harvey 1981, 40–41)

This is somewhat of a reversal of the notion of the personal being political—here Harvey is suggesting that we live our personal lives in accordance with our political beliefs. She is advocating for choosing one's friends and lovers at least partially for their politics. In other words, if someone doesn't agree with her, or if they haven't devoted their lives to political activism, they are not a potential friend.

Freedom Ain't No Bowl of Cherries is a combination of political message and instruction manual for becoming a political activist. Throughout the play each of the characters is confronted with his or her personality flaws and expected to change, or at least improve them. Toward the end both of the marriages portrayed in the play end more or less amicably. Both relationships have already been characterized as destructive and the result of inertia rather than love and devotion, and through a song the audience is told that regardless of what our personal deficiencies are, we must all work for social change.

Harvey's last play, entitled *From Left Field* (1983), attempts to deal more directly with sexism in social interactions. In addition to pointing out how men treat women as sex objects, the songs and dialogue also address the issue of women's compliance with and initiation of some of this treatment. The plot of this play is quite similar to that of *Death Watch?* and *Freedom Ain't No Bowl of Cherries*—the action takes place in a communal apartment of political activists. *Left Field* is also a musical, as was *Cherries,* and the "message" of this play is also a combination of information about various aspects of the military and intelligence goals of the U.S. government with homilies about relationships and sexuality in particular. The plot twist in this play takes place when a visiting female friend of Harvey's decides to pretend to the rest of the collective that she is a man. This masquerade is intended to teach the others a lesson by having them meet the character first as a man, learn to think of her as a man, and then find out that she is really a woman. In this way they will learn that the ways that we think of men and women differently are social constructs, not based in any essential biological differences.

Left Field does not deal with marriage—none of the characters are married; nor does it deal with parent-child relationships. The focus is on issues of cooperative living, such as who does more housework, and so on, and on, the learned behaviors that keep men and women from treating each other honestly and equally. The play ends with Harvey's character announcing that she is pregnant and that the father is the gay man who was played by her homosexual lover. Again, this was a reflection of events that were actually taking place within the community. During this time period (1985–86), two gay members of the community became fathers, with female members with whom they had not necessarily had sex.[20] It is interesting to note that there is no portrayal or discussion of lesbian relationships in this play, or in any of Harvey's other plays, in spite of the fact that there were many lesbians in the community. Lesbians were strongly encouraged (if not required) to have sex with men as well as women, for the same reasons that Harvey gives above.

THE FILMS OF JOAN HARVEY

In addition to her five plays, Joan Harvey also co produced and directed three feature-length documentary films. The first film, *We Are the Guinea Pigs*, was made immediately after the Three Mile Island accident in Harrisburg, Pennsylvania, in 1979. It was based on interviews with residents of the Harrisburg area and of experts on nuclear power plants and nuclear energy in general. The film was distributed and broadcast nationally on the Public Broadcasting System, and also received some international distribution. The organization of production for the film took place through the "film committee," a group that was hand-picked by Harvey, Klein, and Newton. The films were the only projects of the Sullivan Institute/Fourth Wall community that involved some outsiders as technicians—the cinematographer was not a member of the group, nor were some of the other participants. They were also the most widely distributed works that the community ever produced.

Rather than concerning themselves with a critique of the family, or with issues such as male chauvinism and monogamy, the films focused exclusively on the political sphere. The apocalyptic beliefs of the leadership—that we were destined for either nuclear annihilation due to a war with the Soviet Union or environmental disaster due to the use of nuclear power—resulted in films that were intended to be calls to public action.

Harvey's second film was called *From Hitler to M-X*, and addressed the issue of weapons production in the United States. It specifically looked at the development of "first-strike" weapons as the ultimate deception of the citizenry by the U.S. government. It was based on a series of interviews of ex-government officials, activists, and scholars who had researched the government-corporate connections in the production of military hardware and software. This film was also broadcast on some PBS channels.

The last film, entitled *A Matter of Struggle*, was based on interviews of grass-roots activists of all types around the United States. The conception of the film that Harvey had developed was that a depiction of individuals from a variety of ethnic backgrounds in different parts of the United States who were working for improved environmental regulations, rights for Native Americans, justice and opportunity for African-Americans, nuclear disarmament, women's rights, worker's rights, and so on would help viewers to become activists themselves. The groups that were focused on, however, were predominantly those on the radical fringe, many of whom advocated violence as a means of achieving their goals. The three films that were produced by the Sullivan Institute/Fourth Wall community through a nonprofit corporation known as Accord Research and Educational Associates (AREA), considered in conjunction with the plays, can be interpreted as evidence of a continuing shift from a concern with individual emotional fulfillment to a preoccupation with a conspiracy of the ruling classes to destroy the world.

SECURITY MEASURES

From 1979, when the Three Mile Island accident occurred, through 1991, when the community began to disband, security was a major issue in the minds of the community leadership. The initial actions taken in this regard have already been mentioned—the institution of the Emergency Communications System and the evacuation plan. The activities of the Fourth Wall also became a source of concern for the leadership. Harvey and Newton reportedly received death threats by telephone, so a security force was instituted to protect the leadership at home, in the theater, and at the Workshop. In the building where the four leaders of the group lived, there was a twenty-four-hour guard posted at a desk by the front entrance. A video camera was installed outside so that anyone attempting to enter the building could be seen. All individuals who rang the front doorbell had to be screened. At the theater on East 4th street in Manhattan, there was an observation post built above the stage so that two guards could look out at the audience during the shows. The emergency plan that was developed anticipated that a member of the audience would fire a gun at one of the cast members. If anyone in the audience rose quickly during the show, they were watched carefully. If someone did pull a gun, the guards were told to turn all the lights in the theater off and to fire a round of blanks into the audience in order to scare away any potential assassins. At the Workshop, the Fourth Wall's vacation property in the Catskills, an underground editing room was built with a secret exit for Joan Harvey while she was editing *From Hitler to M-X*. The footage for this film was believed to be so damaging to the U.S. government that it was thought that they might attempt to prevent the film from being produced.

THE AIDS RESTRICTIONS AND THE PURCHASE OF 2643 BROADWAY

The trend toward increasing authoritarianism continued for several years, with Saul Newton and Joan Harvey at the top. In 1983 two important events accelerated this trend. One was the decision by the leadership approving the proposal of a few members to purchase a building for occupancy by approximately eighty members. Although the idea of acquiring a building originated with a small group of members, the leadership exercised control over the financial arrangements, the architectural design and renovation, and even the selection of which members would live there. The building that was selected, which was in need of a total renovation, had seven floors, each of which was to be a large communal apartment. The same-sex arrangement was to be kept within apartments, so that, for example, the second floor was all women, the third floor all men, and so on. Although members were told that they would become shareholders in the new building, in fact ownership remained in the hands of a few members designated and controlled by the leadership and no shares were ever issued. Members who resided in the building made out their checks to a corporation composed of these designated individuals, and questions about ownership were discouraged and considered to be an attack on the community.

The second significant event in the life of the community in 1983 was the advent of the AIDS restrictions. The SI/FW community had known about GRID (gay-related immunodeficiency) since 1979, and had cautioned male homosexuals in the group to observe precautions, such as the use of condoms. However, with the spread of HIV infections to the non-gay populations, it was decided that more drastic action had to be taken. The community was effectively sealed off from sexual contact with outsiders (which had been one of the predominant avenues of recruitment). Any member who had sex with a nonmember was expelled from the community. Condoms were required for all sexual contact. Members' shoes were to be removed immediately upon entering any group apartment, and hands were to be washed in a special bathroom designated the "outside" bathroom. No member was allowed to eat in a restaurant or drink in a bar. Other restrictions included wiping dogs' paws after they had been walked, a prohibition against eating in nonmembers' houses, and against travel for pleasure. Business travelers were required to disinfect their hotel rooms before using them, and to bring and cook their own food.

Some of these restrictions were relaxed when it became clear that the AIDS virus was not transmitted through casual contact. The restrictions against sexual contact with outsiders and regarding the use of condoms remained in place, however. Although some part of the community's response to the AIDS epidemic was understandable, other restrictions were, in medical terms, hysterical overreactions that resulted in the increasing isolation of members and an ever-increasingly authoritarian structure within the group itself. For those who remained inside, the notion of leaving became even more difficult to imagine than before. They were convinced that the outside world was full of disease, and that they would never find friends or lovers to replace those they had in the group. In conjunction with this fear, members were often told by therapists that they would become severely depressed or suicidal if they left. Those who left the community were effectively shunned, and those who remained experienced an increasing sense of psychological isolation and fear of the outside world. Many members reported that the idea of physical and/or psychological survival away from the group was inconceivable.

CONCLUSION

During the relatively short period of time from 1979 to 1983, the entire nature of the Sullivan Institute/Fourth Wall community changed radically. From a belief system that preached social revolution and expected it to occur in a relatively short period of time, the leadership embraced an apocalypticism in which the role of the membership became that of saving the world from imminent destruction. While the ideal of the abolition of the nuclear family and its replacement with an extended family of "like-minded others" remained intact, it was pushed indefinitely into the future. The primary goal of the community became outreach—the education of the general public regarding the nuclear (and military) threat. The AIDS restrictions and the hysteria that lead to the further isolation of community members from mainstream society contributed to this mentality.

NOTES

1. I was one of the students in the training institute, and worked for four years after my completion of the course as a computer programmer.

2. The founding of the comedy group is one instance of a common phenomenon that took place during the "hedonistic period" in the community—creative individuals would come together spontaneously and in many instances would produce original and potentially professional works of theater, painting, music, poetry, fiction, and dance.

3. Recruitment into the group often took place in "contingents." For example, one student at Manhattan School of Music recruited other students, so eventually there was a "Manhattan School of Music" contingent. In the 1960s, several abstract expressionist artists became patients of Sullivan Institute therapists. This phenomenon also took place within certain graduate departments, such as Columbia's department of Anthropology, Columbia School of Social Work, and others.

4. The property was called the "Workshop" because it was conceived as a place where the performances for the next season would be rehearsed.

5. This transition can also be viewed from the point of view of the sociology of religion as the move from a "postmillennial" to a "premillennial" group. While during the early years of the Sullivan Institute community, the prevailing worldview was that the most constructive means of effecting social change was to live up to one's "true potential" as a human being, in later years the community came to believe in the necessity of immediate action directed toward the outside world in order to save the planet. My thesis regarding this transition is that it was directly related to changes in the political situation in the external world.

6. A phone tree is an organization whereby one member is contacted and asked to contact several other members, thereby facilitating speedy communication of messages.

7. Four or five children's plays were written by group members and directed by Harvey.

8. She is not meant to be an extreme case, but a representative of a common, if not predominant, social phenomenon.

9. In spite of the fact that most theoretical paradigms in psychoanalysis assume some variation between families, the Sullivanians did not acknowledge much variation in their writings or teachings.

10. There is a chapter in Conditions of Human Growth devoted to this topic.

11. This practice is still common in Canada, and in most European countries, where it has never been found to be much of an impediment to youngsters' ability to become independent.

12. This type of apocalyptic thinking permeated the group in this period.

13. These groups made up the majority of the audience for Fourth Wall plays.

14. Harvey's young daughter was involved with an antinuclear group at this time. The group had plans to occupy the Shoreham nuclear facility on Long Island during a demonstration in which other participants would be elsewhere and unable to provide support for the civil disobedience. Harvey, in a panic that her daughter would be arrested and killed, enlisted the help of the entire SI/FW community. Group members formed small groups, led by designated lieutenants, who watched Harvey's daughter's group go over the fences at Shoreham, and then accompanied them to the police station to lend support for those who were arrested.

15. In These Times, Chicago Ill (October, 1979).

16. It is important to note here that the leadership actually consisted of two married couples—Saul and Joan divorced, Joan married Ralph, and Saul married Helen. The two couples lived together from the 1970s through 1992 when Saul died.

17. The average member of the community lived with several other people in relatively modest surroundings, regardless of his or her income level. For those who were earning high incomes, this was a considerable sacrifice.

18. Harvey herself may have also been a member of the CP/USA, but if she was, no one in the community knew about it.

19. A "security operation" was a term Pearce and Newton (and possibly even Sullivan) used to refer to certain activities an individual could engage in that prevented him or her from growing interpersonally.

20. See Chapter 4, section on "Childbearing and Child Rearing."

The Decline and Dissolution of the Sullivan Institute/ Fourth Wall Community: 1984–92

The "revolutionary" period in the Sullivan Institute/Fourth Wall community resulted in its increasing isolation from mainstream society. The Reagan years had begun and the gentrification of the upper west side of Manhattan was moving quickly ahead. Group members were faced with an uncertain economy that did not reward many of their skills or values. The political climate had changed, while the ideology of the Sullivan Institute/Fourth Wall had not. The brand of old-style socialism that the Fourth Wall advocated was increasingly being discredited by dissidents in the Soviet bloc, and by neoconservatives and neoliberals at home. A large proportion of the academics, writers, musicians, dancers, and artists who had been able to support themselves through the 1970s was no longer able to earn salaries that could keep pace with the rising cost of living inside and outside of the community.

The isolation of the Sullivanian community was not simply caused by changes in the U.S. political climate. The leadership had maintained a stance of superiority, self-righteousness and contempt for the outside world throughout the life span of the group. In the late 1970s, when the antinuclear movement became increasingly active, the Fourth Wall attempted to work in tandem with other political, cultural, and professional organizations on demonstrations and other political actions. Leaders and members of other organizations who came into contact with Fourth Wall leaders during this period report that the Fourth Wall consistently attempted to dominate both dialogue and decision-making processes. Many of these groups eventually ostracized Harvey and other Fourth Wall members in charge of outreach. Political groups who had previous contact with the Fourth Wall were extremely wary. If the Sullivanian leadership was incapable of cooperating with left activist groups, it was certainly not interested in, nor capable of, becoming part of the larger society.

There is no one particular event or time when the decline of the Sullivan Institute/Fourth Wall community can be pinpointed. Rather, it can be viewed as the product of constant interaction between internal and external events, such that the escalation of certain conflicts over time eventually resulted in the disbanding of the community. The demise of the group may have been predicted in 1983 when the AIDS restrictions took effect, because from that time on no new members were accepted. However, it is also possible to argue that since the membership had been dwindling for many years by that time, the decline began even earlier than 1983. In any case, the rate of decline accelerated rapidly after 1985. Prior to the defection of two high-level trainee therapists in March and December of 1985, the membership of the community had numbered approximately 225 individuals. By January 1986 it was down to 213, and by January of 1990 it was 178. In the Spring of 1990, precipitated by the incapacitation of Saul Newton due to illness, the community split into two factions—one led by Joan Harvey and Ralph Klein, the other by Helen Moses. Accusations of embezzlement were traded back and forth between the factions, and members were expected to align themselves with one side or the other. The dissolution of the community had begun.

The departure of the two (previously mentioned) therapists in 1985, along with approximately eight other friends and patients, can be viewed as the beginning of the precipitous decline and dissolution of the community. In order for these individuals to go into voluntary exile, giving up their careers, their living situations, and most of their friends at the same time, strong forces had to be at work. Although the two therapists did not leave at the same time, they were close friends and had planned their departures together. The one who left first (L. C.) had been in the training program since 1972 and had risen through the ranks to become a favorite of the leadership. Due to his high status in the community, he was able to view the functioning of the leadership and their decision-making process close up. The information that he was privy to, and the knowledge of the personal lives of the leadership, led him to view the Sullivanian experiment as a failure and the leadership as corrupt and exploitative. The contacts he had made as one of the few individuals in the community who was responsible for outreach to other political and cultural groups enabled him both to look at the community from the point-of-view of an outsider, and to get aid and support when he was ready to leave. He described some of the events leading up to his departure:

My relationship with Joan was always up and down. When I came back from Europe and she was underground up in the country, we were like confidantes. She told me everything about her life, why she didn't live with Saul, what a total jealous fuck he was. How she hated his guts basically and she thought he was crazy, how much she hated Helen and why she chose Ralph because there was nobody else. She told me all this stuff, and there was a brief period of time when we were really confidantes. Then Saul started to get on my ass in New York and she really felt trapped, and she took his side, and that was really the beginning of the end. That's when I started to think about how crazy this whole lunacy was, I was doing a lot of speed and I tried to talk to her about it and I realized she was addicted to drugs and was not going to be of any help. (L. C. 1988, 19)

In addition to the AIDS restrictions and the purchase of the building, other events within the community pointed to increasing authoritarianism. These events caused dissatisfaction among many members, but those closest to the leadership were in a better position to see inconsistencies and corruption. One significant structural change led to a great deal of internal conflict, as well as demonstrating the change in the focus of the leadership from individual growth to group solidarity and productivity.

A political education committee had existed in the SI/FW community since the early 1980s. Originally, the leadership chose the committee, and "politics classes" were held on a voluntary basis. "House meetings" (weekly meetings of group apartment members) had taken place since the early 1970s as vehicles for addressing the organizational and interpersonal issues that came up in communal apartments, thereby contributing to the maintenance of social control. In 1984 the leadership decided that "house meetings" would become "politics meetings," and that every apartment group would be required to read and discuss certain books selected for them by the politics committee in these meetings. The first books dealt with the Chinese revolution, including some of Mao Tse Tung's writings, and the book *Fanshen* by William Hinton. *Fanshen* was a description of events that occurred in a rural Chinese village in the years immediately following the revolution of 1949. The practice of "going to the gate" as described in *Fanshen*, which referred to the confession of one's bourgeois past and the divestment of one's property, was applauded by the Sullivanian leadership as an effective means of cleansing the community of bourgeois thoughts and customs. The practice of criticism/self-criticism became popular within the Sullivanian community. Although these practices were not new— house meetings had always been a forum for both criticism and self-criticism— the overtly political nature of these practices was.

Simultaneously, Saul Newton and Helen Moses initiated a self-described campaign against male chauvinism along these lines. The men in the community were accused of male chauvinism for refusing to sleep with certain women who had approached them. Some members were ordered to terminate romantic relationships with each other on the grounds that these relationships harmed the individuals involved as well as the other members of the community, who were deprived of their companionship.

It has been hypothesized by some ex-members of the community that one of the precipitating factors of this phenomenon may well have been the fact that the membership of the Sullivan Institute/Fourth Wall community was skewed approximately two to one in favor of women at that time, and that due to the AIDS restrictions, many of these women were unable to find sex partners. The refusal of male members to accede to requests for sexual relations were interpreted by the leadership as male chauvinist. It has also been pointed out that the anti-male-chauvinism campaign took place at the same time that several male members refused requests for "sleepover dates"[1] by Newton's wife, Helen Moses. L. C. recalls his impressions of this phenomenon:

Well, the background of where I was at during that period of time is important to understand my perspective on the male chauvinism thing, because by that time I was already on my way out. . . .

I knew it was insanity right from the beginning. I knew this was going to be a disaster for me personally, a disaster for the men in the group generally, and was a complete farce and had nothing to do with what was going on at the surface.[2] I know how it started was that a bunch of people didn't want to date Helen Moses, and that she started complaining to Saul that it was a male chauvinist group. Now actually I knew about it earlier. I knew there was going to be trouble years before the male chauvinism thing. There were two trips to Europe with Freedom Ain't No Bowl of Cherries. The first one was to England that I was not on. This is when I was dating Helen. . . . She came back from that trip, this was about 6 or 7 months before I went to Finland. . . and she was complaining that the guys on the trip, who were B. M., who was gay, J. H., who was fucking everybody else, I don't know who, everybody also was working 18 hours a day. No one wanted to fuck her on the trip and she was furious. She was livid, out of her mind and in a big fight with Joan about it. Because Joan was saying: "what the hell are you talking about? We're running around like lunatics, going from city to city throughout England, sleeping in sleeping bags and cots." And Helen was like furious that the men were not beating down her sleeping bag door. Furious, I mean, she must have gone for three hours, just telling me how terrible these guys were because no one wanted to have a date with her on this trip. . . . I think she would get terribly jealous of Saul's exploits and so a lot of this needing men to want to fuck her was either to get back at Saul or to make up for it. . . .

I think it was through the political group that met to decide what the hell we were going to do in politics groups. I think it began there, and it came from Helen and Saul. I know that Joan thought the whole thing was totally fucking insane, she was working on one of the films. . . . Helen called this the "cultural revolution.". . . there were going to be these open discussions about male chauvinism, in all the house meetings. And actually, I think it got out of hand, it really got completely berserk. (L. C. 5/15/88, 20–21)

Another male member wrote a piece that he called "Women" a few months before he left the group, which illustrates some of the complexity of the relationship in the community between power, sex, and romantic love: "A lot of my rage at Saul has to do with his making women unavailable to me—or, from the other side, forcing me to treat women—e.g., W. E.—as people, not objects—WOMEN. He took W. E. away—a woman wouldn't have done what W. E. did to me ON HER OWN for her own reasons—out of her own head (S. P. 3/23/86, 5–8).

Here S. P. is referring to the fact that the leadership was able to prohibit certain relationships among patient-members, and the fact Saul had told his lover, W. E., to stay away from him:

[Hallucination from then while fucking with W. E.—Saul holds all our pricks in his hands—Power!—Aargh—disgusting image!] But I then related to W.E. as though she were in his power—deniable to me—but without regard to my relationship with HER. . . .

So, I SHOULD have switched [therapists] before—or would I have gotten it without getting in so deep? Would chauvinism mean much without the experience I had? Would I have changed without it? He [Saul] once said, after a conversation with B. S., looking right at me: "Change is such a hard thing to bring about and keep happening—that I would do anything to make it happen—anything!" He once said to me he started dating W. E. to make me change! Well, it's a theory! (S. P. 3/23/86, 5–8)

Here Saul is depicted as both an exploiter and torturer, but also as a stern yet loving father. This is a powerful example of the feelings Newton was capable of evoking in patients and other members. His absolute power was a predominant cause of these feelings. When general meetings of the Fourth Wall were held, decisions that had already been made by the leadership were often put to a vote. The form this voting took was not that of a secret ballot, which would have protected the identities of dissenting members, but of a show of hands. This method almost always resulted in votes that were unanimously in favor of the proposals put forth by the leadership. Individuals who challenged these proposals, even if only for purposes of clarification, were often criticized by their roommates or therapists. In one case, a member who cast the only dissenting vote at a meeting was "asked to leave" the community a few weeks later. Ostensibly this was not because he had voted against a proposal, but because he was no longer an asset to the group.

L. C. related the male chauvinism campaign to another series of events that were taking place concurrently.

Now I think it was in conjunction with another amazing power move in the group, which I still think was brilliant on Joan's part. . . . And I think this really affected the male chauvinism thing greatly. There was a lot of dissent at one point in the group, particularly around the new building, and me and D. P. and M. B. were the first ones to get hit because we were the first ones vocal against the building, and we were creamed. . . . Independently of us, J. A.'s apartment had a dissent move and they called for a general meeting in the group which got squelched. It was B. S., J. A., J. H., and B. P. It was a whole movement, completely independent of me, D. P. and M. B. I thought this was unbelievable, I thought there were going to be pockets of dissent coming up, and that one really got sat on quickly. Then Joan did this incredible thing of having these nights where you would make fun of other people in the group, which I hated. I don't think there was anything that ever happened that I hated more than those things. And from being a therapist there, you could see that it really worked to take people's dissent, rage, anger, disenchantment, ranging from disenchantment to complete violent horror, rage, disgust at the group. And it channeled it into these nights, people got really into these nights as a way to openly criticize the group, make fun of each other, be violent. It was amazing to watch. (L. C. 5/15/88, 22)

L. C. is describing a series of "writer's nights," in which Fourth Wall members were encouraged to write, direct, and act in original sketches that depicted some other individual or individuals in the community. In one of the skits, two members played the roles of Newton and Harvey running a general meeting of the Sullivan Institute/Fourth Wall community. In the skit they call for a vote of the membership, and when one member dissents, he is carried out of the meeting bodily and dumped. This was meant to spoof the so-called democratic process within the community. However, the mere fact that the leadership allowed this skit to be acted out under the auspices of the Fourth Wall was meant to prove that there was in fact freedom of speech and freedom of criticism within the group. L. C. explains:

It was a brilliant, brilliant maneuver to calm down all the feelings in the group. Well, if we could laugh about this, if we could talk about this openly, then this must be a democratic scene. Nothing changed, it really worked. People were violent about each other when they made fun of each other. It was amazing, and that happened with the male chauvinism. I think that was the beginning of "it's okay to openly, violently rip the other apart in public." It was an interesting form of public destruction of the other. And that was my experience of the male chauvinism thing. That it became a way, under the guise of "rooting out" male chauvinism, for guys to go ape shit on each other at meetings, for women to rip guys apart, for all this latent hostility to just get publicly out in the open. And J. C.'s description always struck me as really, really true, that it quickly turned into, not a discussion about male chauvinism, but it quickly moved into class discussion, "well, it's not the just the men who are oppressing the women, the therapists are a class and they're oppressing, etc." It really became an analysis of the whole group, and that's when they ended it, and Saul put out the word that it had gotten out of hand and we're going to stop this discussion. And that Saul and Ralph [the two male leaders] never came up once in any discussion that I know of. (L. C. 5/15/88, 22)

Some male ex-members stated that one result of the campaign was that they felt obligated to consent to any request for sex by female members, regardless of whether or not they wished to have sex. More important, however, was the release of antagonistic feelings it provided for disgruntled members.

Although the departure of the two therapists, as they themselves have reported it, was not intended to be openly adversarial to the community, it was inevitable that such high-level defections would have a significant impact on both leaders and members. The response of the leadership was to immediately declare that both therapists were CIA members and to attempt to "circle the wagons" in order to defend the rest of the group from this outside threat. In addition to the CIA accusations, the leadership analyzed each of the departures as the result of severe character flaws that the two men did not wish to confront or change. In spite of the attempts to discredit them, however, the act of leaving without "permission" could not be ignored. Many members began to secretly question the absolute authority of the leadership.[3] While some may have had private discussions regarding their doubts, few, if any, told their therapists about these thoughts and feelings. However, several members left the community shortly after the two therapists left. Some of these members had been closely associated with the two therapists, others had not.

Towards the end of 1985, F. F., who had been a member of the community for approximately fifteen years stated that she was ordered by her therapist, Ralph Klein, to cease having any contact with her infant daughter, who was approximately two months old at that time. Previously, two female members had children removed from their custody based on decisions by the leadership.[4] F. F. had been very close to one of the two defected therapists, and called on him to help her flee the community with the child. The act of contacting an ex-member in this way was totally forbidden, and was already an indication that F. F. was ready to defy the leadership. She hired two private detectives to help her physically seize the child, and went into hiding (on her lawyer's advice) after accomplishing this end. As part of her lawyer's strategy to maintain custody of her daughter, he contacted the press. A front-page article appeared in the *Village Voice,* and both television and print media coverage of the story resulted. This was the first time that either a member or an ex-member of this community had been willing to speak to the press, and many individuals recounted their versions of life within the community in support of F. F.'s case:

S. L. v. F. F.[5] . . . has blown open the closed world of the Sullivanians and the Fourth Wall. All the lawyers for S. L., two of whom have either quit or been dismissed, have been infuriated by the judge's ruling that the lifestyle and philosophy of S. L. and his associates are relevant to . . . [the baby's] safety. Judge Schackman may have been influenced by the Sullivanians' eerie behavior on the first day of the hearing. It had hardly begun when Judge Shackman was informed by court officers that some members were circling the courthouse in cars and communicating by walkie-talkie. ("Escape from Utopia," *Village Voice,* April 22, 1986)

S. L. vs. F. F. was settled out of court in F. F.'s favor after testimony by several ex-members of the community, who attested to the Sullivanian community's practice of divesting patient-members of their parental rights. "Miss J." had testified that she had not spent more than three days with her oldest daughter, who was ten years old when she was sent to boarding school, from 1976 to 1985. She had stopped having her daughter come home for vacations at the behest of her therapist, Marc Rice (April 1, 1986, proceedings of the Supreme Court of the State of New York, Index Nos. 2903/86 and 78613/85). In her deposition of February 11, 1986, E. S. described the relationship of parents and children within the Sullivan Institute/Fourth Wall community.

The relationship that parents had with their children was intensely scrutinized. I was very involved with several children as a baby-sitter and on many occasions sat with parents as they talked to either Helen Moses or Saul Newton who dictated the day to day care of their children.

One child that I loved very much, D. M. (now age 6) was the child of J. M. and T. P. J. M. stopped seeing Danny when he was less than one year old and had no relationship with him at all until he was four. He then was allowed by his analyst to see D. M., though only for an hour or two a week. When D. M. was four and a half years old he became intensely afraid of Saul Newton and Helen Moses, who were the parents of his friend M. Everyone else in the Fourth Wall was also scared of these two individuals and D.'s reaction seemed to me to be an honest mimicry of the adults around him. However it was promulgated that T. P. (the mother) was the cause of D. M.'s fear of Saul. For an entire summer he was segregated from all other children in the Fourth Wall's country residence, and consequently had no children to play with. He was told that he had to stop being afraid before he could play with his friends again. In the middle of the summer D. M. was taken away from his mother and given to his father, who had had little to do with him for three and a half years. (1986, pp. 2–3)

It was a combination of this testimony and the strange behavior of community members in and out of the courtroom that led to S. L.'s decision to cede custody to F. F. Within two years of the settlement, S. L. left the community and rejoined F. F. They left New York City with their daughter soon after.

The impact of this case, which was concurrent with the departure of Michael Bray (the second therapist), was far-reaching inside the community. The *Village Voice* article and the television and other newspaper coverage of the case, and of the community, placed the community under intense public scrutiny for the first time in its over thirty-year history.[6] Reporters with television cameras appeared at community residences, videotaping members as they entered and left. The impact of this sudden notoriety was experienced differently by various members.

At approximately the same time as the custody cases were initiated, other ex-members brought legal proceedings against the leadership and management of the building that had been ostensibly purchased in their names. These ex-members were requesting that they receive compensation for their investments in the building after they had been expelled or moved out. The case was settled in the plaintiffs' favor. The leadership presented their defeat in the S. L./F. F. case combined with their loss of the civil case as a declaration of war by ex-members against them. Soon after this, two other ex-members, S. P. and M. B. initiated custody proceedings against their ex-wives in order to remove their children from residence in the community.

The majority of members of the community were shielded by the leadership from knowledge of details of these events, with the exception of the press coverage. Once *The Village Voice* article—which appeared on the front page and was quite long and detailed—was published, a flurry of media activity ensued. Members could not help but be impacted in various ways by the public reaction to the article. Some members were asked at their jobs if they were involved with the Sullivanians, and some children of members were taunted at school by other children whose parents had read the article.

The media exposure affected the membership in several ways. On one hand, it resulted in the leadership creating an ever more insular, separate, and paranoid community. It raised some secret doubts in the minds of members, who could not help but recognize some of the claims made in the article as accurate. It also prompted the leadership to ask the membership for even greater sums of money in order to finance the various court cases that were ongoing. On the other hand, it forced the leadership to mitigate some of their most restrictive practices, such as prohibiting individuals from bearing children and removing certain children from their parents' care.

The ongoing custody cases were viewed by the leadership and by many of the members as a battle between the forces of good and evil. In the S. L./F. F. case, trusted members had been assigned to follow some ex-members who were believed to know the whereabouts of the mother and child who had "escaped."[7] In the S. P./W. E. and M. B./K. B. cases (the two fathers who were suing together), group members were asked to be part of a "dirt squad" assigned to dig up incriminating information about the plaintiffs' characters and the characters of their witnesses. Several members cooperated in a plan to intimidate both defected therapists (one of who was M. B., who was suing for custody of his children) through violence. The first therapist was reportedly accosted on a subway platform by two men in hooded sweatshirts, and threatened with further violence if he continued to assist F. F. with her custody case. M. B. also reported that two men assaulted him in the vestibule of his apartment building; they allegedly beat him and broke his glasses. He stated that he recognized their voices as two members of the community's "security squad."

The S.P./W.E. and M.B./K.B. Cases

Both S. P. and M. B. initially sought joint custody of their children when they left the community, but were denied access to their children by their ex-wives, who were very close with the leadership in different ways. One was Newton's lover and one of his favorites; the other was a therapist who lived with the leadership at 314 West 91st Street. In the M. B./K. B. case, the couple had been married, but decided to divorce for financial reasons.[8] K. B.'s lover, who was also Newton's eldest son, claimed paternity of the children and claimed that he had acted as the "real father." S. P. was married to W. E. when he left the community, so his case included a petition for divorce as well as for custody of their child. It is also important to the eventual outcome of both cases to note that S. P. and W. E. had chosen each other—they had a romantic relationship, whereas this was not the case with M. B. and K. B. They had been friendly acquaintances before K. B. asked M. B. to father her children.

The two cases were to be tried together, but S. P.'s went to trial first. The arguments that were made by S. P. and M. B. in their cases were based on the allegation that W. E. and K. B. had ceded their parental decision-making responsibilities to the leadership. In other words, they argued that the mothers were not really the parents in the sense that they were not making the types of decisions that parents are expected to make on a day-to-day basis. These decisions included weaning, administration of medicines, discipline, "play-dates," school selection, care-giver selection, and decisions about how much time to spend with their children. In order to prove these allegations, it was necessary to offer proof that the Sullivan Institute/Fourth Wall community was an authoritarian group that exercised extraordinary power over the lives of its members.

In the wake of the S. L./F. F. case, which had received so much publicity, the newspapers and talk shows were eager to cover these trials as well. The case received publicity, but was finally settled out of court when S. P.'s wife agreed to leave the SI/FW community. M. B.'s case was also settled, after approximately four years of litigation, when his ex-wife agreed to a joint-custody arrangement and they agreed to move to the same community so that the children could go back and forth with relative ease. In the meantime, the community was in the process of disbanding.

The impact of the custody cases on the Sullivan Institute/Fourth Wall community was manifold. On one hand, the publicity and the large sums of money assessed from the membership for the court cases brought the community closer together in an "us versus them" bunker mentality. On the other hand, the leadership had to disprove some of the allegations that were being made by the plaintiffs and the press to its membership in order to maintain their allegiance. Regulations governing childbearing and mate selection within the community were relaxed. There was a large cohort of women at this time who wanted to have children, and who was nearing their last years of fertility. Several of these women became pregnant during this period, and some of them decided to live with the fathers of their children. This would not have been permitted in earlier periods.

THE FORMATION OF P.A.C.T.

Immediately following the *Village Voice* article in 1986, several concerned relatives of group members contacted the "Cult Hot Line" at the Jewish Board of Children and Family Services. Many of them had just realized for the first time what their child or sibling or cousin was involved in. They were seeking more information about the Sullivan Institute/Fourth Wall community, as well as advice as to how to best help their children and relatives. A meeting was organized at which some practitioners—social workers, psychologists, and psychiatrists—spoke about cults in general, and about the Sullivanians in particular. Ex-members also attended and spoke to the families; they also attempted to answer questions about particular individuals and about the practices of the group in general.

This meeting was reportedly experienced by family members as extremely helpful, both in terms of teaching them more about the beliefs and practices of the community, and in terms of helping them feel that what they had experienced as their own personal pain was also shared and understood by many others. Several of the parents who attended this meeting decided to form an organization that would provide support and information to family members of individuals in the Sullivan Institute/Fourth Wall community, and would also actively attempt to extricate their loved ones from the group. Some ex-members of the community became active in this organization as well. It was named "People Against Cult Therapy," or PACT.

The newly formed organization issued this (excerpted) statement of purpose:

We are PACT. We are primarily the families who have lost children to a cult.

We suffered as our children cut us off—abusively, angrily—but with little explanation. Sometimes they came back to get money, only to quickly reject us again. For years, more than 15 years for some of us, we dealt with our pain as uniquely and personally our own. Only in 1986 did most of us learn that our grown children had been trapped into a psychotherapy cult known as the 4th Wall, or the Sullivanians, one of the estimated 3,000 boutique-sized (75–250 members) mind-altering cults currently flourishing in the United States.

Why our children? There is no definitive answer. We thought of them as average, capable, middle-class children—maybe a bit above the average in intelligence and sensitivity. One characteristic, however, runs in common. At the time they were recruited, most of our children were going through a period of personal stress or anxiety—perhaps a failing marriage, or feelings of alienation, or a sense of falling out of touch with what they felt was their true potential—and they wanted to do something about it. . . .

When we formed PACT, we were essentially a support group, and that still plays an important role for us. Meeting other parents and families who have suffered pain similar to ours, and sharing our stories and information has proven of great value.

But PACT has evolved into more than merely a support group. Our ultimate objective is to break the chains by which the Sullivanian Leadership shackles its members. To that end, we serve as a catalyst to bring the Leadership to judgment for their illegal, unethical, and unprofessional acts. We serve as an information clearinghouse to increase the knowledge and awareness of the real nature of cults. We serve to assist ex-Sullivanians to re-establish themselves in society, and to support them in appropriate litigation against a Leadership that has literally stolen years of their lives. And we are prepared to help those members of the cult who are left when the leadership finally implodes. (excerpted from "We are PACT," 1986)

The founding of PACT served to polarize even further the stance of the Sullivan Institute/Fourth Wall community against the outside world—especially those outsiders who were perceived as enemies. Some children of PACT members contacted their parents (an act that was seen by PACT as a successful outcome of their actions), if only to threaten them with even further alienation from them if they did not sever their ties to this organization. However, given the fact that many of these parents and other family members had not seen or heard from their children in years at that point, it was not always enough to threaten to cut off further contact. One member contacted her father and threatened to bring charges of sexual abuse against him if he continued to be affiliated with PACT. Other members promised to see their parents periodically, but *only* if they would drop out of PACT.

Just as in the case of the publicity that was focused on the Sullivan Institute/Fourth Wall community, the existence of PACT had some contradictory results. On one hand, it served as proof of the leadership's claims that the outside world was hell-bent on destroying the community. This justified requests for additional funds from the membership in order to fight the court battles, as well as exacerbating tensions between members and ex-members and family members. On the other, it forced the leadership to relax some of the most restrictive rules it had enacted, if only to prove to PACT that conditions within the Sullivan Institute/Fourth Wall community were not as repressive as they claimed.

THE DISSOLUTION OF THE COMMUNITY

In the late 1980s the decline of the community accelerated. The causes were multiple, but two important factors stand out. The first was the deterioration of Saul Newton's physical and psychological condition. He was alleged to have made sexual advances towards several children, including his daughter, as well as one (or more) of the young (approximately 12–13 years old) girls that lived in the building shared by the leadership. Newton was also alleged to have beaten his young son as well. He was more confused and forgetful than he had been previously. In 1989 Helen Moses, who was Newton's wife at the time, arranged for him to be moved out of the building into an apartment with a female patient of hers:

... I think that when he started getting Alzheimer's was when he started molesting his kids. And now I see that was why Helen wanted J. L. to take on the responsibility of moving him out of 91st street because he had actually beaten one of his children.

... He had beaten M. But the stuff with T. had been going on for a while. . . . That was first told me by S. N. because he was after T. and C. N. and C. C. Neither one of the other mothers confronted Helen and Saul with this. All they did was they told their kids that they didn't have to sleep over there. (W. D. 7/14/93, 18)

This type of behavior was not out of character for Newton—he was reported to have physically assaulted Joan Harvey as early as 1970. By the mid-1980s, and possibly before, he was alleged by many female members to have consistently demanded oral sex from many of the women who lived and worked in his house, sometimes violently. Based on these reports, it is reasonable to surmise that his sexual demands and abuse extended to even more women than those who have reported it. It is also possible that the accusation that he was "molesting" his daughter or her friends was trumped up to move Newton out of the house as the symptoms of Alzheimer's disease progressed.

Once Newton was moved out of 91st street, he was no longer part of the leadership of the community. He was in a state of semi-exile and reportedly saw little of his wife or children. Apparently his wife, Helen Moses, began telling her younger children almost immediately that Newton had not been their "real father." Although he had been in a debilitated state for some period of time prior to moving, the move was symbolic of his final loss of power. The immediate repercussions of his absence were felt immediately in the form of a split within the leadership between Joan Harvey and Ralph Klein (who were married), and Helen Moses. Each of these two camps had their followers, composed of "trainee therapists" and patients, so each of them had a power base within the community. This had always been true to some extent, but the leadership had maintained its unity until this time. The public splintering of the leadership was the beginning of the final dissolution of the group:

L. F. had come into a bunch of money because she had come into a co-op on 110th street. Saul told her that she didn't have any right to that money, so she gave it to the Fourth Wall. The money was laundered through the building. She and I were in essentially the same position. When I gave my mammoth loan to the building of $100,000, I didn't realize that I owed taxes on that money. She didn't realize that she was going to sooner or later get hit for taxes on this other money, capital gains. So she realized that this was coming her way and she went to Joan and said that she wanted something in writing that her taxes would be covered. And Joan hit the roof, and called her every name in the book. Somewhere along this point, E. C. and A. G.—after having been a faithful slave for years doing everything Ralph Klein told her to do—received a letter from Ralph, some kind of legal document saying he had nothing to do with the finances of the building. E. C. shows up on A. G's doorstep and says "You're in trouble. You'd better get a lawyer." So here A. G. is trying to cover her butt. (W. D. 7/14/93, 18)

The split in the membership reportedly began in the spring of 1990 when a high-ranking member began to spread rumors that she had been defrauded of monies that she had given to the leadership:

But at the time in the building, she was spreading rumors or telling the truth—who the fuck knows?—about how the money had been mismanaged by Joan. And so camps started happening, and people started having house meetings about it. . . . Either you were on Joan's side or you were on Helen's side. There was nothing in between. And, of course, I knew my alliance. I picked Joan's side. And people would make these orations in these meetings. I'm not kidding. People would get up and speak for . . . And crying. It was like watching David Koresh on a TV movie. M. T. got up once and made a 45-minute speech. M. F. got up and spoke for Helen, a 45-minute speech and started crying. 'You don't know this and this and this that's going on.' M. T. said "Joan has saved everybody's life. I can't believe people are turning against her. And look what you were and where you've been, and if it hadn't been for Joan . . ." It was an unbelievable speech. . . .

. . . All the people who were semi in the leadership, not big, big leadership, but people who were anybody spoke. At the very last minute I remember . . . Joan came and then Helen came and B. P. came and everybody came to these meetings... There were very few people who spoke for Helen. G. T. spoke for Helen, of course. And M. F. spoke for her. But I'm not talking about a five-minute speech here. I'm talking about people sobbing hysterically for half an hour about how their lives have been saved and changed, how you would have been in the gutter and fucked up and on drugs and liquor and in some halfway house. (L. D. 6/1/93, 15–16)

The split polarized the community down to the last member—individual living units were divided in half depending on which residents adhered to which faction. One ex-member recounted an extremely bitter situation in which members of the two camps in her apartment appointed negotiators in order to resolve how to divide up their living space. More members left the group at this point, with much less animosity than had previously been the case. Since there was no centralized leadership at the time, it was no longer possible for members to maintain a united front against those who were leaving. The entity that these people were leaving was different from the one that previous members had left.

The second overarching factor in the decline of the SI/FW community was connected to the departure of several high status members, and the attempt by the community to explain these defections as resulting from severe psychological flaws on the part of those ex-members. Even while remaining members were denigrating those who had left, many were secretly wondering if perhaps they should leave as well. Women who were concerned that they would not be allowed to bear children in the community also exerted considerable pressure on the leadership. This put the leadership in an awkward position: if they refused to allow members to have children, they were proving that the accusations of the media, PACT, and other ex-members were true. Once they allowed more members to have children, however, they furthered the process of disintegration by creating more potential family units.

During this period there was conflict within the Fourth Wall as well as in relation to childbearing, custody, and cohabitation. Some of the most involved members of the theater company began to challenge Joan Harvey's "absolute monarchy." Harvey had stated that she wanted input from the membership regarding the direction of the Fourth Wall. This resulted in several members writing letters to her about what they felt should be changed. According to one ex-member, Harvey was not particularly pleased with the response to her request, but was somewhat honor-bound to listen to and act on some of the suggestions. One of these was that the company produce the plays of some other members, as opposed to those of Harvey alone. In the fall of 1990 the company began rehearsing a play by a high status member. Although the play itself had not been written by Harvey, she undertook its direction, with very little input from the playwright. The result of this decision was that the playwright was dissatisfied with the results Harvey was getting, and wanted to remove his play from production by the Fourth Wall. Although he was not able to attain this goal, there was increasing dissatisfaction with the theater productions and decreasing member participation.

During this time period, the building on 100th Street and Broadway, which had been purchased by Sullivan Institute/Fourth Wall community members, became insolvent due to the departure of many of its residents from the group. Some of those who left asked for their money back; others did not. Those who did try to get some of their investment back discovered, however, that the building was not actually a cooperative in the legal sense. A corporation had been established, but shares had never been issued to individual "owners." It was on this basis that some ex-members were able to take legal action to recoup their investments. Over the last few years of the community's existence, the building was foreclosed and remaining members were not compensated at all.

In December of 1991, Saul Newton died in a hospital in Brooklyn. From the apartment at 98th street that he was removed to in 1989, he was taken to a nursing home where he allegedly became violent and attacked another patient. He was then taken to Mt. Sinai's geriatric psychiatry unit, where he reportedly received few visitors. An obituary appeared in *The New York Times:*

Saul B. Newton, a psychotherapist who ran an unorthodox commune in Manhattan that was assailed by ex-members as an abusive cult died on Saturday at Methodist Hospital in Brooklyn. He was 85 years old and lived in Manhattan. . . .

"He was both hated and loved," said Esther Newton, his eldest daughter, who was not involved in his therapeutic community. "His ideals were lofty—the results are for others to judge," she said. "He was very bright and creative, charismatic and definitely difficult, handsome, attractive to women and tyrannical." (December 23, 1991)

A memorial service for Newton was organized by his eldest daughter, Esther, and three of her cousins. The only members of the Sullivan Institute/Fourth Wall community who attended were Newton's eldest son, K. B., and K. B. and M. B.'s two children. Helen Moses, who was Newton's wife at the time of his death, had already begun divorce proceedings and had plans to marry another member. She subsequently moved to Westchester with her children and her new husband and changed her last name and the children's last names. Her rationale for abandoning her husband at his deathbed was that he had been an abusive husband and leader of the Sullivan Institute/Fourth Wall community. She apparently perceived herself as a victim of Newton's charismatic hold on the group, and was possibly personally abused by him as well.

According to L. D. and several others, Joan Harvey and Ralph Klein were able to maintain a small group of approximately thirty patient-members. They, along with Moses and Marc Rice, a secondary member of the leadership, were charged with professional misconduct by former patients and supervisees. The New York State Office of Professional Discipline heard these charges. Harvey and Klein decided to give up their professional licenses rather than contest them. This did not stop them, however, from seeing patients, only from receiving third-party payments. In 1997 Helen Moses and Marc Rice (also a therapist) had their licenses revoked. Helen Moses was fined $15,000 as well.

Although the building at 100th street was foreclosed, many ex-members of the Sullivan Institute/Fourth Wall community still live at 240 West 98th street, a large building on the upper west side of Manhattan that has been the residence of various group apartments for at least twenty years. Some of these people still maintain close relationships. Most ex-members retain some of the friendships that they had formed within the group, and some are forced to maintain relationships with ex-spouses with whom they have had children. Although many have left New York City, and still more have left the upper west side, there is still a network of ties that keeps many individuals in communication with each other.

The effects of the Sullivan Institute/Fourth Wall community live on in the lives of the ex-members and ex-leaders. For those people who did not consciously leave the community, they have had to deal with the dissolution of their chosen way of life and the loss of a cohesive and in many ways supportive community. For many of those who chose to leave before the community dissolved, the task of reconstructing social networks and family ties is ongoing. Most ex-members have decided to reincorporate themselves into mainstream society in one way or another. This reintegration process can be extremely difficult and disorienting for people who have spent up to thirty years within the community. Many have been forced to make career changes, often taking jobs that they were not trained for and do not particularly want. Others have had serious psychological problems, and many are struggling financially due to large sums spent in the community.

NOTES

1. In this case a euphemism for a request for sexual relations.

2. L. C. stated that what he meant by his comment here is that the purpose of the anti-male-chauvinism campaign was not to honestly deal with male chauvinism as it existed in the Sullivan Institute/Fourth Wall community. Rather it was a ploy, designed to ridicule and intimidate some of the men in the group who had not made themselves available to Helen Moses, or who had challenged the leadership in other ways.

3. The authority of the leadership had been questioned before; however, in this case, a number of factors contributed to create a more unstable situation than previous dissent. These factors will be discussed in the concluding chapter.

4. Legally speaking, these women decided to put their infant children up for adoption, but the reason they made this decision was that they were told that they would cause severe psychological damage to their children if they decided to care for them.

5. In the Village Voice article, the husband and wife's real names were used, but I have changed them here to protect their identities.

6. In 1975 New York Magazine published an article by David Black entitled "Totalitarian Therapy on the Upper West Side," but the article was written by an outsider whose only access to the community was several weeks of therapy with a Sullivan Institute psychotherapist. No additional television or print coverage ensued.

7. I was one of the ex-members who were followed.

8. It was common practice for community members to marry one another in order to obtain health insurance coverage.

Why Members Joined and Why They Stayed: Theoretical and Practical Considerations

INTRODUCTION

Perhaps the most obvious and important question to emerge from this research is *why* highly educated, middle-class young adults would allow their lives to be dictated to such an extent? What would cause individuals who seemed highly functional—at least on the surface and for the most part—to give over so much control to others, especially against the advice of families and friends? Although there is no one answer to this question because each individual who joined the Sullivan Institute/Fourth Wall community came from a different set of circumstances, a few explanations can be offered that account for a great deal of this phenomenon.

The explanations include psychological theories about the development of the self, and sociological critiques that question the very idea of an autonomous individual. Before proceeding to a discussion of these themes, however, it is important to review the self-reported reasons members of the SI/FW community have given for their involvement, and place these within the overall context of the times. Participant-observation, interviews, and retrospective written accounts indicate two primary reasons why individuals joined the community and two primary reasons why they stayed.

REASONS FOR JOINING THE COMMUNITY

Most individuals joined because they were looking for a therapist, or because they were looking for a group of friends, lovers, or a community. The primary means of recruitment was through members entering into psychotherapeutic treatment with a therapist from the Sullivan Institute. As discussed in chapter 4, reasons for entering psychotherapy were extremely varied, but not particularly different from the reasons why any individual might seek therapy. Some people were at transitional periods in their lives—having just moved to New York City and needing to find friends and social support, wanting to end a marriage, or having problems with parents. Others were experiencing severe anxiety or depression, such as W. D., who said that she was having a nervous breakdown when she was referred to Ralph Klein by her English professor at Bennington College (W. D. 7/14/93, 2). L. C. had lost both his parents, and his only sister had moved out of the country. M. B. was alcoholic and was having difficulty adapting to life in New York City with his new wife. M. J. was raising two children alone and trying to finish graduate school; W. K. was shy with women and wanted to have a more expansive social life.

Analysis of demographic data from an aggregate perspective leads to some interesting findings. For example, individuals who became members of the Sullivan Institute/Fourth Wall community were overwhelmingly young (20–30), white, middle- to upper-class, and highly educated. The majority of members and leaders were Jewish, but there were also large percentages of Protestant and Catholic members.

Patients were drawn from the artistic community (Kenneth Noland, Jules Feiffer, Jules Olitsky, Jackson Pollack), the academic community (anthropology, history, psychology, sociology, and English Literature), the performing arts (Judy Collins, Joan Harvey), and other related professions such as architecture and set design. The group, which was quite small in the late 1950s and early 1960s, was described by one onlooker as a bunch of would-be bohemians (D.S. 7/20/93). This is an interesting perception in terms of developing an understanding of what their involvement in the Sullivan Institute community would have meant to therapists and patients.

In order to get a sense of how members differed from others in their cohort at this point in history, it is necessary to examine what kinds of changes in social structure and life choices were taking place for other individuals of the same demographic group.

In this regard, the structure of European-American middle- and upper-class family and social life in general was changing drastically and would continue to change rapidly during the period from 1958 to 1990. Many young people—20 to 30 years old—were delaying marriage for a variety of reasons. Some were concerned about the declining economy and wanted to finish their schooling and get a job before choosing a partner. Women were entering the workforce as a matter of course, and some were expecting to establish themselves in a career before having children, with or without a partner. People who had been involved with the civil rights, antiwar, women's, gay, African-American, Puerto Rican, and other movements concerned with social justice felt themselves at somewhat of a loss after the war in Vietnam ended. As Tipton (1982) concludes, part of this feeling of loss was a loss of moral grounding.

In addition, the U.S. economy began to experience structural economic changes in the 1970s that have been widely discussed. The manufacturing economy was declining and the service economy was providing more, but lower-paying jobs. There was an oversupply of individuals with advanced degrees, so many graduates of M.A. and doctoral programs were forced to take low-paying jobs in other fields. One of the functions that the Sullivan Institute/Fourth Wall community performed for its members was that of help in retraining individuals for jobs in areas that were experiencing growth and therefore looking for new employees.

The question arises as to whether one could delineate a profile of the type of person who would have become a member of the Sullivan Institute community. The research and personal experiences drawn upon here suggest that there were a few different reasons why people joined the group. One hypothetical member profile is that of the individual who feels the need for psychotherapy and is simply in the "right" place at the "right" time and is referred to a Sullivanian psychotherapist. Of course, this individual might or might not have then chosen to join the community, but chances are that he or she would have been encouraged to do so by the therapist. Another profile is that of the individual who has had prior political or countercultural involvement, or both, and is interested in a life that includes some continuity with the values that this lifestyle implies. Still another profile is that of an individual who experienced the political and cultural movements of the 1960s on the sidelines, and who was eager to experience some of the defining aspects of these lifestyles closer up. Many people that did become members belonged to more than one of these profile groups—these were the most common routes to membership.

REASONS FOR REMAINING IN THE COMMUNITY

In terms of remaining within the community, both the therapy and the group living situations reinforced members' decisions to stay. For some of those who joined in the 1960s and 1970s, the community had an initial impact on their lives that they still characterize as positive, although the experience may have soured for them later. Several individuals who left in the 1970s went on to become extremely successful musicians, writers, dancers, psychologists, artists, anthropologists, and members of many other professions as well. Some of these people attribute at least part of their later success to their therapists and friends in the group. Others are more angry and bitter about their experiences, especially those that stayed later. After 1979, as stated in chapter 6, the emphasis on individual fulfillment had been transmuted into a subservience to the group—rationalized by a belief system that predicted the nuclear destruction of the planet unless immediate action was taken. Many members who stayed past this point were expected to change careers in order to donate more money and time to the Fourth Wall Repertory Company and Accord Research and Associates. Based on interview data, it seems that a higher percentage of ex-members who left in the 1980s and 1990–92 feel that much of the Sullivanian experience had negative repercussions.

The Issue of the Self

One explanation for members' involvement revolves around the concept of the self, these days often known as the "narcissistic," "fragmented," or "protean" self. The enlightenment vision of the autonomous self was a concept that was meant to have a universal application, but in fact applied only to a tiny segment of the European population. Autonomy implies power and freedom; these are both ambiguous terms, but by most definitions not possessed by many individuals in early modern Europe or today. It was used to refer to those men who, after receiving considerable education and wealth, became leaders who were willing to challenge established ideas and to attempt to create a social world of their own making. Many critiques have been put forth regarding this notion of autonomy, but for the purposes of this discussion, the most relevant ones are those put forth by the Frankfurt School theorists in the 1930s and 1940s, and some aspects of the feminist critique, which did not emerge until the 1970s.

The Frankfurt School

The Frankfurt theorists and feminist theorists share a critical stance toward notions of enlightenment rationality and the autonomous individual. They approach this question from different perspectives, however. The Frankfurt theorists: Adorno, Horkheimer, Fromm (in the 1930s), and later Marcuse take both Marxist and Freudian theory as their starting point. The historical context for their interest in this question is the success of the fascist movement in Germany. They hypothesize that the combination of rapid industrialization with the German's loss of World War I and the extreme economic instability following these events resulted in a society in which the family structure has been fundamentally altered. The strong, authoritative role that fathers played as heads of households—which were also the basic economic units of their societies—has been replaced by "weaker" fathers who work outside the home and are subservient to others. This, they posit, has resulted in the inability of most boys to internalize a strong superego.[1] As a consequence of the lack of strong paternal authority in the home, and of extreme economic instability, many are likely to seek out a powerful authority figure outside the home to fill the gap in their psyches.

The Frankfurt theorists reasoned that Hitler was obviously such a figure for many of Germany's disenfranchised young men. The danger lies in the inability of the individual to control the external super-ego especially when a charismatic leader appeals to the id through the superego.[2]

This analysis is problematic for several reasons. It can easily lead to the conclusion that the patriarchal father as a force in familial relationships is the source of individual autonomy. Even if this had been true for small segments of the population during the historical period immediately prior to the 1930s, 1940s and 1950s during which Adorno, Horkheimer and others were living, it would not be possible nor desirable (for most) to return to this period. It can be argued that this type of male autonomy has always been achieved at the expense of both men and women—resulting in a polarization of roles (dependency/autonomy) that benefits neither in the long run. It is inaccurate to characterize any individual as existing outside the social/familial/cultural context into which he or she has been socialized.

Furthermore, even if we accept Adorno and Horkheimer's thesis of the decline of the individual as an accurate analysis of the impact of socioeconomic transition on the early twentieth-century family, we cannot return to a time before this period in the hope of recovering a stronger individual. The question that arises is: What could happen in the future to bring this (presumably desirable) goal about? The return of the individual family as the primary economic and social unit is not forthcoming. It is also doubtful that social change will bring about a family in which the father again becomes the unquestioned ruler.

The Feminist Critique

Another critique of enlightenment rationality and the ideal of individual autonomy is that put forth by Jessica Benjamin:[3] "Feminist theory has already exposed the mystification inherent in the ideal of the autonomous individual. As our discussion of Oedipus showed, this individual is based on the paternal ideal of separation and denial of dependency. The feminist critique of the autonomous individual closely parallels the Marxian critique of the bourgeois individual, elaborated by the Frankfurt theorists" (1988, p. 187). Benjamin not only critiques traditional notions of individuality, but also attempts to integrate notions of intersubjectivity, as addressed in the work of Habermas, into psychoanalytic theory. This attempt is based on both an empirical and a normative component.

On the empirical level, she puts forth an explanation of human development—based on research—that describes the child's process of "individuation" as dependent on the recognition and affirmation of his or her independence by significant others. This state of affairs presents itself as a paradox—in order to develop a healthy[4] sense of independence and selfhood, the infant is dependent on the primary care-givers. The empirical component of this theoretical analysis holds that unless infants are recognized and affirmed in their movements toward self-reliance and agency, they will encounter developmental difficulties. Care-givers do not always provide positive recognition to infants— sometimes they react negatively and sometimes they react apathetically. The prescriptive, or normative, component of Benjamin's analysis is derived directly from Winnicott's concept of "good enough" parenting. She asserts that in order to raise healthy children we must provide an environment in which they are responded to with empathy *enough of the time*.[5]

Given the socioeconomic conditions, in which most parenting takes place, empathic response to babies is often impossible—it is an ideal that we can hope to attain someday. What is striking to outside observers of authoritarian groups is that members have often cut their ties with traditional social networks, and no longer make important decisions about their lives in concert with family, social class, religion, or friends from their prior lives. This is important for understanding the assumptions implicit in many analyses of authoritarian groups and other social configurations. If we are to assume that each individual needs to be able to make decisions based on an autonomously formed opinion, we must take into account the fact that the overwhelming majority of people in the world cannot and do not wish to make decisions with reference to moral frameworks that exist outside their immediate sociocultural milieu.

Subjectively, individuals within the Sullivan Institute/Fourth Wall community may have actually experienced themselves as having become *more* autonomous than they were before. Certainly the influential people and forces in their lives became more centralized. If we view this freedom in the negative sense, they were "free" from the traditional bonds of family, cultural, and class expectations. Additionally, they believed they had *chosen* [6] to affiliate with the Sullivan Institute/Fourth Wall community. This was not the case with regard to their family or other influential socioeconomic conditions of their lives.

In a sense, Pearce and Newton would have agreed wholeheartedly with Benjamin regarding the illusory nature of "bourgeois" or "patriarchal" autonomy. They specifically stated that they were attempting to create a situation in which individuals could "grow up" without the constraints their parents and subcultures had placed on them. This "solution" to what was perceived as a very real problem resulted, however, in a "scientifically" engineered community in which power was centralized to a much greater extent than it is in the lives of most middle- to upper-class urban dwellers in the late twentieth-century United States.

Within the community, power was articulated quite differently than it is for people who are not intensely involved in a quasi-total institution or organization. There were many fewer intermediaries between a discourse of "right" action and the individual who would carry that action out. The smaller scale of the group made the linkages between the top and bottom of the social hierarchy more readily visible. It also made "slipping between the cracks" much more difficult.

Domination, for Benjamin and other feminist theorists, results from a situation in which mutual recognition fails to occur. Instead, roles in the relationship are sclerotized: one party becomes "the recognized" (the dominant partner) and the other becomes "the recognizer." In this respect, Benjamin referred primarily to male-female relationships. However, in the Sullivanian community this more traditional form of domination was replaced by a primary relationship to a therapist in which mutual recognition occurred—in an extremely delimited form. The patient was "recognized" as "sick" or "crazy," and the therapist was recognized as "healthy" and in possession of the "cure."

Some feminist theorists hold that because we live in a society in which instrumental reason is paramount, we tend to think dualistically about subject and object, the action and the acted upon. Benjamin believes this dualism is based in the social world: "The idea of rationalization forms a bridge between intellectual history and the history of social and economic relationships. It describes the essence of modern social practice and thought. It is, in Foucault's sense, a discourse. My argument is that it is a gendered discourse, that the instrumental orientation and the impersonality that govern modern social organization and thought should be understood as masculine" (1983, 187). This same duality is visible when we look at the Sullivanian community's promise of total freedom and self-fulfillment through its "technologies of the self" (described fully in chapter nine). The SI/FW community was an experiment in cultural engineering—in the sense that Pearce, Newton, and the other founders of the Sullivan Institute believed they could create a new culture, and thereby a new type of individual, by applying certain scientific principles. While this was a progressive notion on the surface, the use of certain techniques to achieve radical personality change produced extreme anxiety in some individuals, not to mention psychic discomfort and pain. In order to achieve liberation, patients were told they had to suffer—in the form of acute anxiety and the loss of important relationships.

This "end justifies the means" rationale, familiar to all of us in one form or another (economic success, religion, social movements, graduate education, tenure proceedings, etc.), can be quite dangerous: It subsumes the well-being of the individual to that of the group. While some people knowingly put themselves at risk, both psychically and physically, and are capable of extricating themselves from dangerous situations, others may neither know the risks nor be able to remove themselves if they should feel it necessary to their well-being.

The paradox in human nature that allows communities like the Sullivan Institute to exist is that people need significant others to recognize and affirm their independence, while at the same time maintaining affective ties. Benjamin refers to this concept as the basis for intersubjective theory, and the key to eliminating subject/object dualism in psychoanalytic theory. (Benjamin 1988, 49)

Heinz Kohut and the Concept of Narcissistic Personality Disorder

How individuals became involved with the Sullivan Institute/Fourth Wall community can also be analyzed from the perspective of the psychoanalytic concept of "narcissistic personality disorder." This concept—initially formulated by Heinz Kohut—has been expanded on in the past twenty-four years by his students and other academics and clinicians who have taken up his interest in the development of the self as it relates to an individual's internal world. Kohut's theoretical insights, and those of his colleagues, form a body of work that has "precipitated a firestorm of controversy, challenging fundamental precepts about both the etiology and treatment of psychopathology" (Baker and Baker 1987, 1). One of the cornerstones of this work was the hypothesis that [parents' empathic responsiveness to their children] is distorted in a specific way. These actual failures are unintended and beyond the parents' control, having as their root cause the psychological limitations of the parents themselves.

. . . developmental arrests which inevitably resulted from parental shortcomings most comprehensively and helpfully explained psychopathology.

Repeated empathic failures by the parents, *and* the child's responses to them, are at the root of almost all psychopathology. (Baker and Baker 1987, 1–2)

Kohut viewed failures of empathy on the part of parental figures as part of normal human interaction. He referred to those needs that humans have that must be at least partially met by another person, as *self-object* needs: "Kohut tried to distinguish self-object needs from object needs. In the latter, the other person functions as an autonomous object, an independent center of initiative. Objects are valued for who they are. Self-objects are valued for the internal functions and the emotional stability they provide. The self-object need being met is more important than who meets it" (Baker and Baker 1987, 2). In terms of a developmental sequence, Kohut posited that self-object needs in infancy must be externally met, primarily from the mother. Throughout childhood, increasing distance from the mother is tolerated; the father and parental substitutes are accepted. In adolescence the peer group becomes an important self-object, and in adulthood the number of potential self-objects is expanded again to include friends, spouse, colleagues, and others.

He also hypothesized that healthy adults are able to develop endopsychic structures that assume many of the functions required of external self-objects: "The person becomes more internally competent, less externally needy, and more flexible in meeting the remaining self-object needs" (Baker and Baker, 1987, 3).

Based on his clinical experiences, Kohut developed three new categories of transference. He called these the "mirroring," "idealizing," and "twinship/alter ago" transferences (Baker and Baker 1987, 3–5).

The mirroring transference pertains to the need of the developing infant to be responded to with delight by his or her parents and care-givers. This response is the precursor to the development of healthy self-esteem and self-assertiveness. Therefore, children who were not responded to positively *enough of the time,*[7] those who have "experienced repeated and significant mirroring failures" from parenting figures, may not develop internal structures to maintain self-esteem (Baker and Baker 1987, 3):

The "idealizing" transference relates to the human need to "merge with, or be close to, someone who we believe will make us safe, comfortable and calm." As with other self-object needs, there is a developmental process of maturation of the idealizing needs. Initially there is a wish to merge with the idealized parental imago; then there is a wish to be very near a source of such power; eventually the mature person is satisfied knowing that friends and family are available in times of stress. The intensity of the self-object needs decreases as the internal capacities increase. . . .

As with mirroring, a good enough parental environment is necessary for the idealizing developmental line to mature successfully. Minor failures create the need for internal structures, while basic success creates a secure enough environment to permit growth. (Baker and Baker 1987, 4)

The third type of self-object needs that Kohut refers to are the "twinship/alter ego" needs. By this he meant the need to feel a degree of alikeness, of commonality with other people. In early years this need may be for a "merged" quality—the sense that one feels identical with the other and that differences are intolerable. With maturity, one should be able to identify with a person or group and also tolerate differences.

For Kohut, a healthy self was one that could maintain some consistency of behavior and experience despite considerable stress. Baker and Baker assert, "the healthy self can internally regulate self-esteem, calm and soothe the self, and so forth." (1987, 5) He explains his divergence from the concern with biological drives of Freudian theorists by pointing out that the psychopathologies Freud attempted to analyze are nowhere near as prevalent today as they were in Vienna during Freud's lifetime. In the modern historical period, Kohut argues, the predominant psychopathologies and neuroses are "the results of a deadening distance to which children are exposed, leading in adulthood to a different kind of psychopathology, the disorders of the self, and leading, also we hope to a new set of explanations which in the long run will help us to overcome the leading psychic disturbances of our time" (Kohut 1985, 168).

The above description of Kohut's theory of the self and of the self-object transferences is intended to give the reader a sense of how he viewed the formation of the self. Using this concept can be useful in understanding how it was possible for Sullivanian psychotherapists to manipulate patients by using the therapeutic transference. Cushman puts this quite well: "As an adult one's sense of self can be threatened in a number of ways: object loss, separation anxiety, loss of status or prestige, a change in one's prescribed role, environmental stress, sociohistorical dislocations, regression due to group influences, or an attack on one's cultural frame of reference. Many of these threats to the self are produced by the techniques employed by restrictive groups" (1986, 6). This means that the recruitment-indoctrination process in restrictive groups stimulates narcissistic conflicts or causes a narcissistic crisis in recruits that impels them toward a regressive, dependent relationship with a charismatic leader who functions as self object, thereby soothing and lending cohesion to their fragmented state.

Perceived Advantages of Membership in the SI/FW Community

As I have tried to show in preceding chapters, the social and historical context within which the Sullivan Institute/Fourth Wall community arose was one in which "psycho historical dislocation" (Lifton 1987) could and did arise among large numbers of young adults. A group that offered both a critique of the traditional institutions of marriage and the family, and a context in which the individual could become part of a new "family" that would support his or her (transformed) values and goals, was extremely attractive to many people. Even for those who were not experiencing an incipient crisis of self-esteem or self-definition, involvement with the therapy could lead to a crisis and was designed to do so.

For those who joined, the advantages were quite significant. They could live in the narcissistic glow of the leadership—taking on their connection to the leaders as a source of self-esteem. Members felt that they were part of a special, elite group that had access to knowledge and self-awareness that few others had.

Many imagined themselves as the forerunners of the future—as an exemplary group in the present and possibly as the leaders of world civilization "when the revolution came." Sexual partners were easily obtained—this was a source of increased self-esteem for many patient-members. Living situations were to a great extent preordained by the leadership, so those who preferred not to live alone could find roommates with whom they shared many beliefs and aspirations.

The lifestyle of the community provided the individual with an integrated, cohesive sense of self. The analysis one's therapist provided was reinforced by roommates, friends, and lovers—all of whom who were all in the same therapy. House meetings, in which members listened to individual life histories and commented on them, provided additional validation for the therapist's conclusions—giving roommates "feedback" about their problems, which would then be discussed with one's therapist. It also gave members a sense of "symbolic immortality" [as Lifton (1987) put it], in that they felt they were part of a social experiment that would bring the culture to its next logical evolutionary plane.

Later, with the radical changes brought about within the community by the leadership's experience of the Three Mile Island nuclear accident an apocalyptic vision emerged in which the community became oriented around educating the world about the dangers of nuclear war and the capitalist economic system. These conceptions imbued group members' lives with meaning.

Belonging to the Sullivan Institute/Fourth Wall community also provided its members with a feeling of membership and solidarity. Whitsett (1992) connects this experience with Kohut's conception of the "twinship/alter ego" transference, and holds that "While the mirroring and idealizing transferences may explain strong ties to the leader and therapist, the twinship transference contributes a great deal to understanding the strong ties to the group. It particularly explains attachments in those cults where members have minimal direct contact with the idealized leader" (Whitsett, 1992, 368). The exclusivity and isolation of group members from outsiders easily led to the conception and feeling that those within the group were similar to oneself, while those outside were different. The longer a member remained within the group, the more likely he or she was to feel this separation quite strongly.

Therefore, in answer to those who have asked how such a bright, capable, and well-liked person could join a group like that, one answer is that not all individuals who became members of the Sullivan Institute/Fourth Wall community were initially experiencing a narcissistic crisis. Many were attempting to come to terms with sweeping economic, social, cultural, and political changes that were taking place in the post–World War II period— factors that deeply affected their lives as young adults. In addition, the technology of Sullivanian psychotherapy as developed by Pearce and Newton was sophisticated and effective in terms of breaking down a new recruit's sense of self, and participating with him or her in the rebuilding of the self in such a way that the individual became dependent on the therapy and the community for the fulfillment of needs for recognition, friendship, romantic love, and family.

CONCLUSIONS

As to the question of whether there were certain characteristics that individuals who became involved with the group shared, some conclusions can be made. Although some patients had experienced significant narcissistic wounds prior to joining, the charismatic leadership of Newton and others combined with the "technologies of the self" employed by the psychotherapists were primary causes of member involvement. It is also arguable that the socio- and psycho-historical dislocations of this particular historical period produced some individuals who were more likely to be in search of "totalistic" or "high control" groups. Based on the research presented herein, it seems that all these factors contributed—in different proportions for each person—to making the Sullivan Institute/Fourth Wall community a cohesive and relatively long-lived group.

If, as Mead and many others suggest, the self is formed only in a social context and is constantly changing, I would suggest that membership in the Sullivan Institute/Fourth Wall community provided a context within which many individuals formed a sense of themselves that they believed would enable them to lead rewarding lives, to experience greater intimacy, to be more successful in their chosen careers, to raise children in a supportive environment, and to experience a general feeling of belonging and purpose. Some aspects of community life have been judged by some participants in retrospect to have been successful. Many others are now considered to have been harmful.

This leads us to the question of whether there were perpetrators and/or victims in this situation. If we conclude that life within the confines of the Sullivan Institute/Fourth Wall community became increasingly restrictive and regimented, how do we account for this development? Is it an inherent characteristic of charismatic groups? Were Newton and Pearce, and later Harvey, Moses, and Klein hucksters who were attempting to enslave their patients and take all their money? Or were they believers who were trying to help as many people as possible?

All of the ex-members interviewed for this project held the leadership responsible for unethical—and in some cases—criminal behavior. This includes those who stayed until the dissolution of the community in 1992. There is a group of ex-members who are still patients of Harvey and Klein, and these people are thought to maintain their support for the actions of the leadership and the direction of the community in general. As mentioned earlier, Helen Moses now considers herself to have been a victim of Saul Newton.[8] Very few individuals, including those who were in the Sullivan Institute training program, consider themselves responsible for any wrongdoing. There are notable exceptions—the case of two of the trainees who, after leaving the community, testified against the leadership in custody cases, and openly referred to themselves as participants. (They also filed charges with the New York State Office of Professional Discipline.)

There are no simple answers to these questions about responsibility. They are moral and ethical questions that are constantly debated with regard to different situations. As a sociologist I can only attempt to shed light on the motivations of the individuals involved and on the events that occurred within this community.

At the social structural level, the community fulfilled basic human requirements such as the need for community, support networks, a sense of purpose, and for professional contacts. In the post-1945 period that most group members came of age, the rate of social change was so fast—and the breakdown of traditional communities, social roles, and mores so complete—that many, if not most, urbanites were less affiliated than ever before. I believe these factors were extremely important in accounting for the success of the Sullivan Institute/Fourth Wall community.

NOTES

1. They do not deal explicitly with how this affects girls.

2. "The superego of a very high-minded person can also gain satisfaction for the id by attacking people who are considered to be immoral. Cruelty masquerading as moral indignation is not unknown and has even been practiced on a large scale." (Hall 1954, 48)

3. She does so in her first article, "The End of Internalization: Adorno's Social Psychology" (1977), which directly addresses the Frankfurt School theorists, and in her book The Bonds of Love (1988).

4. I am using "healthy" here to mean a balance of independence and dependence—sometimes referred to as interdependence,

5. Benjamin is not asserting that care-givers must be empathic all the time, only that they be so on a regular basis without significant interruption.

6. A great deal of controversy exists regarding this point—many members who would have at one time maintained that they joined the community of their own free will would now hold that they were strongly urged by their psychotherapists to join. And some number would even say they were coerced.

7. Kohut points out that he is using a concept of "good enough" parenting, which refers to the fact that all parents are unresponsive some of the time, and that this is not a cause of psychopathology.

8. At least she is reported to have said this on several occasions.

Chapter 9

Conclusions

INTRODUCTION

Accounting for the paradox between the libertarian promise of the Sullivan Institute/Fourth Wall community and the highly authoritarian outcome of its practices requires consideration of the various elements that factored into this development. These elements involve primarily the historical context in which the community formed and functioned (the macro level), and the basis, structure, and implementation of power, including the importance and technology of discourse (the micro level). The rise and fall of this experiment can be viewed as a microcosm of the of the rise and decline of both the New Left and the counterculture. It can also be viewed in the context of the "dialectic of enlightenment"—the paradox that Adorno and Horkheimer discuss in their book of that name (Adorno & Horkheimer, 1949)—in the sense that the attempt to supplant irrational sources of moral authority (religion, the family) with rational ones (psychoanalytic and political theory) resulted in an outcome that was more repressive in many ways than before.

THE USE OF POWER

A powerful mix of formal and informal power was utilized to maintain the cohesiveness of the Sullivan Institute/Fourth Wall community for thirty-five years, and impart a strong sense of belonging and "chosenness" to its therapist- and patient-members. At the formal level, the tools of power included: the therapeutic relationship and misuse of the transference, the creation of a discourse that was used in specific ways to shape individuals in terms of their internal self-conceptions and their actions toward others, and the institution of community structures that supported these uses of power. At the informal level, the role of charisma is examined.

Power: The Formal Level

The Therapeutic Relationship

Central to the existence of both the discourse and the community itself was the therapeutic relationship. This relation could be considered the constitutive element of the entire enterprise. As discussed in chapter 5, the therapeutic relationship Sullivanian psychotherapists developed with their patients engendered extreme psychological dependency. This was accomplished in several ways: through misuse of the transference; through the evocation of existential fears of loss, abandonment, and death; and through providing patients with a total social environment.[1] Patients were told that leaving either therapy or the group was equivalent to psychological death, and those who chose to do so were ostracized.

The Creation of a Sullivanian Discourse

A specific discourse was created that dominated the lives of the therapists and patients who became members of the SI/FW community. This discourse sprang from a radicalization of certain aspects of neo-Freudian psychoanalytic theory, and was in keeping with the social and intellectual trends prevalent at this time among both the intellectual elite and mainstream U.S. culture.

In the context of this discussion, I will use the word "discourse" to refer to concepts elaborated by Michel Foucault, and later by Edward Said and others. A discourse will refer to a body of expert knowledge, accumulated in relation to specific institutions (often the state or religious bodies), that is used to actively disseminate conventional wisdom regarding that specific area of knowledge.

Said (1979) used this concept in relation to Orientalism, the elaborate scholarly and diplomatic edifice constructed by Western Europeans to understand and colonize the Middle East, and later the Far East. While the concept of discourse may appear metaphysical—in the sense that it is not overtly related to people, institutions, and economic processes—it is not. Rather, it is a way of formulating an extremely complex relationship, within the cultural sphere, between those who have been empowered to speak in the public arena with the economic, political, social, and cultural forces that put them in this position.

In the case of the Sullivan Institute/Fourth Wall community, the concept of a discourse can elucidate exactly how the founders of the group were able to create a cohesive and long-lived community that provided many of its members with a framework in which to conduct meaningful and purposeful lives. Pearce and Newton took Sullivan's theory and added to it a more radical interpretation of the role of parents in constraining their children from becoming mature adults. They incorporated the counterculture's emphasis on ecstatic experience through the use of alcohol and barbiturates, wild parties, and their attitude about sexual experimentation.

The expressive ethic that Tipton (1982) refers to was certainly in evidence—

not only in the emphasis on the ecstatic, but also in the importance placed on artistic, literary, kinetic, and musical expression. Like many other parts of the human potential movement that began in the late 1960s, the radical Sullivanians believed that the important thing for the individual was self-expression. It did not matter if you were trained or talented, the only way to grow and learn was to simply do it.

The Content of the Discourse

The basis for the new discourse that became the framework for the SI/FW community was as follows:

1. The belief that the human personality is formed through interaction with the early primary care-taking figures.

2. The conception of the human personality as being composed of a self-system, an integral personality, and a central paranoia:

   The self-system is composed of those experiences that the parents (and care-givers) allowed one to experience consciously—in other words, those experiences that did not make them anxious.

   The central paranoia is that part of the personality that discourages the individual from having those experiences that cause the parents anxiety.

   The integral personality is the progressive, growth-oriented part of the personality that incorporates both the "me" and "not me" experiences. It is constantly pushing the individual to reintegrate those experiences that were forbidden by the early caretakers or parents.

3. The extension and reification of developmental stages developed by Sullivan. Each stage—the early infancy, late infancy, juvenile, preadolescent, adolescent, and adult—had a set of developmental goals that were either attained or somehow prohibited or impeded by one's care-takers or parents. In Pearce and Newton's book, Conditions of Human Growth, each stage is described in terms of specific abilities that should be acquired. At the end of each such description, there was a section called "residuals of infancy, childhood, preadolescence, adolescence," and the like, which detailed the most commonly unattained psychological functions for that particular stage.

4. The belief that the traditional nuclear family was inherently unsuitable to raise the modern individual to "true" maturity. The mother, as primary caregiver, was thought to be too limited in her own experiences and abilities (due to societal repression) to allow her child to develop the necessary interpersonal skills, or to have the variety of experiences necessary in order to move smoothly through the requisite developmental stages. In other words, maternal envy was posited to prohibit the infant and child's ability to accumulate the experience necessary to grow.

5. The belief that in order to "jump start" the growth process, and circumvent

the initial repressive influence of the nuclear family, a community of like-minded others, with whom one would make up for these lost experiences, was necessary.

The Break with the Larger Psychoanalytic Community

While the initial discourse developed by Pearce and Newton shared the same origins as those of many other communes, social movements, and trends within the mainstream of the psychoanalytic and human potential movements, it quickly became completely isolated from these sources. Pearce had the credentials—and the relationship to the institutions of expert knowledge—to challenge the status quo. However, her colleagues considered some of her methods unethical, and she lost a great deal of her initial legitimacy in the eyes of mainstream psychoanalysts with whom she had previously been affiliated.

Pearce's and Newton's isolation was largely self-imposed. Other members of the profession did not initially shun them, but because they were extremely critical and dismissive of all mainstream practitioners, and because they were promoting a social "scene," they quickly became outcasts. They were no longer part of any referral network, nor were they participants in any kind of theoretical or clinical dialogue with their peers in other psychoanalytic institutes. Through the charismatic quality that she and her husband possessed, however, Pearce and Newton were then able to form a community of individuals who adhered to their theoretical and practical vision.

One of the results of the near-total isolation from the intellectual community from which they had sprung was the lack of further development of their theory. Such development is usually based on the constant critique, research, and refinement that usually take place in theoretical endeavors. The Sullivan Institute ceased holding classes in 1981, even though they technically still had students. New perspectives, when they were incorporated, seemed to come from the idiosyncratic interests of the leadership, such as Saul Newton's and Helen Moses' interest in the writings and theory of Mao Tse Tung. Neither Pearce, Newton, nor any of the other psychotherapists in the Sullivan Institute attempted to develop their psychological theory any further by adding new insights gained by other theorists in their discipline.[2] Any member who attempted to inform himself or herself by reading and grappling with other theorists was actively discouraged. So while they had rebelled against the intransigence and conservatism of the New York psychoanalytic establishment (which they felt included Freudians as well as neo-Freudians), they soon became every bit as rigid and resistant to outside input as they accused those institutions of being.

The theoretical paradigm Pearce and Newton formulated was universalistic—claiming to account for both the development of the individual, and the political and socioeconomic factors that created the context for this development. Although politics and socioeconomics are only alluded to in Conditions of Human Growth, they are very present in both verbal and written statements that were made both in the formative period of the community and in the later periods.

The Technology of the Discourse

In order to explain why the Sullivan Institute founders were so rigid and disinterested in dialogue with any other part of the psychoanalytic profession, we must look at several factors. While Weberian theory would tell us that this was the result of the routinization of charisma—or of rationalization—it may not be the case in a community of this size. In this case, I believe it may be more appropriate to use the concept of "reasons of state." That is, once founded, the Sullivan Institute community had a self-perpetuating logic that stipulated that staying in the community and severing all or most outside ties was the fastest route to maturity (for those pronounced "together" enough). Rejection of all other theoretical perspectives was necessary because the leadership maintained that patients who wanted to "grow" should stay with Sullivan Institute therapists.

Theory does not, however, become discourse without a relationship to powerful institutions—in the sense that it must be accepted and conveyed to specific individuals and groups. In the case of the SI/FW community, there were several sites where this process took place. The primary sites were the therapy session, the group apartment, and later on, the Fourth Wall Repertory Company. The study of this group is made more complex by the fact that the leaders were self-reflective in terms of their awareness of the interaction of power and ideology. They consciously promoted the creation of new identities or selves for members, and used their influence as experts to enable this process.

The Structure of Power: A Three-tiered Pyramid

The implementation of power relations was highly specific and hierarchical within the community and can be conceptualized structurally as a three-tiered pyramid. The leadership, which began as Pearce and Newton, but later became a foursome, was the pinnacle of this pyramid. The therapists, who disseminated the discourse from the top to the bottom of the pyramid, were the middle tier, and the patient-members, who were recipients for the most part but also acted to modify and resist the discourse, formed the lowest tier. This structure was not, however, totally rigid. As mentioned earlier, other individuals were able to rise to the middle tier through obtaining responsible positions in the Fourth Wall Repertory Company or becoming a friend or lover of one of the leaders.

Initially, Newton and Pearce occupied the top leadership positions. However, other therapists (who, during the 1950s and 1960s were all licensed with M.D.s or Ph.D.s) commanded a high level of respect and were also considered leaders. With the inception of the training program and the addition of patients to the Sullivanian Institute community in 1970, however, the three-tiered structure was developed, and power became more concentrated at the top—then occupied by Newton, Harvey, Moses, and Klein. The conception of the middle tier as trainees, and their lack of formal training as clinicians, made them extremely vulnerable to direct control by the leadership. Several trainees have subsequently reported that their supervision sessions with the four training analysts often consisted of their giving information about specific patients and receiving orders about dealing with particular situations.

The structure of the new community was initially the same as that of a fairly traditional psychoanalytic institute. As was noted earlier, the structure of psychoanalytic institutes, where students are required to undergo their own training analyses in addition to being supervised closely on their cases, can lead to an atmosphere in which both students and training analysts feel restricted. The characteristic of the Sullivan Institute that differentiated it from the mainstream institutes in the United States at that time was that patients were introduced to each other and encouraged to become friends, lovers, and often roommates. In addition, the data I have collected indicate that Saul Newton began to have sexual relations with both his own patients and patients of other Sullivan Institute psychoanalysts—and encouraged the other training analysts to do the same. From these initial divergences, the community of patients and therapists arose—and was considered extremely unethical and disreputable by the majority of the psychoanalytic community in New York City.

The Sullivanian discourse became a way of thinking for members—a template that permitted certain thoughts and interpretations and prohibited others. The repercussions of any challenge to the discourse by members were quite serious. Initially, one might simply be reprimanded. If the leadership perceived a significant challenge to its hegemony in the form of any disagreement with its world view, however, individuals could be criticized, told to move out of their apartments, "thrown out" of therapy, expelled from both therapy and the community, and physically threatened or attacked.

Until the Village Voice article of 1986, the SI/FW community managed to avoid the spotlight of media exposé, with only one exception (a New York Magazine article in 1975). As discussed earlier, the combination of defections by important individuals in the group's hierarchy, and the publicity generated by the Voice article and subsequent custody cases, began the process of delegitimating the discourse, and eventually destroyed the community.

The process of dissolution can also be viewed in historical terms. It became increasingly unacceptable to the majority of people to disavow romantic relationships. The communitarian experiments of the 1960s and 1970s receded and the economy declined. As mainstream society became increasingly individualistic and materialistic, and as communism appeared to be on the verge of extinction, it became ever more difficult to live in a community that demanded its members give up all privacy, individual decision-making power, and a great deal of their money as well.

The Relationship of the Discourse to the Individual

While the general historical and cultural context discussed above provided the basis for the development of this discourse, it could not have taken place without the existence of the particular type of power structure that characterized the Sullivanians. Individual members, whatever their position in the hierarchy of the SI/FW community, thought of themselves in terms of Pearce-Newton theory. This took place through various institutionalized mechanisms, the most central of which was the therapeutic relationship. In this context we are able to see the impact of discourse on the individual psyche in a very detailed and specific manner.

The relationship of discourse to the individual depends on the relationship of each person to the custodians of expert knowledge. In terms of the individual's ability to impact on received wisdom, this can take place only insofar as we may become experts ourselves, or are able to challenge the credentials of the experts.

During the period from 1970 to 1979, when the community was experiencing relatively rapid growth, many new patient-members were not aware of the hierarchy. They had little contact with the leadership, and related to their own therapists as the ultimate authorities in their lives. Although the group did have a reputation among certain social networks in Manhattan, as stated by David Black in his 1975 New York Magazine article,[3] not all individuals would have known this.

After the takeover of the Fourth Wall and the Three Mile Island accident, however, the leadership became much more visible. It was during this time that Newton and Harvey held general meetings and spoke directly to the membership at large. As the artistic director of the Fourth Wall, Harvey also spent a great deal of time at the Workshop[4] in Accord, New York, and at the theater in Manhattan, directing and acting in new productions. These changes had a transformative impact on the community—it was no longer a loose aggregate of therapists and patients, but a cohesive group with a purpose.

One ex-member who was interviewed for this project used the analogy of an early modern kingdom to describe the hierarchical structure of the group. He imagined Saul Newton and Jane Pearce (and later Joan Harvey, Helen Moses, and Ralph Klein) as absolute monarchs accorded all the ceremonial (and material) privileges thereof. These included a castle and summer residences, ladies-in-waiting, palace guards, courtiers and courtesans, royal musicians, artists, doctors, lawyers, and other court intellectuals, and several strata of servants. The peasants were those members who supported the royalty through payments for psychotherapy, donated labor, and labor at below market rates (such as baby-sitting).

Of course the analogy is far from perfect; the economic relationships involved were quite different, for example, but the notion of the Sullivanian community as a premodern social world is instructive. Within the group conceptions of public and private spheres that we can usually apply to mainstream culture did not exist. One's personal relationships, or one's so-called personality flaws, were not always private. Individuals were constantly falling in and out of favor, and could be exiled at the whim of the leadership. Ideas about autonomy and individuality were quite different from the mainstream in all its variations. The experience of individuals living in this context can be compared to life within a reclusive sect, as well as life in certain times and places, such as post-revolutionary China, the USSR, or Eastern Europe.

148   Sullivan Institute/Fourth Wall Community

POWER: THE INFORMAL LEVEL

The Role of Charisma

At the informal level, the charismatic appeal of Saul Newton was, from the earliest days at the William Alanson White Institute, vital to the coming together of the founders of the Sullivan Institute. It was also vital in maintaining the group and inspiring high levels of commitment. Together with the theoretical sophistication, the validity of their critique of the U.S. psychoanalytic establishment, and sophisticated "technologies of the self" employed by the therapists, the Sullivanians attracted a dedicated following.

The role of charisma in the exercise of power has been of interest to sociologists since Weber, and to social philosophers before his time. In this case, the question that arises is how much the community functioned as a result of the charismatic hold of Newton and others on the membership, and how much it did so as a result of the discourse and structure of the group. Actually, it would be more precise to say that the charisma of Newton (and some others) was connected in specific ways to the discourse and structure of the community as it developed over the years. While the source of Newton's hold over Sullivan Institute teachers, students, and patients did not spring from a unique access to revelation per se, he was viewed by many of his peers, his students, and his patients as an individual who had privileged access to the true nature of reality. This special status was due to his working-class background, his experiences as a labor organizer, and his participation in the Spanish Civil War and World War II.[5]

In the early years of the Institute community, most members were in personal contact with Saul (which is what everyone involved, including his children, called him). Later, many patients who began therapy in the late 1960s and 1970s had not met or learned much about him prior to their entry. While membership did not necessarily depend on a personal relationship with him, Newton exercised power over the community by direct control over the other psychotherapists within the Sullivan Institute, and indirect control over patients of the therapists he supervised. As noted, he also spoke directly to general meetings of the entire membership in later years.

Furthermore, he was involved in a continuous process of choosing and rechoosing favorites among women at every level of the group hierarchy, often elevating these women to higher positions and jettisoning those he abandoned. For example, Jane Pearce's power and authority were slowly delegitimated after her marriage to Newton ended. By 1978 she was neither an active leader nor a member of the community, and did not receive any new patients through the Sullivan Institute.

As already mentioned, Saul became involved with Joan Harvey—and then Helen Moses—during the late 1960s. After his divorce from Harvey, she married Ralph Klein. From the mid-1970s on, these four individuals comprised the leadership structure, which remained intact until the dissolution of the Sullivan Institute/Fourth Wall community in 1992.

While Newton's charismatic hold diminished over the years, as he grew older and more infirm, Harvey's, Moses' and Klein's increased. When Harvey became the artistic director of the Fourth Wall Repertory Company and was in day-to-day contact with a much larger percentage of the membership than any of the other three, she expanded her coterie of followers to include stage managers, costume designers, lighting and sound technicians, and musicians. Moses, on the other hand, consolidated a more traditional female role of experienced mother and expert on health issues.

It is important to attempt to understand Newton's and Pearce's intentions when they founded the Institute and the community. With regard to Pearce, who had spent decades on medical and psychoanalytic training, both ex-patients and colleagues report that she believed very strongly in the project of the Sullivan Institute and the community. Newton, on the other hand, seems to have been a much more motivationally complex personality. Whereas Pearce had dedicated her life to the study and further development of Sullivan's psychoanalytic theories, Newton had very little formal academic training. He met Pearce while working in the bursar's office of the William Alanson White Institute. He was charismatic, intimidating, and sexually voracious—according to several informants who knew him in the late 1950s. He was also a self-described communist who had taken part in partisan fighting against Trotskyites during the Spanish civil war—bragging that he had killed Trotskyites as well as fascists. He often made publicly violent threats, and according to direct observation and the reports of ex-members, he practiced both verbal and physical violence against women. It is impossible to retrospectively ascertain what inspired him to co-found the Sullivan Institute. He certainly enjoyed being the center of controversy, and reveled in being considered a disreputable maverick. The in-fighting in the psychoanalytic profession may have inspired him, and he may very well have viewed himself as the right person to help Pearce develop a more radical formulation of Sullivan's theories. For Newton, being seen as an upstart who had no respect for tradition may very well have been a source of pride.

GENERAL APPLICATIONS OF THE RESEARCH

It is hoped that this research will contribute to an understanding of the technologies of discourse in mainstream culture, as well as those of other subgroups. Its basis for doing so lies in its ability to chart the dissemination of the discourse in a small community and follow its development from a theory held by certain individuals into an instrument for forming and maintaining an entire community of participants in a coherent way. The detailed study of the evolution of a specific discourse that became hegemonic for a marginalized, reclusive group—and its uses in the production of identities (or selves)[6]—within this group, could be useful in understanding the mechanisms by which specific discourses come to influence us in mainstream society. In addition, it raises another relevant question: To what extent is society composed of subgroups in which certain discourses become hegemonic, as opposed to consisting of one homogenous group of creators and recipients of various discourses? Or do both conditions exist at the same time? In other words, do mainstream discourses exist that have some effect on all members of a particular culture, and do subcultural discourses adopted by smaller groups share some cultural/political/ socioeconomic /ethnic characteristics?

The rise and fall of the Sullivan Institute/Fourth Wall community also raises some fascinating questions regarding the viability of enlightenment rationality as a replacement for the traditional normative structures of religious faith and its expression in the social structures of church/denomination and family. Given the fact that the founders of the Sullivan Institute were predominantly of Eastern European Jewish descent (even Jane Pearce was half Jewish), a group that has long been immersed in secularism and scientific scholarship, the attempt to create new cultural forms in a social laboratory is in keeping with a cultural and intellectual heritage that also resulted in the kibbutzim of the newly-formed Israeli state. The connection between secular Judaism and the radical Sullivanians deserves further research.

The combination of a rational-scientific discourse with the charismatic powers of Saul Newton resulted in the formation of a community that slowly became a repressive group. While this was not the only possible outcome of the initial formation of the group, it may have been the only one that enabled it to maintain its cohesive structure. Other possibilities existed, but probably would have resulted in the splintering of members into many smaller units that eventually could have reintegrated themselves into the mainstream culture of the late-twentieth-century United States. What remains now is the experience of hundreds of ex-members whose understanding of this phenomenon, along with the insights of outsiders, could be used to draw valuable conclusions about the social issues and problems that face post traditional societies.

NOTES

1. By total social environment, I mean a combination of a living situation, friends, lovers, employment or employment assistance and support, summer house roommates, academic tutoring and support, and inexpensive child care.

2. Saul Newton is rumored to have been embarking on a new theoretical work in the years before he died, but I have not been able to find out its content as of this writing.

3. He had posed as a prospective patient in order to collect information for his article "Totalitarian Therapy on the Upper West Side" (December 15, 1975).

4. The "Workshop" was an old resort/bungalow colony in the Catskills that the Fourth Wall purchased with the intention of using it as a summer retreat in which to work on new productions. Community children also spent a good deal of time there in the summers, and members were often expected to spend their vacation time there either rehearsing new productions or maintaining the buildings and grounds.

5. This romanticization of the "working classes," and of war as well, was part of the cultural context of the earlier part of the twentieth century. Especially for certain segments of the middle and upper classes, the experiences of African Americans and of the white lower and working classes were fascinating, first of all because they were foreign, and second because Marx and others had pinpointed the lower classes as the true agents of progressive social change in industrial capitalist society.

6. Throughout the text I have used these terms interchangeably, although they do not have exactly the same meaning. Identity is usually used to refer to the various roles

an individual plays in a complex society. Self usually has a deeper meaning, based on the individual's self-conception. In a community like the SI/FW community, the two meanings are closer together due to the fact that is more like a traditional society.

Appendix A:
A Review of the Literature

UTOPIAN COMMUNITIES AND DYADIC INTIMACY

This is one aspect of membership in new religious movements that has received attention. Stuart Wright (1986) investigated the relationship between dyadic intimacy and commitment in three groups—the Unification Church, the Hare Krishna (ISKON), and the Children of God/Family of Love. All three of these movements had strict prohibitions of different kinds on romantic relationships. He found that in cases where strong dyadic ties were formed, either without the group's knowledge or before the couples became members, the risk of defection was much greater than when members remained single with no strong romantic attachments. Research into the practices within the SI/FW community affirms these findings. Romantic relationships were considered unhealthy, and individuals who became involved in this way could be threatened with expulsion and/or told to end the relationship. In contrast to Wright's findings, however, data regarding the SI/FW community shows that strong friendship, as well as romantic love, could also threaten members' commitment to the group.

PSYCHOTHERAPY CULTS

While both Temerlin and Temerlin (1982) and Singer (Singer and Temerlin 1977; Singer 1990) have encountered and treated individuals who were members of similarly structured groups, neither they nor any other researcher has had the prolonged contact and experience with this type of therapeutic relationship that has been possible in this research.

SEX-ROLE AND FAMILY TURMOIL IN THE 1960S

Aidala (1985) has analyzed data gathered by a nationwide survey of communal groups during the period from 1974 to 1976 and then followed up this research more recently in 1982. Based on her findings, she has concluded that during the period beginning in the 1960s, a period of "sudden economic, social, and demographic changes . . . have eroded the taken-for-granted legitimacy of prevailing institutions" (1985, 287). Gender roles, because they are directly affected by these factors, are often thrown into disarray during these turbulent periods. New religious movements, or quasi-religious movements, provide clear-cut definitions and regulations regarding gender roles. Therefore, she argues that during these periods individuals who have a low tolerance for ambiguity in regard to their intimate relationships will seek out these groups. Individuals who have out-and-out rejected traditional gender roles are more likely to join communes that allow role experimentation rather than providing specific structures.

Research data on the SI/FW community so far partially validates these conclusions, but with some interesting exceptions. Aidala does not include secular groups in her categorization of groups that have strictly defined gender roles. The SI/FW may be one of the few self-described secular groups that had such strict requirements regarding gender roles—specifically regarding sexuality, marriage, procreation, and child rearing. Although these rules were in some ways extremely egalitarian with regard to men and women, they were nonetheless rigid. In addition, many individuals who became members of the SI/FW community had previously rejected traditional gender roles. Aidala does not account for this possibility, as stated above—she concludes that those individuals who have engaged in a great deal of sexual experimentation prior to joining a commune, and who have rejected traditional gender roles, are more likely to join a secular commune with no specific regulations regarding these roles. While some aspects of her thesis may be challenged by the SI/FW community data, much of it is confirmed. Aidala's work is among the most useful for both its breadth and depth of understanding of the communal experience. Some other researchers have also offered useful data in regard to women's search for structured gender roles (see Kauffman 1985; Davidman 1990).

Jacobs (1989) offers insight into the processes that result in both conversion and deconversion into new religious movements/cults. She interviewed defectors from patriarchal or charismatic groups in the 1970s, concluding that the communities provided alternate families for individuals who were both affected by the notions of ideal family put forth in the 1950s and disillusioned with their own families, specifically their fathers. Research in the SI/FW community shows that while some members may have initially entered into Sullivanian psychotherapy with negative feelings and thoughts about their families, the therapy itself was the instrument through which many individuals became convinced that the problems they were experiencing were caused by their parents. Therefore, it is possible that in addition to providing alternatives to the traditional family, these groups themselves were part of the overall historical trend at that time that was challenging the discourse and beliefs about the post–World War II family.

CAN PSYCHOTHERAPY BE VIEWED AS RELIGIOUS?

Sociologists vs. Psychologists

The largest body of literature addressing groups that share many of the characteristics of the Sullivanians is the subfield of the sociology of religion that specializes in the study of "new religious movements" or "cults." Although the SI/FW community never defined itself as religious, and in fact was specifically atheist in its beliefs and practices, its members nevertheless displayed aspects of faith and commitment that bear striking similarities to groups such as the followers of Bhagwhan Shree Rajneesh, members of the Unification Church, and the Children of God, to name just a few. When we look at the ways in which members of the SI/FW community were expected to demonstrate their faith, both in the leadership and in the precepts espoused by the community, the line between religious communities and therapeutic ones becomes increasingly blurred.

The label "new religious movement" has been applied to certain new (and marginal) groups at least partially in response to a controversy over the use of the word "cult" and the implications of that label (Robbins and Bromley 1992). While there is a separate category of groups referred to as "psychotherapy cults," they are much fewer in number than the groups that define themselves as religious. While some studies have looked at these groups (Temerlin and Temerlin 1982; Cushman 1986; Singer, et al. 1990), few monographs have examined them in depth.

Within the academic community, there is disagreement about the nature of communities such as that of the Sullivanians. A schism[1] has taken place, more or less along disciplinary lines, between sociologists and psychologists in regard to how to name ("cult" vs. "new religious movement") the communities, and how to analyze them. Barker (1986) also notes that the sheer quantity of research undertaken by sociologists stands in contrast to the actual proportion of the U.S. population that are members of a cult/new religious movement.

The focus of the disagreement between (most) sociologists and (most) psychologists, psychiatrists, and social workers that study these phenomena is on the conversion process. While sociologists for the most part view conversion as a function of a variety of societal and personal factors (see Fichter 1987; Singer 1977; Tipton 1982; Bromley and Richardson 1983; Barker 1984; Robbins 1991; Snow and Machalek 1984), psychologists, psychiatrists, and social workers view it from the point of view of "undue influence" on the individual (Singer 1977; Cushman 1986; Hassan 1988; Whitsett 1992). This research will attempt to bridge the gap between these disparate perspectives by attempting to integrate both psychological and sociological understandings of the SI/FW community. This type of analysis is not only useful in terms of a contribution to interdisciplinary research, but is also necessary in order to comprehend the particular nature of the SI/FW community. In the context of religious studies, it is possible to neglect the psychodynamic components of membership in an authoritarian community, and focus on social and behavioral factors alone.

However, the use of psychoanalytic techniques in the SI/FW community demands the examination of intrapsychic as well as contextual factors.

While I will examine the issue of conversion and its causes, namely, "mind control" versus "free will," I also focus on these issues in terms of the everyday life of the SI/FW community, as well as on the level of discourse or ideology. A study of the development of a universalistic (and totalistic) theoretical paradigm into a discourse within the context of a small community can add to general knowledge regarding the mechanisms through which specific discourses are created, become legitimated and accepted, and finally lose their hegemony as they are replaced by other, competing discourses. Although the Sullivan Institute/Fourth Wall community cannot be taken as an analog of U.S. society as a whole, a study of the means by which a particular discourse was developed and instituted there on a small scale can certainly find a reflection of the whole contained in a part. Some theorists (Robbins and Bromley, 1992) have argued that new religious movements (including communities like the SI/FW) can be viewed as laboratories of social experimentation. This work examines not only the day-to-day experiences of members and leaders, but also what they believed—how they justified their actions, and the relationship between these aspects of the community. Many scholars focus on coercive practices only in terms of conversion and deconversion; they "neglect analyses of group practices that sustain and restrain committed members" (Cartwright and Kent 1992, 347). I focus specifically on the construction of hierarchies and the way in which power was distributed. I hope to shed light on the factors that lead individuals to join a community, on the reasons they decide to remain in an authoritarian situation, as well as on those factors that result in individual decisions to leave or to stay.

Additionally, this book documents the life cycle of a community that had hardly been written about before 1986 (Conason and McGarrahan 1986). Due to its fairly recent dissolution and the death of Saul Newton, the primary leader, it is now possible to write about the early period, the "heyday," and the decline of the SI/FW community, giving the reader an opportunity to learn about the factors that led to both rise and fall.

Power and Intimate Relationships

Power in the SI/FW community consisted to a large extent of the control of affective ties, including those that characterize the family. Sociologists of religion, feminist scholars, as well as historians have pointed out the necessity of controlling intimate relationships in utopian communities.

In many respects, the strongest emotional tie for many, if not most, SI/FW community members was the relationship with their therapist. One crucial difference between the therapeutic relationship within the community and the majority of relationships between patients and "mainstream" therapists is that Sullivanian psychotherapists regularly broke the rules of the American Psychological Association's Code of Ethics, which require therapists not to treat their friends, lovers, colleagues, or students. Since members of the SI/FW community were in frequent and often prolonged social contact with each other, they were consistently breaking this rule and were perceived as unethical by most of the psychoanalytic community.

The Failure of Universalizing Thought

In addition to contributing to an understanding of the processes that resulted in the formation of the SI/FW community and its authoritarian characteristics, this work attempts to add to a deeper understanding of the aporetic aspects of both psychoanalytic and Marxist thought. Several theorists have chosen to view new religious movements/cults as "laboratories of social experimentation" (Kanter 1972; Straus 1979; Robbins and Bromley 1992). It is hypothesized in this research that the attempt to actualize a blend of psychoanalysis and Marxism in the SI/FW community demonstrated some of the failings of both of these radical enlightenment projects. Additionally, it is hoped that the experience of this community can be used to show the need in theory, and in society as well, to abandon the ideal of one single reason and to take up instead the notion of many rights, or of communicative rationality. (Habermas 1984)

It has long been recognized that the structure of psychoanalytic institutes can lend itself to sectarian hierarchies and totalizing thought processes among students and faculty (Kohut 1976; Roustang 1982; Lifton 1989). In the case of mainstream psychoanalytic institutes, however, the individuals involved do not live together or socialize only with each other. In the SI/FW community, the ethical norms of mainstream psychoanalysis were abrogated in that training analysts, trainee analysts, and patients were part of a residential, social, and (sometimes) economic community. This led to an extreme form of the same process. Nevertheless, in both cases, the potential for totalizing thought processes to develop when a community forms around a particular set of ideas is great. The cause of this phenomenon is not simply structural, however, it is also historical. The adoption of a medicalized confessional discourse that contains specific definitions of health and sickness that apply to every individual, regardless of differences in the subjective experiences of particular patients, has become a form of power. As Foucault points out (Foucault 1978), the confessional mode developed by the Catholic Church and later incorporated by pedagogical, medical, and psychoanalytic practitioners made it necessary to confess every detail of one's thoughts, feelings, and actions in order to be saved. In the process of doing this, the individual's self-perception is interpreted in specific ways, and his or her self-concept is affected. It will be shown by this research that this is exactly what took place in the SI/FW community, but that all psychoanalysis carries within it certain elements of this dynamic.

In the context of Marxist theory, there are two elements that were utilized by the SI/FW community and that have been put into practice in much larger contexts as well that, it is hypothesized here, led to its authoritarian nature. The first is the notion of a particular subject of the revolutionary process, namely, the proletariat. This led to Lenin's notion of the vanguard party and therefore to a rigid, antidemocratic hierarchical structure. The second is Marx's utopian notion of an end of the dialectic, that is, a time when all contradictions will be resolved, when the state will "wither away." This can lead to (and has led to) a belief in a "perfect society," and in many cases to the attempt to create the "new socialist man," as in Maoist China.

In both cases the reincorporation of a nineteenth-century view of science into psychoanalysis and Marxist thought has led to the acceptance of the notion of one universal truth. Perhaps the knowledge of those who have lived these experiments can inform future attempts, both to improve society and to improve our understanding of it.

NOTES

1. Perhaps this is hyperbole, but it is true that individuals on opposite sides of this debate seem to have a great deal of animosity towards each other.

Appendix B:
Details of the Research

INTERVIEWS CONDUCTED

I conducted the following interviews:
S. P.—3/23/86
D. W.—4/27/88
E. C.—4/30/88
M. J.—5/1/88
S .B.—5/5/88
W. K.—5/9/88
L. C.—5/15/88
L. D.—6/1/93
W. D.—7/14/93
G. S. —10/16/93
G. P.—6/23/93
F. N.—6/29/93
A. M.—7/7/93
D. S.—7/20/93
E. G.—6/30/94
M. B.—7/11/94

In addition to these interviews, Richard Ofshe, Ph.D. conducted three interviews in his capacity as an expert witness for the Bray/Dobash custody case. I was given permission by the interviewees to use these interviews for this research.

Bibliography

Bollinger v. Bollinger, 40 N.Y.2d 543, 387 N.Y.S.2d 821 (1977).

Aidala, A. 1985. "Social Change, Gender Roles, and New Religious Movements." *Sociological Analysis* 48, 286–314.

Baker, H. S., M.D. and Margaret N. Baker, Ph.D. 1987. "Heinz Kohut's Self Psychology: An Overview." *The American Journal of Psychiatry* 144, 1–9.

Barker, E. 1984. *The Making of a Moonie: Choice or Brainwashing?* New York: Blackwell.

Barker, E. 1986. "Religious movements: Cult and anticult since Jonestown." *Annual Review of Sociology* 12, 329–46.

Bellah, R. N. 1976. "The New Consciousness and the Berkeley New Left." In Glock, Charles Y. and Bellah, Robert N. (Eds.), *The New Religious Consciousness* (77–92). Berkeley: University of California Press.

Bellah, R. N., R. Madsen, W. M. Sullivan, A. Swidler, S. M. Tipton 1985. *Habits of the Heart: Individualism and Commitment in American Life.* New York: Harper & Row.

Benjamin, J. 1988. *The Bonds of Love: Psychoanalysis, Feminism, and the Problem of Domination.* New York: Pantheon.

Black, D. 1975. "Totalitarian Therapy on the Upper West Side," *New York Magazine* (37).

Bromley, D. and J. T. Richardson 1983. *The Brainwashing/Deprogramming Controversy: Sociological, Legal and Historical Perspectives.* Lewiston, NY: The Edwin Mellen Press.

Carter, L. F. 1990. *Charisma and Control in Rajneeshpuram: The Role of Shared Values in the Creation of a Community.* Cambridge, UK: Cambridge University Press.

Cartwright, R. II. and S. A. Kent 1992. "Social Control in Alternative Religions. A Familial Perspective." *Sociological Analysis* 53, 345–61.

Chapman, A. H., M.D. 1976. *Harry Stack Sullivan: His Life and His Work.* New York: G. P. Putnam's Sons.

Chapman, A. H. and C. Miriam C.M.S. 1980. *Harry Stack Sullivan's Concept of Personality Development and Psychiatric Illness.* New York: Brunner/Mazel.

Cushman, P. 1986. "The Self Besieged: Recruitment-Indoctrination Processes in Restrictive Groups." *Journal for the Theory of Social Behavior* 16, 1–28.

Davidman, L. 1990. "Women's Search for Family and Roots: A Jewish Solution to a

Modern Dilemma." In T. Robbins; D. Anthony (Eds.), *In Gods We Trust: New Patterns of Religious Pluralism in America* (385–407). New Brunswick, NJ: Transaction.

Dickstein, M. 1989. *Gates of Eden*. New York: Penguin Books.

Elman, R. 1991. "Newton's Laws." The Society for Psychoanalytic Psychotherapy Bulletin, 6, 31–35.

Fichter, J. H. 1987. *Autobiographies of Conversion*. Lewiston, NY: The Edwin Mellen Pres.

Foucault, M. 1978. *The History of Sexuality: An Introduction*. New York: Vintage Books.

Freud, S. 1966. On the History of the Psycho-Analytic Movement. New York: W. W. Norton.

Ghent, E., M.D. 1989. "Credo: The Dialectics of One-Person and Two-Person Psychologies." *Contemporary Psychoanalysis*, 25, 169–211.

Gilbert, J. 1986. *Another Chance: Postwar America, 1945–1985*. Chicago: The Dorsey Press.

Gitlin, T. 1987. *The Sixties: Years of Hope, Days of Rage*. New York: Bantam Books.

Glock, C. Y., R. N. Bellah 1976. *The New Religious Consciousness*. Berkeley and Los Angeles: University of California Press.

Goffman, E. 1959. The Presentation of Self in Everyday Life. New York: Anchor Books.

Goffman, E. 1961. Asylums: On the Characteristics of Total Institutions. Garden City, NY: Anchor Books.

Greil, A. L. and D. R. Rudy 1990. "On the Margins of the Sacred." In T. Robbins and D. Anthony (Eds.), *In Gods We Trust: New Patterns of Religious Pluralism in America* (219–32). New Brunswick, NJ: Transaction.

Guntrip, H. 1973. Psychoanalytic Theory, Therapy and the Self. New York: Basic Books.

Habermas, J. 1984. *Reason and the Rationalization of Society*. Boston: Beacon Press.

Halberstam, D. 1993. *The Fifties*. New York: Villard Books.

Hale, N. G., Jr. 1995. *The Rise and Crisis of Psychoanalysis in the United States: Freud and the Americans, 1917–1985*. New York and Oxford: Oxford University Press.

Hammond, Phillip E. 1992. *Religion and Personal Autonomy: The Third Disestablishment in America*. Columbia, SC: University of South Carolina Press.

Harvey, J. 1974. Seminar at the Sullivan Institute for Research in Psychoanalysis, notes taken by M. Cohen

Harvey, J. 1980a. Seminar at the Sullivan Institute for Research in Psychoanalysis, notes taken by M. Cohen.

Harvey, J. 1980b. In The Beginning...

Harvey, J. 1981a. *Ride a Red Horse*.

Harvey, J. 1981b. *Death Watch?*

Harvey, J. 1982. Freedom Ain't No Bowl of Cherries.

Harvey, J. 1983. *From Left Field*.

Hassan, S. 1988. *Combating Cult Mind Control*. Rochester, VT: Park Street Press.

Isserman, M. 1987. *If I Had a Hammer... The Death of the Old Left and the Birth of the New Left*. New York: Basic Books.

Jacobs, J. 1989. *Divine Disenchantment*. Bloomington: Indiana University Press.

Jacoby, R. 1975. *Social Amnesia: A Critique of Conformist Psychology from Adler to Laing*. Boston: Beacon Press.

Jacoby, R. 1983. *The Repression of Psychoanalysis: Otto Fenichel and the Political Freudians*. New York: Basic Books.

Jacoby, R. 1987. *The Last Intellectuals: American Culture in the Age of Academe*. New York: Farrar, Straus and Giroux.

Kanter, R. M. 1972. *Commitment and Community*. Cambridge, MA: Harvard University Press.

Kauffman, D. 1985. "Women Who Return to Orthodox Judaism: A Feminist Analysis." *Journal of Marriage and the Family*, August, 543–51.

Kohut, H. 1985. "Creativeness, Charisma, Group Psychology: Reflections on the Self-Analysis of Freud." In C. B. Strozier (Ed.), *Self Psychology and the Humanities: Reflections on a New Psychoanalytic Approach* (171–211). New York: W. W. Norton & Company.

Kurzweil, E. 1989. *The Freudians: A Comparative Perspective*. New Haven: Yale University Press.

Lifton, R. 1985. "Cult processes, religious liberty and religious totalism." In T. Robbins, and W. Shepherd (Ed.), *Cults, Culture and the Law*. Chico, CA: Scholars Press.

Lifton, R. J. 1987. "Cults: Religious Totalism and Civil Liberties", *The Future of Immortality and Other Essays for a Nuclear Age* (209–19). New York: Basic Books.

Lifton, R. J. 1989. *Thought Reform and the Psychology of Totalism*. Chapel Hill: The University of North Carolina Press.

Neufeld, A. 1989. "One Step Away from Mother: A Stepmother's Story." In Maglin, Nan Bauer and Nancy Schniedewind (Eds.), *Stepfamilies: Voices of Love and Anger* (77–92). Philadelphia: Temple University Press.

Newton, S. 1979. Notes from a Sullivan Institute class 1/17/79.

O'Neill, N., and G. O'Neill. 1972. *Open Marriage: A New Lifestyle for Couples*. New York: M. Evans.

Ofshe, R. 1988a. Interview with Michael Bray.

Ofshe, R. 1988b. Interview with Michael Cohen.

Ofshe, R. 1988c. Interview with Amy Siskind.

Pearce, J. M. D., and Newton, S. 1963. *The Conditions of Human Growth*. New York: The Citadel Press.

Pearce, J. M. D., and Newton, S. 1970. "Establishment Psychiatry—and a Radical Alternative."

Perry, H. S. 1982. *Psychiatrist of America: The Life of Harry Stack Sullivan*. Cambridge, MA: The Belknap Press.

Racker, E. 1968. *Transference and Counter-Transference*. New York: International Universities Press.

Richardson, J. T. 1993. "Definitions of Cult: From Sociological-Technical to Popular-Negative." *Review of Religious Research* 34, 348–56.

Robbins, T., and D. Bromley. 1992. "Social Experimentation and the Significance of American New Religions: A Focused Review Essay". *Research in the Social Scientific Study of Religion* (1–28). Greenwich, CT: JAI Press Inc.

Robbins, T., and R. Robertson. 1991. "Studying Religion Today: Controversiality and 'Objectivity' in the Sociology of Religion." *Religion* 21, 319–37.

Roszak, T. 1969. *The Making of a Counter Culture: Reflections on the Technocratic Society and Its Youthful Opposition*. New York: Doubleday & Company.

Roustang, F. 1982. *Dire Mastery*. Baltimore: The Johns Hopkins Press.

Said, E. 1979. *Orientalism*. New York: Vintage Books.

Singer, M. 1977. "Therapy with ex-cultists." *National Association of Private Psychiatric Hospitals Journal* 9, 15–18.

Singer, M. 1979. "Coming out of the Cults." *Psychology Today* 72–82.

Singer, M. T., M. K. Temerlin, and M. D. Langone. 1990. "Psychotherapy Cults." *Cultic Studies Journal* 7, 101–25.

Snow, D., and R. Machalek. 1984. "The sociology of conversion." *Annual Review of Sociology* 167–90.

Stark, R., and W. S. Bainbridge. 1985. *The Future of Religion: Secularization, Revival, and Cult Formation*. Berkeley: University of California Press.

Straus, R. 1979. "Religious Conversion as a Personal and Collective Accomplishment." *Sociological Analysis* 40, 158–65.

Sukenick, R. 1985. "Up from the Garrett: Success Then and Now." *New York Times Book Review*, January 27, 30.

Sullivan, H. S., M.D. 1954. *The Psychiatric Interview*. New York: W. W. Norton & Company, Inc.

Temerlin, M. K., and J. W. Temerlin. 1982. "Psychotherapy Cults: An Iatrogenic Perversion." *Psychotherapy: Theory, Research & Practice* 19, 131–41.

Tipton, S. M. 1982. *Getting Saved from the Sixties: Moral Meaning in Conversion and Cultural Change*. Berkeley: University of California Press.

Veysey, L. 1973. *The Communal Experience: Anarchist and Mystical Counter-Cultures in America*. New York: Harper & Row.

Wallis, R. 1974. "Ideology, Authority, and the Development of Cultic Movements." *Social Research* 41, 299–327.

Weber, M. 1968. *Economy and Society; An Outline of Interpretive Sociology*. Edited by Guenther Roth and Claus Wittich. Translators: Ephraim Fischoff [and others]. New York: Bedminister Press.

Whitsett, D. P. 1992. "A Self Psychological Approach to the Cult Phenomenon." *Clinical Social Work Journal* 20, 363–75.

Wright, S. 1986. "Dyadic Intimacy and Social Control in Three Cult Movements." *Sociological Analysis* 47, 151–59.

Index

About the Author

AMY B. SISKIND is an independent scholar. She has taught at the State University of New York, Purchase, Hunter College, and New York University. She has published numerous articles on the topic of new religious movements, utopianism, and the phenomena of high control groups. Her works span the disciplines of sociology, psychology, and history.